Chi-Yun Shin is Senior Lecturer in Film Studies at Sheffield Hallam University, and is on the editorial board of the *Journal of Japanese and Korean Cinema*.

Mark Gallagher is Associate Professor of Film and Television Studies at the University of Nottingham.

'A truly groundbreaking collection, this book will do for East Asian noir what the French did for Hollywood noir in the 1950s: name it, define it and make sure it is firmly ensconced in global film history. Fans and scholars have done much to call attention to Asian horror. Now it's time, courtesy of this collection, to discover the pleasures and pain of the Asian noir universe.'

David Desser, Professor Emeritus of Cinema Studies, University of Illinois, and co-editor of the *Journal of Journal of Japanese and Korean Cinema*.

'So you think you know what a noir film is? Time to think again. East Asian Film Noir is an exciting read for anyone interested in noir as well as East Asian film, and not just because it firmly inscribes East Asian films into the noir canon. Equally important is its gutsy challenge and expansion of the existing definitions of noir itself. The essays comprising this rich collection do address the works of directors like Wong Karwai, Akira Kurosawa and John Woo, known for their homages to the downbeat postwar American crime films originally identifi ed by French critics as noir. But the extra reward offered by this is the willingness of the authors to extend the limit of cases, such as Kurosawa's samurai film Yojimbo, or the Ghost in the Shell anime films, Taiwanese art films like *Rebels of the Neon God*, and Chinese independents like Jia Zhangke's *Xiao Wu*. By the time you get to the end of this collection, you may well be rethinking the whole idea of noir, and not just in East Asia.'

Chris Berry, Professor of Film Studies, Kings College.

EAST ASIAN FILM NOIR

TRANSNATIONAL ENCOUNTERS AND INTERCULTURAL DIALOGUE

EDITED BY CHI-YUN SHIN AND MARK GALLAGHER

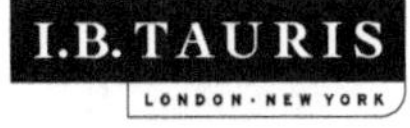

Published in 2015 by
I.B.Tauris & Co. Ltd
London • New York
www.ibtauris.com

Tauris World Cinema Series

ISBN: 978 1 78076 008 7 hb
978 1 78076 009 4 pb
eISBN: 978 0 85773 573 7

A full CIP record for this book is available from the British Library
A full CIP record is available from the Library of Congress

Library of Congress Catalog Card Number: available

Typeset by Newgen

Contents

Illustrations

Chapter 9

Chapter 10

Chapter 11

Chapter 12

Acknowledgements

Both editors wish to thank Philippa Brewster and Anna Coatman at I.B.Tauris and series editor Lúcia Nagib for their support of this work. We also jointly thank all contributors for their insights, professionalism and agile responses to editorial suggestions.

Chi-Yun Shin would like to thank Mark Gallagher for breathing life back into the project with such enthusiasm and attention to details. Love and thanks also to her husband Richard Argent for ushering Imogen and Meredith out of Mummy's study when needed! Special thanks to the Department of Humanities at Sheffield Hallam University for providing support for the publication of this book.

Mark Gallagher thanks Chi-Yun Shin for launching this exciting project, for responding to ceaseless entreaties to let me help shape it, and for being a knowledgeable, easygoing collaborator. Thanks also to the University of Nottingham's Centre for Contemporary East Asian Cultural Studies for support of activity around the project. Finally, special thanks to Elaine Roth for enduring long periods of breathless commentary on the romantic, violent, erotic, unnerving, hilarious, grim, enlightening, paralysing, dizzying, contemplative and other manner of dynamic film output that prowls the dark streets and rugged paths of East Asian noir.

Note on Names and Romanization

Mainly for ease of use and to avoid any confusion, all Japanese, Korean and Chinese names in this book are presented in the Anglophone order, that is, given name first, surname last. We use this format to achieve consistency and also to correspond with naming conventions used by the Internet Movie Database (IMDb) website. As for the transliteration, all Korean names and titles have been romanized according to the Revised Romanization system (the South Korean government's official system) rather than the McCune-Reischauer system, while the romanization of Japanese *(Romaji)* is largely left to contributors' preference. The presentation of Chinese is rather more complicated, but the Wade-Giles system is mainly used for Taiwanese films, while the *pinyin* system is used for films of Hong Kong and Mainland China. However, as a general rule of thumb, again for ease of use, characters' names appear in spellings supplied by films' English-language subtitles.

Notes on Contributors

Suzanne Arakawa is a lecturer at California State University, San Bernardino, where she teaches English as well as film and media studies courses. Her publications focus on spatial practices in Asian-American and American literature and film, with an emphasis on detective and crime genres. Her current research focuses on the outlaw Japanese-American body in literature and film. She is also revising a mystery novel manuscript titled *Spandau Memories*.

Mark Gallagher is Associate Professor of Film and Television Studies at the University of Nottingham. He is the author of *Another Steven Soderbergh Experience: Authorship and Contemporary Hollywood* (University of Texas Press, 2013) and *Action Figures: Men, Action Films and Contemporary Adventure Narratives* (Palgrave Macmillan, 2006) and has published extensively on US, East Asian and global film and television. He is now working on a book on the actor Tony-Leung Chiu-Wai.

Erin Yu-Tien Huang is Assistant Professor of East Asian Studies and Comparative Literature at Princeton University. She is currently working on her book manuscript, entitled *Capital's Abjects: Chinese Cinemas, Urban Horror, and the Limits of Visibility*, where she examines the relationship between capitalism and urban horror in post-1980s Chinese film cultures.

Kyu Hyun Kim is Associate Professor of Japanese and Korean History at the University of California, Davis. He is the author of *The Age of Visions and Arguments: Parliamentarianism and the National Public Sphere in Early Meiji Japan* (Harvard University Press, 2007) and has written many articles on modern Japanese history, Korean colonial experience, Korean cinema and popular culture. He has also been a contributing editor to www.koreanfilm.org since 1999.

Philippa Lovatt is Lecturer in Media and Communications at the University of Stirling, where she teaches Global Creative Industries. She has published in *Screen* and *The New Soundtrack* and is co-editor of *Asian Cinemas: A Reader and*

Guide (2nd ed., Edinburgh University Press, forthcoming). She is also a film programmer and recently curated a season of independent Chinese films for Takeaway China, an annual festival of film and photography in Glasgow.

Daniel Martin is Assistant Professor of Film Studies at the Korea Advanced Institute of Science and Technology (KAIST). His recent research concerns the international circulation of films from South Korea, Japan and Hong Kong. He is the co-editor of *Korean Horror Cinema* (Edinburgh University Press, 2013), and his research has been published in *Cinema Journal*, *Acta Koreana*, *Film International*, *Asian Cinema* and several other journals and edited collections.

Dolores Martinez is Reader Emerita in Anthropology at SOAS, University of London and Research Associate at ISCA, Oxford. She is the author of *Remaking Kurosawa: Translations and Permutations in Global Cinema* (Palgrave Macmillan, 2009), editor of *Modern Japanese Culture and Society* (Routledge, 2007) and *The Worlds of Japanese Popular Culture: Gender, Shifting Boundaries and Global Cultures* (Cambridge University Press, 1998), and co-editor of *Documenting the Beijing Olympics* (Routledge, 2010). She also has published extensively on gender, religion and the anthropology of Japanese society.

Daisuke Miyao is Professor and the Hajime Mori Chair in Japanese Language and Literature at the University of California, San Diego. He is the author of *The Aesthetics of Shadow: Lighting and Japanese Cinema* (Duke University Press, 2013), *Cinema is a Cat: Introduction to Cinema Studies* (Heibonsha, 2011) and *Sessue Hayakawa: Silent Cinema and Transnational Stardom* (Duke University Press, 2007), and Editor of the *Oxford Handbook of Japanese Cinema* (Oxford University Press, 2014).

Dan North is an independent scholar based in The Hague, Netherlands. He is the author of *Performing Illusions: Cinema, Special Effects, and the Virtual Actor* (Wallflower Press, 2008), editor of *Sights Unseen: Unfinished British Films* (Cambridge Scholars Publishing, 2008), and co-editor (with Bob Rehak and Michael S. Duffy) of *Special Effects: New Histories, Theories, Contexts* (BFI, 2015). He is currently writing a book about the history of puppetry on film, and continues to blog at *Spectacular Attractions* (drnorth.wordpress.com).

Hyun S. Park is a postdoctoral fellow at Yonsei University. After finishing her PhD at the University of California, Irvine with a project investigating the political aesthetics of Korean modernism, she served as a postdoctoral fellow at the University of Southern California. She is currently working on a book manuscript tentatively titled *Korean Modernism at the Margin: Visualizing Affect, Body, and Exteriority in Modern Literature and Film.*

Chi-Yun Shin is Senior Lecturer in Film Studies at Sheffield Hallam University. She has published on contemporary East Asian cinema (in areas including gender, genre, remakes and reception) and Black British Diaspora cinema in a range of journals and anthologies. She is also co-editor of *New Korean Cinema* (Edinburgh University Press, 2005) and is currently working on transmedia stardom and fandom in Korean Idol drama.

Andy Willis is a reader in Film Studies at the University of Salford. He has published a range of articles and co-edited multiple books on popular cinema from around the world, including *East Asian Film Stars* (Palgrave Macmillan, 2014) and *Defining Cult Movies: The Cultural Politics of Oppositional Taste* (Manchester University Press, 2008). He is also co-author with Peter Buse and Nuria Triana Toribio of *The Cinema of Alex de la Iglesia* (Manchester University Press, 2007).

Introduction

A Very Rough Guide to East Asian Film Noir

Mark Gallagher

This collection's title, while straightforward, immediately raises some large questions about film industries, film circulation and film culture. One might reasonably ask: does film noir exist in East Asia? Do East Asian filmmakers make films noirs? And if so, how widespread is recognition of a category we can call 'East Asian film noir'? This introductory essay and the 12 chapters that follow offer some answers to the first two questions. For the third, we might look to present-day cinephile discourse to note how little East Asian cinema is seen to matter in the ongoing construction of the expansive category of film noir. As Chi-Yun Shin and I prepared this manuscript for publication, the UK's *Sight and Sound* magazine published a lengthy feature entitled 'Twenty-First Century Noir', highlighting a dozen films for particular celebration and name-checking scores of other titles, from classical US noir, the so-called neo-noir of the 1960s and 1970s, and more.[1] The dozen seen to exemplify contemporary noir included nine US films and one each from the UK, France and Turkey, the last selection giving the overall cluster extra global resonance thanks to Turkey's position at the boundary of Europe and Asia. But East Asia – home of two of the world's three largest economies and film markets (China's and Japan's, with South Korea the eighth-largest film market worldwide as of 2012) – does not register at all as a producer of notable noir works. Nick James' article names just one East Asian film, the South Korean *Peppermint Candy* (1999), noting it only for a time-shifted structure that anticipates *Memento* (2000), which leads the list. James argues that 'the noir legacy now seems central to the pleasure of this era of cinema',[2] though from *Sight and Sound*'s selection of films, East Asia makes no contribution to the era, or at least to its pleasure for viewers and critics.

James' appraisal offers only fresh evidence that film noir is primarily a critical category, and as such, its limits are as infinite, or as narrow, as critics' own visions. Always retroactively conceived, film noir has been understood as a discrete Hollywood production cycle ranging from the mid-1940s through to some time in the 1950s, as a form of generic expression, as an international filmic sensibility, and as a discourse loosely joining innumerable texts and a range of production and reception phenomena. For 1950s French cinéaste-critics and later commentators in the USA and elsewhere, film noir was distinguished by varying narrative characteristics and motifs, ambivalent treatment of socially marginal individuals and groups, formal components including particular lighting and compositional choices, and a cynical or fatalistic sensibility usually seen as reflective of the wartime and postwar cultural malaise avowedly afflicting filmmakers and films. As a discursive construct, film noir's boundaries, forever elastic, have been extended to take in so-called neo-noir from the late 1960s to present as well as international precedents, variations and other homologous or analogous forms. However defined and categorized, film noir in many guises offers a compelling frame through which to view individual works, looming political and cultural contexts, film-industrial and reception activity, and wider circuits and frictions of global screen-media flow.

This collection looks at a range of cases that have been explicitly framed as film noir or East Asian noir or that acquire legibility as noir texts through reception discourse and other critical activity. Contributors look at historical cases to understand textual production in the long wake of Hollywood's celebrated 1940s and 1950s noirs, and at contemporary cases to understand the terms on which national, regional and transnational cinemas conceive artistic expression. Classical noir's downbeat sensibility finds compelling expression in later films from Japan, South Korea and greater China (the mainland, Hong Kong and Taiwan) that both participate in and are excluded from circuits of global-noir traffic past and present. Across this book, conceptualization and articulation of an internationally situated 'East Asian film noir' helps raise questions around the politics of representation, authorial activity, positioning in genres and modes, and local and cross-cultural reception.

This introduction addresses briefly the cultural, industrial and discursive contexts that both join and distinguish the cases, seeking to draw conclusions about noir's global reach and local expressions. Film noir is an industrial phenomenon, a tool for artistic expression, an aesthetic strategy and resource, a mode for social and political commentary arguably symptomatic of particular historical conditions, and a nodal point for international artistic and critical dialogues. What, then, do we mean by the term 'East Asian film noir'? What can the category include, and what are its parameters? What can we do with East Asian film noir as an organizing rubric? In total, how does the positing of the category enrich understandings of regional and global film history, aesthetics, production, circulation and reception?

To approach these questions, a selective critical history of film noir is in order. Noir's origins and its consolidation as a critical if not industrial category have already been exhaustively recounted, and many chapters here draw on notable scholarship on the subject. In their 1955 monograph *Panorama du Film Noir Américain*, French critics Raymond Borde and Étienne Chaumeton laid some ground rules for film noir, delineating a narrow range of settings, subject matter and character types in US films from the end of the 1930s through to the early 1950s.[3] Other French and American writers weighed in on the category as well, with filmmaker (though then chiefly critic) Paul Schrader's 1972 essay 'Notes on Film Noir' codifying noir further.[4] These works propose fairly narrow, subjective taxonomies – Borde and Chaumeton declare film noir to involve crime, not policing, so the 1950s US cycle of procedural noirs would exceed their definition; and Schrader stresses the influence of German Expressionism but ignores French Social Realism, and adds his idiosyncratic view of noir's expressive use of water, in effect ruling out the many ostensible noirs with arid Texas or Mexico settings. Explorations such as Janey Place and Lowell Peterson's 1974 essay 'Some Visual Motifs of Film Noir' aimed for a more systematic aesthetic analysis of noir works.[5] These works and later collections such as Alain Silver and James Ursini's *Film Noir Reader* kept noir in the critical eye though continued to approach it as chiefly an aesthetic regime, one sometimes asserted as a reflection of cultural and historical circumstances, particularly the end of World War II.[6] Parallelling this critical work, with the advent of feminist psychoanalysis, texts such as Ann Kaplan's edited collection *Women in Film Noir* and Frank Krutnik's *In a Lonely Street* looked to noir as a site for compelling, often troubling gender representation, putting industrial history aside in favour of ideological critique.[7] Scholars eventually began to map crime cinema after US film noir's classical heyday, though such works as Foster Hirsch's *Detours and Lost Highways* retained notions of noir as chiefly a category of American cinema, if open to occasional embellishment from filmmakers such as Hong Kong's John Woo.[8] These works too largely perpetuated the 'film noir – genre or mode?' debate, mostly put to rest in scholarship after the 1998 publication of James Naremore's *More Than Night: Film Noir in Its Contexts*, which compellingly argued for noir as a discursive phenomenon uniting filmmakers, films and interested viewers.[9]

Scholars such as Naremore also raised awareness of film noir's iterations outside the USA in precursor works and later traditions. *More Than Night* gives space not only to noir's depiction of exotic Asian characters and locales, but also to contributions of East Asian filmmakers – including Akira Kurosawa, Seijin Suzuki, John Woo and Kar-Wai Wong – to noir films and discourse.[10] David Desser's essay 'Global Noir: Genre Film in the Age of Transformation' name-checks dozens of other East Asian works, offering a quite capacious definition of global noir but emphatically seeing noir as a heterogeneous international phenomenon.[11] Andrew Spicer's collection *European Film Noir* takes a partly taxonomic approach but overall convincingly emphasizes the range of films and cycles legible as noir in France, Germany, Britain and more.[12] By the time of such collections as Mark Bould et al.'s *Neo-Noir*, film noir's internationalism appears beyond dispute, with many of its essays taking on cases outside US cinema.[13] Scholars thus began to investigate particular formations of a noir cinema in East Asia. Hyangjin Lee's 'The Shadow of Outlaws in Asian Noir' in the *Neo-Noir* collection,[14] and previously Joelle Collier's 'The Noir East' and Theresa Geller's 'Transnational Noir', both in anthologies on contemporary East Asian cinema, looked to 1990s cases to develop arguments about regional inflections of noir.[15]

East Asian film noir is not a strictly contemporary cultural formation, though. Film noir has long been distinguished by its internationalism: in the constitution of its production teams, in its wide circulation and reception, and of course in its emergence as a set of US cultural productions brought together retrospectively by a French critical taxonomy. Arguably, this collection's subtitle, 'Transnational Encounters and Intercultural Dialogues', is somewhat redundant. Film noir – whether in its core US form, its European precursors and variations, or its newer East Asian and other regional offshoots – has always been explicitly transnational and intercultural. Still, our subtitle underscores the vast array of cultural experiences and critical perspectives that shape film noir as we know it, and that will continue to inform debates about noir's defining features, its political and cultural appeals, and its value for screen producers and consumers.

Film noir's internationalism does not involve only transnational homages, borrowings and cross-cultural dialogue. (Many of our contributors do profitably trace such intersections, though.) We can also identify indigenous forms of a broadly constituted film noir within the artistic and national-cinema traditions of the East Asian territories this volume addresses. For example, our first contributor, Daisuke Miyao, turns his attention to works that include the Kon Ichikawa-directed 1958 film *Conflagration* (aka *Enjo*), which showcases amorality, corruption, bad blood and irrational violence amid sacred spaces. The film, adapting a Yukio Mishima novel and based on historical events, appears not as an homage to US noir or even as part of a parallel crime-film or black-melodrama tradition. Instead, *Conflagration* can be said to represent a use of cultural and artistic materials to reconstitute what could define a dark cinema or film noir.

For many commentators, film noir both in its classical form and with its neo-noir descendants is tightly bound up with experiences of modernity such as city life.[16] Many of our contributors draw from Edward Dimendberg's *Film Noir and the Spaces of Modernity*, which brings urban studies' and cultural studies' insights to bear on 1940s and 1950s US noirs, offering models for investigation of other noir cities.[17] The urban focus of much classical noir finds ready parallels in many East Asian noirs across historical periods. Expanding cities such as Seoul and Shanghai, or long-bustling metropolises such as Tokyo and Hong Kong, have become common settings for cinematic imaginings of crime, vice, deception, eroticism and other situations generating psychological and physical tension. Correspondingly, many of our contributors investigate films that use as backdrops such vibrant cities as Tokyo, Seoul, Shanghai, Beijing, Hong Kong and Taipei, cities often caught at moments of chaotic transformation. But just as classical US noir's corpus includes period variations such as the Victorian noir of *Gaslight* (1944), and geographic relocations such as the border noir of *Border Incident* (1949) and *Touch of Evil* (1958) or the wilderness noir of *On Dangerous Ground* (1952), East Asian noir can be seen to encompass films with rural or historical settings. Suggestive examples from across East Asian cinema might include: in Japan, the just-mentioned *Conflagration*, about the destruction of a centuries-old temple located in Osaka but far from its urban centre; in China, the peasants-behaving-badly drama *Blind Mountain* (2007), underground filmmaker Yang Li's follow-up to the similarly themed *Blind Shaft* (2003), which Philippa Lovatt investigates in this volume; and in South Korea, the historical detective film *Duelist* (2005), whose original title translates as *Detective* and to which Daniel Martin draws our attention here as well.

The ability of film noir – in its US form, its global variations and the specifically East Asian works covered here – to build stories of inequity, disharmony and betrayal in rural as well as urban locations and in films with both past and present-day settings shows noir as a site for the articulation of a range of social, psychological and temporal tensions. These tensions are not exclusive to the spaces of urban modernity, but show more broadly the condition of films *made under* modernity. Such films use dark materials to register ambivalence or outright alarm about modernity's capacity to jeopardize social contracts. Exported to or expanded to include East Asia, noir can register the social experiences and aftermaths of war, colonization, occupation and dictatorship.

The fact that noir can express such culturally specific experiences indicates not just its elasticity but also its deep indigenization in the hands of particular filmmakers. East Asian noir, especially in its raw Chinese incarnation – exemplified by no-frills productions such as Xiaoshuai Wang's *So Close to Paradise* (1999) – is less transplanted Hollywood noir than a cinema of distress and of the dispossessed. Elsewhere, as perhaps in such glossy fare as Hong Kong's *Infernal Affairs* series (2002–2003) or the stylized urban crime films of Japan's Seijin Suzuki in the 1960s or Hong Kong's Johnnie To since the late 1990s, East Asian noir inhabits spaces that partake of the fruits of modernity and economic growth. Yet as most of our contributors argue, East Asian noir repeatedly represents modernity's casualties, telling stories of the disenfranchised and marginal. This power dynamic does take us back to the explicit awareness of social injustice in classical noir (to say nothing of its precursors in 1930s French Social Realism), even as it urges us to acknowledge the regionally specific conflicts and social formations that contribute to an expanded global-noir discourse.

Approaching noir as including only films about private eyes in fedoras and trench coats bedevilled by amoral femme fatales, then, results in a quite limited global definition, based chiefly on homologies and transnational borrowings. On the other hand, figuring noir as comprising a downbeat sensibility and tonality suggests many different pathways that a noir cinema may follow, not restricted to contemporary urban crime stories but open to many local narrative types, thematic preoccupations, settings and iconographies.

To probe the significance of East Asian noir as a genre, mode and discourse, this collection looks not only to cases easily discernible as central to an East Asian noir category – Hyun S. Park's investigation of 1960s South Korean noir, for example, notes the popularity of explicitly noir films during the period – but also to a range of limit cases. These potential outliers pose challenges to narrow conceptions of film noir or East Asian noir. One can learn something of noir's international reach by considering films that might appear to transplant classical noir templates into other production and cultural environments, that is, surveying private-eye and dirty-cop and fallen-woman films set in Asia's urban metropolises. For example, the Akira Kurosawa-directed *Stray Dog* (1949) can easily be yoked into an international corpus of postwar hardboiled noir, just as stylized, narratively complex Hong Kong thrillers such as *Overheard* (2008) or *Accident* (2009) can fit smoothly into consensus views of present-day neo-noir urban thrillers. From South Korea, Chan-wook Park's dark art melodrama *Oldboy* (2003) appears so obviously representative that its poster image graces the cover of the 2009 anthology *Neo-Noir*. Investigations of such works can produce insights surrounding cultural specificity as well as global connections. At the same time, to look at a more expansive catalogue of works, styles and influences can reveal still more about East Asian noir's field of activity, even if paradoxically registering features and preferences that East Asian noir shares with its other international counterparts.

Any effort to corral the 12 essays in this book, and the designation 'East Asian film noir', into a unifying whole involves reduction, simplification and omission. To do so would also presume the existence of a shared, identifiable object of study and point of reference, that is, that our contributors are all talking about the same film noir, let alone the same East Asia. Contributors mostly retain notions of East Asian noir as set in East Asian locales and produced by East Asian companies and filmmakers. Yet as Suzanne Arakawa's consideration of films set in Los Angeles' Little Tokyo may remind us, East Asian film noir can be understood still more expansively in terms of diasporic populations or via putatively 'foreign' perspectives on East Asian places. Thus, we could logically draw such films as the Josef Von Sternberg-directed *The Shanghai Gesture* (1941) and *Macao* (1952) from the catalogue of classical noir (or proto-noir in the case of 1932's *Shanghai Express*, also directed by Von Sternberg) and into the field of East Asian film noir. And too, US neo-noirs such as *Year of the Dragon* (1985), with its controversy-arousing representation of New York's Chinatown, or *Blade Runner* (1982), with its vision of a dystopically Asianized Los Angeles, powerfully inform the category of East Asian noir as well. Such a view can move us beyond implicitly essentialist framings of East Asian noir as something constructed exclusively by, for and in East Asia. Taking the full measure of the category may help us see how contemporary films such as *Cloud Atlas* (2012) – with one of its six stories depicting a sci-fi noir cartoon future's 'Neo-Seoul' populated not only by an infinite number of distressed Doona Baes but also at least one troublemaking Xun Zhou[18] – participate in the international discourse of East Asian film noir alongside a range of indigenous and other diasporic works.

The very notion of limit cases implies that a particular textual or discursive category has a discernible centre, a baseline articulation alongside which others can be measured. For East Asian film noir, one might be tempted to identify those films and filmmakers most visibly transplanting the tone, storytelling, thematics and styles of classical or contemporary European and US noir to East Asian locations. While our contributors do address such repositionings of familiar noir and neo-noir signposts, they also look to indigenous textual forms that take film noir in original, unexpected directions. If much classical US noir emerges from traditions of social-realist filmmaking – with fatal-coincidence plots such as that of *Detour* (1945) part of a tradition of films of lower middle-class misfortune that includes non-noir precursor works such as the USA's *I Am a Fugitive From a Chain Gain* (1933) and *Fury* (1936) or France's *La bête humaine* (1938) and *Le jour se lève* (1939) – then we could reasonably locate many East Asian works in a similar noir genealogy. Indeed, chapters here include coverage of films such as *Xiao Wu* (aka *Pickpocket*, 1997) and *Beijing Bicycle* (2001), films easily categorizable as social realism and largely devoid of the stylization and sexual tension (to name just two features) we might regard as characteristic of and perhaps even requisite for film noir. These Mainland Chinese films' petty crimes are far from the premeditated murders, double crosses, crimes of passion and more that motor Euro-American noirs. But different cultural and cinematic traditions produce their own range of deviant acts, transgressions and injustices; their own figures of virtue and vice; their own tough men and hard women, devils and dupes; their own oppressive authorities and liminal underworlds. To admit even a category such as film noir into the East Asian context may do violence to, or at least upset or ignore, a broad swathe of historical forms and cultural traditions. Still, we believe the category gives us purchase on a rich dialogue in global cinema uniting a host of filmmaker preoccupations, textual features and viewing pleasures.

As many chapters in this collection demonstrate too, such varied categories as martial-arts films, period dramas, melodramas and more are all legible as noir if we accept an expansive definition of the category. To do so helps shift the understanding of noir from its Eurocentric and US-centric 'origin', and challenges the idea that East Asian filmmakers are necessarily influenced by or indebted to 1920s German Expressionism, to 1930s French Social Realism, to 1940s and 1950s US filmmakers, to French critics of the 1950s and 1960s, or to any other particular aspect of proto-noir, classical noir or loosely understood neo-noir traditions. Such an expansive view links to this book's interest in using noir to revisit films and clusters not easily assimilable into reflexive views of noir. Putting urban thrillers into an already understood taxonomy produces little insight, but moving toward limit cases of noir helps demonstrate the utility and richness of the film-noir category, and of the sensibility and discourse that create and consolidate that category.

The Geography of East Asian Film Noir

Moving well beyond familiar signposts of global and East Asian noir, our contributors address a diverse range of films and contexts, both historical and contemporary, mostly within the East Asian region but with detours to Los Angeles and Ho Chi Minh City, among other locations. We have organized the book around points of geographic origin and return, emphasizing films' and filmmakers' provenances and cultural allegiances. This structure does raise questions about national cinemas as distinguishing categories. Categories of national cinema are often arbitrarily defined and largely fail to take account of the global circulation of people, artworks and ideas. As Dolores Martinez's chapter in the first section suggests, one of the key values of a concept such as East Asian noir is the way it casts light upon processes of indigenization. Indigenization is a hallmark of any transplanted cultural tradition, and it takes us to many unexpected places. We might use Martinez's model for reframing the Akira Kurosawa-directed *Yojimbo* (1961) to make sense of a very different East Asian work, the 2009 Chinese film from director Zhang Yimou, called either *A Woman, a Gun and a Noodle Shop* or *A Simple Noodle Story*. Zhang's film is a period comedy and costume drama that also happens to be a remake of the Coen Brothers' neo-noir *Blood Simple* (1984), which gets its title from a line in Dashiell Hammett's 1929 novel *Red Harvest*. The Coens' screenplay is credited in the Chinese film, but viewers would probably not see the films as mirror images in any way. Zhang's film hardly leaps out as a noir of any stripe. But like Martinez's chapter and the *Yojimbo* adaptation case (which also involves Hammett's *Red Harvest*), it raises the question of whether the cinematic realization of a noirish source – like a Dashiell Hammett novel – invariably results in something we could term film noir. And if not, then at what stage do we accept that the work ceases to be eligible for the category of film noir? The answer matters only if our job is purely taxonomic. As might be evident from our regional and global focus, though, we seek to open out categories rather than enclose them further.

This collection's parallel framing in terms of national cinemas raises other taxonomic concerns but offers valuable distinctions as well, as national cinemas do in part respect geography, history and culture. Organizing the book's chapters in terms of geographically and politically defined regions emphasizes that the texts and contexts here arise from specific locations and are the product of particular social and political histories, artistic traditions and industrial practices. The collection's geographic divisions ask us to think through not just the noirness of the films, filmmakers and situations in question but also crucially their East Asianness. Each chapter here frames some material as culturally specific, including individual filmmaker sensibilities, generic traditions and sociocultural conditions. Our contributors also use categories such as gender, constructs such as otherness and the uncanny, and critical models from film studies, urban studies, history, post-structuralism and more to bridge divides and draw connections. Thinking in terms of film noir, we can see thematic and aesthetic preoccupations identified by critics, and a range of industrial cycles, famously in the USA but also in many other production traditions, that give us a set of questions or a range of dilemmas that guide our investigations of films and filmmakers. But we can also of course push at the boundaries of the noir category to ask different questions and get to different forms of knowledge. Thus, the question can become not 'what is East Asian noir?' but 'why does it matter?'

Japan: From Post-World War II Crime and Drama to Anime Dystopias

The collection begins with 'Out of the Past: Film Noir, Whiteness and the End of the Monochrome Era in Japanese Cinema', in which Daisuke Miyao investigates the return to black and white cinematography in a pair of 1950s Japanese films, *Tokyo Twilight* (1957) and *Conflagration*. With Japan's film industry having largely shifted to colour production by the late 1950s, Miyao argues that the films use black and white cinematography to revive political dialogues with the past as a means to generate social critique. The films' aesthetics not only create historical dialogues with past Japanese film and culture but also establish homologies with the diffuse, international noir mode and discourse.

We might regard Miyao's chosen films as limit cases even for the loose constellation of Japanese or East Asian noir. One might presume the core texts of Japanese noir to be films such as Akira Kurosawa's *Stray Dog* or *High and Low* (1963), not Yasujiro Ozu's sombre family drama or Kon Ichikawa's adaptation of a modernist novel. Our next contributor, Dolores Martinez, does take us to the work of director Kurosawa, but directs her most sustained attention to another possible limit case, *Yojimbo*, a samurai film with a US detective-novel source, Hammett's *Red Harvest*. Owing to its location, iconography and more, *Yojimbo* for most people belongs squarely in the domestic samurai-film tradition, not that of US or Japanese or East Asian noir. In 'Kurosawa's Noir Quartet: Cinematic Musings on How to Be a Tough Man', Martinez investigates Kurosawa's reconception of Hammett's novel as both a remodelled noir and an intervention into discourses of Japanese and Western masculinity. Martinez's chapter sees *Yojimbo* as a dialogue about comparative masculinities, staged both on the platform of a detective-novel source and a mutating samurai-film tradition.

Representation of masculinity is central too to Suzanne Arakawa's 'The Japanese Los Angeles of *The Crimson Kimono* and *Brother*'. Looking at two US-set films (one a late-1950s US independent release, the other a contemporary international coproduction) that foreground the experiences of Japanese and Japanese-Americans in Los Angeles, Arakawa argues for both noir and neo-noir's capacity to deal with persistent questions of race, gender and local and national identity. Most of the films investigated in this collection are set in East Asia and thus showcase Asian characters who belong to a majority race. Arakawa's chapter invites us to consider inflections of Asianness in locations that position Asian men as minority figures, whether as assimilated but still racially hypervisible Asian-Americans (in *The Crimson Kimono*) or as transplants or visitors with powerful ties to a Japanese homeland (in *Brother*). Arakawa's chapter illuminates the transformations of space, and the expressions of both cultural friction and solidarity, that occur amid Los Angeles' Japanese enclaves in late-classical US and contemporary transnational films.

The section's final contributor, Dan North, also grapples with Japanese media's dynamic intertextuality and cross-media adaptation. North's '*Ghost in the Shell*: The Noir Instinct' shows the robustness of noir constructs across textual forms and media. Japan's science-fictional, cyberpunky *Ghost in the Shell* series has received critical attention from scholars of manga, anime, video games and more. North addresses the ways noir discourse powerfully informs particular film and television iterations of the series. *Ghost in the Shell*'s open-ended narrative and aesthetic universe, argues North, uses noir signposts alongside a range of other intertexts to create provocative intersections among past, present and future. His chapter thus demonstrates ways the repertoire of noir ideas and images can be leveraged anew to show technology, crime and policing tugging at constructions of identity in a post-post-modern future fiction.

South Korea: From Postwar Modernity to Crime and Detection on a Global Stage

As for Japan, one might posit the existence of a South Korean variant of noir as partly a consequence of the cultural encounters engendered by the longtime stationing of US military forces (if not an outright occupation as in the case of Japan), beginning with the USA's post-World War II military governance of southern Korea and continuing with an effectively permanent US military presence after the Korean War.[19] As in the USA, Europe and elsewhere in East Asia, South Korea's cultural products of the post-World War II era show symptoms of the dominant global context of the Cold War. They also register locally specific responses to ongoing conditions of urbanization and modernization. Attuned to these contexts and conditions, Hyun S. Park's 'Allegorizing Noir: Violence, Body and Space in the Postwar Korean Film Noir' interrogates the representation of the noir body, particularly the bodies of economically and socially marginalized women who in early-1960s Korean thrillers fall prey repeatedly to punitive male violence. Park takes as her case studies two 1964 films, *Black Hair* and *The Devil's Stairway*, both from director Man-hee Lee (aka Yi Man-hŭi), finding in them provocative critiques of local social conditions and gender politics.

To tease out the allegorical dimensions of screen violence and the wider significance of her cases' figurations of bodies and space, Park turns not only to scholarship on Korean film and culture but also to diverse models such as that offered in Anthony Vidler's 1992 work *The Architectural Uncanny* and to more venerable if no less useful models from philosophers Walter Benjamin and Georg Simmel. We might ask how these thinkers, and invocation of such concepts as Foucauldian biopolitics, help us understand films' specific position in and dialogue with South Korea at a moment in its history. With the importation of any theoretical superstructure from Europe, or the application of the blanket category of film noir anywhere outside US cinema, historical and international critical models provide means to draw connections across time and space. Park does so while recognizing the ways bodies appear in these 1960s films as particular to South Korean politics and culture. The European critical models also help change the conversation so critical activity does not simply become a matter of identifying noir tropes in Korean cinema – there's a hardboiled detective, there's a femme fatale, there's a set of Venetian blinds – but of thinking of specific conditions of the body in South Korea's social experience. Park's chapter hints at how films we group under the noir rubric look through multiple lenses: as templates for pursuit of ideas such as biopolitical engagement and the architectural uncanny, as part of a loose global tradition of film noir, and as part of South Korean indigenous cultural expression.

Our next contributor, Kyu Hyun Kim, brings the discussion to contemporary Korean cinema and trains his eye on a series of works from celebrated popular filmmaker Seung-wan Ryoo. In 'The True Colours of the "Action Kid": Seung-wan Ryoo's Urban Film Noir', Kim investigates the repeated engagements of acclaimed director Ryoo – who is routinely framed in film journalism and scholarship as an action filmmaker – with noir narratives, iconography and discourse across his diverse filmography. By moving beyond the narrow appraisal of touchstone films (*Oldboy* or *A Bittersweet Life* [2005], for example) that are overwhelmingly apprehended as East Asian or global noirs, Kim's study shows how a particular filmmaker draws from the expansive catalogue of noir subjects and resources to create compelling, original screen art.

Finally in this section, Daniel Martin also provides case studies around the work of a contemporary director, this time demonstrating the divergent understandings of films' generic positions that arise in local and international reception contexts. Martin's 'A Mess of Contradictions?: Korean Noir in Myung-se Lee's *Nowhere to Hide* and *Duelist*' highlights both noir's elasticity and its perceived boundaries, demonstrating how figures such as police and detectives can locate films within noir contexts even as other features such as period settings can call forth reception formations more attuned to action and martial-arts genres. Martin shows how Lee's films attain narrative momentum and signification through a core of noir features, alongside a range of events and attributes that take the works into culturally specific hybrid modes. Looking particularly at English-language criticism of Lee's 1999 and 2005 films, Martin reveals the curious dynamic by which critics seemingly impose rigid genre definitions on both films, finding *Nowhere to Hide*'s comic elements incommensurate with their expectations for noir works while ignoring *Duelist*'s explicit use of noir and detective-film templates. His chapter's reception study reminds us that generically hybrid works may encounter rather less hybridized responses in particular release contexts.

Three Chinas (Mainland China, Hong Kong and Taiwan), Many Noirs

Japan has long been recognized as the site of one of the world's most vibrant film traditions, and South Korea has, particularly in recent decades, shown itself to be host of a dynamic cinema disproportionate to the nation's size. But any inclusive account of East Asian cultural production must address the output of greater China, home to three distinct and influential filmmaking traditions: those of the long-colonized but partly autonomous Hong Kong, the disputed territory of Taiwan, and the increasingly modernized and globalized Chinese mainland. Chapters in this section look at figures and cases within each of the so-called 'three Chinas' as well as cases that bridge the territories and also flourish internationally. The five chapters in this section attest both to the diversity of filmmaking traditions across Chinese territories as well as to greater China's expanded significance within both East Asian and global film cultures.

Considerations in this section of Mainland Chinese underground films and works from the Taiwanese New Wave remind us of the adamantly local components of works we can bring into the configuration of East Asian film noir. As suggested above, that configuration is repeatedly manifest as a cinema of distress, attuned to the marginal and dispossessed, those modernity leaves behind. Erin Yu-Tien Huang's investigation of the banal urban dystopia that Ming-liang Tsai's *Rebels of the Neon God* (1992) makes of contemporary Taipei calls up this culturally specific rendering of and response to modernity, as does Philippa Lovatt's attention to the marginalized workers and criminals of the underground mainland films *Xiao Wu* and *Blind Shaft*. Also emerging from Chinese underground film, *So Close to Paradise* director Wang moved to straighter social realism and away from ostensibly noir configurations with his next film, *Beijing Bicycle*. Still, as Chi-Yun Shin demonstrates in her study of mainland star Xun Zhou, *Beijing Bicycle* introduces a noir-adjacent mystery woman in the form of Zhou into its own realist take on modernity's discontents.

Leading the section with attention to early-1990s cinema, Huang's 'From Urban Crime Thriller to Silent Ghost Story: *Rebels of the Neon God* and Taiwanese Neo-Noir' pursues a theoretical investigation of Asian marginality and modernity that in part complements Park's theoretically informed approach to Korean cinema in the preceding section. Huang's chapter illuminates *Rebels of the Neon God*'s minimalist-noir aesthetic, which director Tsai uses in his debut feature to render the subjectivities of the disempowered young people who will inherit Taiwan's future. Huang shows that works framed as auteurist art cinema also acquire legibility according to globally resonant generic and discursive frameworks, and that both modes allow filmmakers to execute complex political critiques. Mobilized in particular by the idea of 'de-spectacularization of crime', Huang's chapter positions *Rebels of the Neon God* as a document of teen alienation in the *Rebel Without a*

Cause (1955) vein and as a species of film about the most quotidian of crimes, petty theft and vandalism. Moreover, her comparative analysis of Edward Yang's *Terrorizer* (1986, aka *The Terrorizers*) locates Tsai's film as part of a dialogue in Taiwanese cinema; and with the reference to Dana Polan's and Edward Dimendberg's scholarship, as part of a film-critical discourse about global noir and space. These framings and the further overlay of the 'silent ghost story' category take us in other directions than if we simply tried to put Tsai's film or other works from Taiwanese or Chinese cinema into a tidy 'neo-noir' box.

Turning to Hong Kong cinema in the wake of its return to Chinese rule, Andy Willis's 'Film Noir, Hong Kong Cinema and the Limits of Critical Transplant' devotes sustained attention to critical reception, assessing how reviewers for different regions' major publications frame films according to Western or global categories such as film noir, to Chinese traditions such as *wuxia pian*, and in other ways. Willis looks in particular at reviews of Hong Kong crime films of the 2000s. He finds reviewers frequently asserting the existence of a Hong Kong noir cinema but questions these largely anecdotal categorizations, arguing that English-language critics' Hollywood-centric frames of reference motivate them to deform locally resonant films to conform to subjective templates of US or global film noir. Identifying the pitfalls of a facile 'critical transplant', Willis's reception study, like Martin's in the previous section, illuminates the culturally situated but still flexible lenses through which critics and other viewers receive films of distinct national and regional origins.

Next, in 'Life is Cheap: Chinese Neo-Noir and the Aesthetics of Disenchantment', Philippa Lovatt takes on the 2003 mainland independent, and by virtue of its subject, de facto underground film, *Blind Shaft*, which she puts in dialogue with 1997's *Xiao Wu*, the debut feature of the now hugely acclaimed director Zhangke Jia. Both films form part of the output of Mainland Chinese cinema in an era of burgeoning artistic freedom alongside ever more refined state controls. Lovatt points to these surrounding contexts and to wider mainland political phenomena such as calls for reform of labour practices in China's dangerous mining industry, the industry at the centre of *Blind Shaft*. Functioning as what Lovatt terms 'docu-noir', *Blind Shaft* interests her for its at times startling illustration of mainland living conditions as well as its strong resonances with the tone and worldview of classical noir and global neo-noir. Stylistically and thematically linked to film noir, *Xiao Wu* and *Blind Shaft* in their settings, subject matter and aesthetics are also unmistakably Chinese, again indicating the intersecting processes of intercultural dialogue and local expression that underpin East Asian noir.

To look at global cultural production under the rubric of film noir can encompass not only individual works, filmmaker sensibilities and local and regional cultural contexts, but also the activities of key performers who choose repeatedly to work on productions that intersect in different ways with noir templates. In 'Tony Leung's Noir Thrillers and Transnational Stardom', Mark Gallagher examines the association of global star Leung (aka Leung Chui-Wai) with noir-indebted films, particularly in international arthouse contexts and in English-language reception. A popular star in Mainland China and his native Hong Kong, Leung has acquired an overseas reputation strongly dependent on his roles in period and contemporary noir thrillers, showing how extra-regional star personas contribute to films' legibility as noir works. This study – of a select group of Leung's performances, filmmakers' emphasis of certain performative features through storytelling and cinematography, advertising that links films in which Leung appears to familiar signposts in Hollywood and arthouse noir, and English-language critics' narrow frames of reference – demonstrates that just as individual films and recognized directors feed into generic and other classifications, star performers too can serve as co-determinants of dominant categories and screen phenomena.

Star personas established and consolidated in a body of films can also intersect with constructs associated with film noir even when the preoccupations of the films in question lie predominantly elsewhere. In our final chapter, 'Double Identity: The Stardom of Xun Zhou and the Figure of the Femme Fatale', Chi-Yun Shin looks at stardom within the Chinese context, investigating the performances and persona of the regionally acclaimed mainland star Zhou. Shin tracks Zhou's stardom from early roles in *Suzhou River* (2000) and *Beijing Bicycle*, films with thematic or ideological connections to noir cinema, through characterizations in non-noir works such as the musical *Perhaps Love* (2005) and the martial-arts fantasy *Painted Skin* (2008) and its sequel (2012). Zhou has appeared in films from dozens of directors and in a range of genres, including Mainland Chinese films, Hong Kong works and many international coproductions. Her diverse filmography may obscure the regularity with which she embodies variations on a pair of dominant noir archetypes: the uncanny double and the femme fatale. Her repeated casting in roles that speak to these noir staples shows other manifestations of film noir influences in East Asia. As Shin's chapter shows us, Zhou's persona incorporates a floating noir character template that enables the star's individual roles to speak to questions of identity and desire that the films may not otherwise powerfully articulate.

The 12 chapters that comprise this collection take a range of approaches to the constituent features, industrial status, cultural location and political efficacy of film noir. Because film noir is a contested object – if even an object at all – our contributors approach noir from a range of different perspectives. Readers may not leave this collection convinced that 'East Asian film noir' exists as a coherent object of study or category of cultural expression. As suggested above, to create that coherence would involve artificially smoothing over a range of cultural differences, and imposing a Euro-American critical formation onto cultures with different histories and works with many different agendas. This book offers a range of approaches to a rich group of cultural productions. We hope that grouping them as a particular strand of output – as East Asian noir, not just films from across geographic East Asia from the late 1940s to the early 2010s – provides a compelling organizing principle and gives rise to points of intersection and synthetic insight. Individual essays differ in their understanding of film noir as genre, as mode, as discourse or as other categories, but we believe all make productive interventions into understandings of noir's global and intercultural footprint, detailing just some of the rich and ongoing history of East Asian filmmakers' engagements with the forms and discourses of global cinema.

Notes

1 James, Nick, 'Twenty-First Century Noir', *Sight and Sound*, February 2013, pp. 56–64.
2 Ibid., p. 56.
3 Borde, Raymond and Étienne Chaumeton, *Panorama du Film Noir Américain, 1941–1953* (Paris: Flammarion, 1988 [1955]).
4 Schrader, Paul, 'Notes on Film Noir', *Film Comment* 8.1 (Spring 1972), pp. 8–13.
5 Place, Janey and Lowell Peterson, 'Some Visual Motifs of Film Noir', in Alain Silver and James Ursini (eds), *Film Noir Reader* (New York: Limelight, 1996), pp. 65–75.
6 Silver, Alain and James Ursini (eds), *Film Noir Reader* (New York: Limelight, 1996).
7 Kaplan, E. Ann (ed.), *Women in Film Noir* (London: British Film Institute, 1998 [1978]); Krutnik, Frank, *In a Lonely Street: Film Noir, Genre, Masculinity* (London: Routledge, 1991).
8 Hirsch, Foster, *Detours and Lost Highways: A Map of Neo-Noir* (New York: Limelight, 1999).

9 Naremore, James, *More Than Night: Film Noir in Its Contexts*, rev. ed. (Berkeley: University of California Press, 2008).
10 Ibid., pp. 225–229.
11 Desser, David, 'Global Noir: Genre Film in the Age of Transformation', in Barry Keith Grant (ed.), *Film Genre Reader III* (Austin: University of Texas Press, 2003), pp. 516–536.
12 Spicer, Andrew (ed.), *European Film Noir* (Manchester: Manchester University Press, 2007).
13 Bould, Mark, Kathrina Glitre and Greg Tuck (eds), *Neo-Noir* (London: Wallflower Press, 2009). Also addressing global contexts, see Fay, Jennifer and Justus Nieland, *Film Noir: Hard-Boiled Modernity and the Cultures of Globalization* (London: Routledge, 2010).
14 Lee, Hyangjin, 'The Shadow of Outlaws in Asian Noir: Hiroshima, Hong Kong, and Seoul', in Mark Bould, Kathrina Glitre and Greg Tuck (eds), *Neo-Noir* (London: Wallflower Press, 2009), pp. 118–135.
15 Collier, Joelle, 'The Noir East: Hong Kong Filmmakers' Transmutation of a Hollywood Genre?', in Gina Marchetti and Tan See Kam (eds), *Hong Kong Film, Hollywood and New Global Cinema: No Film is an Island* (London: Routledge, 2007), pp. 137–158; Geller, Theresa L., 'Transnational Noir: Style and Substance in Hayashi Kaizo's *The Most Terrible Time in My Life*', in Leon Hunt and Leung Wing Fai (eds), *East Asian Cinemas: Exploring Transnational Connections on Film* (London: I.B.Tauris, 2008), pp. 172–187.
16 For stimulating consideration of the intersections of cities and noir sensibilities or expressions in global cultural formations, including popular cinema, see Prakash, Gyan (ed.), *Noir Urbanisms: Dystopic Images of the Modern City* (Princeton: Princeton University Press, 2010), especially Prakash's introductory essay, 'Imaging the Modern City, Darkly' and Li Zhang's 'Postsocialist Urban Dystopia?', on contemporary Chinese cinema.
17 Dimendberg, Edward, *Film Noir and the Spaces of Modernity* (Cambridge, MA: Harvard University Press, 2004).
18 For an insightful reading of the Asian presence in *Cloud Atlas*, see Wheeler, Christopher, 'Facing the Future in *Cloud Atlas*'s "Neo-Seoul"', *HanCinema*, 17 November 2012, <http://www.hancinema.net/hancinema-s-film-talk-facing-the-future-in-cloud-atlas-s-neo-seoul--49839.html>, accessed 23 February 2013.
19 For more on the film-cultural engagements made possible by the US military presence in South Korea, see Klein, Christina, 'The AFKN Nexus: US Military Broadcasting and New Korean Cinema', *Transnational Cinemas* 3.1 (May 2012): 19–39.

PART I

JAPAN: FROM POST-WORLD WAR II CRIME AND DRAMA TO ANIME DYSTOPIAS

Chapter 1

Out of the Past: Film Noir, Whiteness and the End of the Monochrome Era in Japanese Cinema

Daisuke Miyao

Introduction

Everybody seems to know what film noir is and talks about its iconic features: such nightmarish visual styles as contrasty lighting and diagonal composition; such puzzling narrational styles as voice-over and flashback; such obsessive characters as femmes fatales and hard-boiled private eyes; such biographical legends as European émigrés being the creators. At the same time, everybody seems to know that any of those characteristics are not enough to define film noir. It is very difficult to find films that satisfyingly include all of those things if we want to be exclusive. If we aim for an inclusive definition, the list will be nearly infinite. As such, the images of film noir float around like a mirage, but are impossible to grab. In other words, as James Naremore and Hideyuki Nakamura argue, film noir exists as a discourse but there is no film noir film *per se*.[1]

Originally, the term film noir was used by pre-World War II French film critics in order to criticize some French films, including *Port of Shadows* (*Le quai des brumes*, 1938) and *La bête humaine* (1938), for being morally unfavourable. Charles O'Brien points out that the term 'film noir' first appeared in French journalism as early as 1938–39 as a term of contempt. According to O'Brien, the term originally suggested 'an essentially affective response to a group of films that seemed to transgress the morality of the national culture'.[2] In 1939, Georges Altman, a film critic at *La Lumière*, noted about 'film noir': 'THE PUBLIC is embarrassed. The "critics" are outraged in a fit of morality. Everyone who thinks the cinema is just a dubious form of entertainment or an abject form of pleasure simply cannot understand'.[3] Nakamura points out that critics used the term 'film noir' appreciatively to evaluate the same films as 'poetic realism' and/or 'avant-garde' that could shock and confuse the viewers for artistic purposes.[4] Film noir emerged as a discursive term to assess certain types of films from the perspectives of morality or art.

Then, after World War II, the term film noir was applied by French film critics to describe a certain tendency in some Hollywood films – *The Maltese Falcon* (1941), *Double Indemnity* (1944), *Laura* (1944), *Murder, My Sweet* (1944) and *The Woman in the Window* (1944), to be more specific. What the French critics recognized and highly valued was the same quality of 'poetic realism' and/or 'avant-garde' that they appreciated in some pre-war French films and hoped postwar French films to achieve in order to defend the French film industry from the Hollywood invasion.[5] Again, film noir appeared in postwar France as a discursive term.

In this chapter, I am going to discuss two films, *Tokyo Twilight* (*Tokyo boshoku*, 1957), directed by Yasujiro Ozu, and *Conflagration* (*Enjo*, 1958), directed by Kon Ichikawa. These films were produced and released around the years when many critics regard the classical era of film noir to have come to an end. They conspicuously use certain visual and narrational styles, such as contrasty lighting and flashbacks, that are commonly regarded as the iconic devices of film noir. However, being aware that film noir is a discursive construct, I am not going to directly associate the styles of these films with film noir. Without resorting to the category of film noir, I am going to discern shared stylistic elements in these films and point out the historical significance of the use of such styles in late-1950s Japan.

I would argue that *Tokyo Twilight* and *Conflagration* consciously engaged with the transition of filmmaking in Japan, from black and white to colour. When these two films were produced, many Japanese filmmakers had already made the switch from working in black and white to working in colour. Under such technological conditions, the choice of black and white cinematography in these films stood out. Perhaps black and white cinematography had the effect of reminding the contemporary audience of the past. Close textual analysis of *Tokyo Twilight* and *Conflagration*, in conjunction with biographical examination of the cinematographer in the case of the latter, will reveal that these two films critically comment on the history of Japan in the late 1950s. In particular, with the use of black and white cinematography, both films refer to the cinematic styles and the social conditions of pre-World War II Japan in the 1930s. What I suggest is cross-historical readings, or considerations of present (a 1950s present) cases in terms of past (1930s) aesthetics. Through this approach, we can see that *Tokyo Twilight* and *Conflagration* question the postwar reconstruction of Japanese politics and its economy. Rather than praising the rapid restoration of the governmental system and the rapid economic rise as the beginning of a new era of Japanese history and Japanese cinema in 'colourful' manners, these two films emphasize the problematic continuity of the political and economic conditions and discourses in Japan from the 1930s through to the 1950s in dark and contrasty tones of black and white. In the following pages, I discuss how black and white cinematography in both cases provides the basis for historical dialogues, comparisons and critiques.

Tokyo Twilight: White in the Streets

By the end of the 1950s, it was clear that black and white filmmaking was coming close to an end in Japan. Film historian Hidenori Okada calls the latter half of the 1950s the 'golden age' of Japanese cinema and considers various technological innovations to be among the major elements that supported cinema's success.[6] In particular, Okada regards the popularization of colour films as 'the most noteworthy' issue because it 'could fill in the gap' between Hollywood, where Technicolor had been in use since the pre-war years, and Japanese films.[7] Okada identifies the year 1958 as the decisive moment in the development of colour filmmaking in Japan because three 'big names' of Shochiku's Ofuna studio – Ozu, Keisuke Kinoshita and Minoru Shibuya – finally started to tackle colour filmmaking in their own manners that year, and their films helped to 'standardize' colour filmmaking in Japan.[8]

Ozu directed his last black and white film, *Tokyo Twilight*, in 1957. The plot of *Tokyo Twilight* centres on two sisters and their father who live in Tokyo. The story is set in winter. The younger sister Akiko (Ineko Arima) is pregnant because of an affair but cannot tell her family. The elder sister Takako (Setsuko Hara) has run away from her husband and returned with her child to the home of her father, Shukichi Sugiyama (Chishu Ryu), a middle-aged banker.

During the film's production, Ozu and his crew were most likely aware of the popularity of the Hollywood films that French critics called film noir. In a scene at Café Étoile, where a detective in civilian clothes (Seiji Miyaguchi) patrols the nighttime street and questions Akiko, who wanders the city of

Tokyo and waits for her unfaithful boyfriend around midnight, we see a poster of Robert Mitchum, iconic actor of film noir, on the wall. Therefore, it might be easy to consider the contrasty lighting adopted in this scene to be the film's mimicry of the prominent style of lighting in film noir.

However, the most striking thing about *Tokyo Twilight* is not its reference to film noir but its obsessive emphasis on whiteness. The contrasty lighting appears only to enhance the whiteness of white objects in this film, including masks, gloves, snow and electric lamps. Such emphasis on whiteness connects *Tokyo Twilight* not to the other post-World War II films that Ozu directed but to his silent films of the 1930s, including among others *That Night's Wife* (*Sono yo no tsuma*, 1930), which depicted the city of Tokyo as an extremely attractive but seriously problematic space that captured the rhythms and tone of modern life. In this regard, Ozu's silent films were in line with the 'street films' produced in Weimar Germany, including Karl Grune's *The Street* (*Die Straße*, 1923). *The Street* was released in Japan in 1925. These Weimar 'street films' have also been called German Expressionist films by many and are regarded as one of the major origins of the styles of film noir. I have no intention of calling *Tokyo Twilight* Ozu's film noir because of its reference to the 'street films' but want to stress that Ozu tried to create a connection between the pre-World War II past (early-1930s Tokyo) and the post-World War II present (late-1950s Tokyo) by way of lighting. As I have discussed elsewhere, Ozu's 'street films' of the 1930s not only look like Weimar street films but also engage directly with the contested discourses on the politics and economy of Japanese modernity, primarily with recourse to the technology of lighting.[9] Taking the viewers back to the period of the 'street films', with the help of conspicuously white objects on the screen, *Tokyo Twilight* engages directly with the contested discourses on the politics and economy of Japan that were still observed in the late 1950s.

Like the opening of *That Night's Wife*, *Tokyo Twilight* begins with a glimpse of a big city at nightfall. In the two opening shots, except for one tiny street lamp in the second shot, all the buildings and objects are in dark silhouette. In the third shot of a side street, which is obviously photographed in a stage set at Shochiku's Ofuna studio, we see a brightly lit neon sign showing the letters 'ON'. It is obviously a segment of advertising neon, an obstructed view of something like 'SALON'. But since we only see the 'ON' part on the screen, which is conspicuously bright and white, it looks as if Ozu has declared, 'Turn ON the light!' As if being drawn to the white light, Sugiyama goes into a bar on the side street. Even though the bar is lit only by a single light from the ceiling, the white cook's dress that the hostess wears reflects the light and is shiningly white. What Sugiyama talks about with the hostess and the only other customer at the bar is white objects – the snow of a skiing ground where the hostess's daughter is, and the pearls that oysters produce. In other post-World War II films directed by Ozu, such hard lighting was rarely adopted, and whiteness was not emphasized in such a conspicuous manner. The nighttime scene at Sugiyama's house that follows the opening is a good example. When Sugiyama comes home, his daughter Takako is waiting. There is a very similar scene in *Late Spring* (*Banshun*, 1949). While the dinner scene between the father (Ryu) and the daughter (Hara) in *Late Spring* is rather flatly lit, the strong white light from a lamp on the ceiling is clearly visible in *Tokyo Twilight*.

The visual elements of whiteness look scattered all over in the narrative of *Tokyo Twilight* as such. At key moments, whiteness is connected to a major thematic motif of the film, surveillance. Wherever Akiko wanders on the side streets of Tokyo, there are white lamps or white objects whose whiteness is enhanced by hard light. At Café Étoile, whose neon sign at the storefront has a shining white star at the centre, a white table lamp is visible

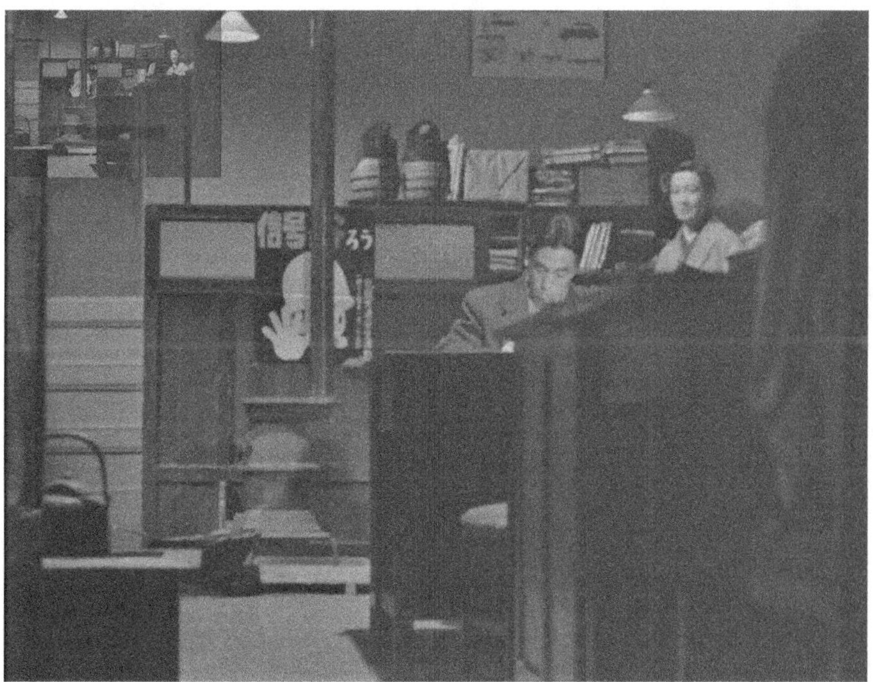

Figure 1.1 In *Tokyo Twilight*, a sign shows a cartoon policeman making a 'stop' gesture with a gigantic white glove

in almost every shot. The detective who questions Akiko wears a large white mask, which covers almost half of his face and emphasizes his surveilling eyes. Spotlighting coming from below enhances the whiteness of the mask, especially in medium shots of the detective. In the following scene at a police station, Takako comes to pick up Akiko. Takako wears a mask as large and white as the detective's. Behind Takako and the detective, a poster on the wall warns how dangerous a railroad crossing is. In the poster, a cartoon character of a policeman makes a 'stop' gesture with a gigantic glove, which is shiningly white.

Right next to the railroad crossing, where Akiko eventually dies from an accident, is an advertising board for the Kinpodo Eyeglasses Store. Two big eyes with glasses ominously gaze at the crossing. The gaze is emphasized by being lit by two electric lamps set right above the board. These two big, electrically lit eyes are most likely a reference to the same motif in *The Street*. In *The Street*, as in *Tokyo Twilight*, there is a scene in which gigantic, electrically lit eyes appear in the nighttime street. They are electric advertising signs for an optometrist. A huge pair of electrically blinking eyes seems to follow the hapless adventurers of the street. Yet, at the same time, these eyes expressionistically connote the inner dispositions of the protagonists (and the viewers of the film). It is as if the protagonists are captured in their own gazes, or, simultaneously, their subjective points of view are taken over by anonymous ones in the street.

The Street makes no explicit reference to the general political and economic conditions of the time in Germany, nor does *Tokyo Twilight*, but both films depict the street as a perilous site. The major difference between *The Street* and *Tokyo Twilight* is that while the street in *The Street* is depicted as harmful because of its seductive allure, the side streets on which Akiko wanders in *Tokyo Twilight* are not attractive at all but filled with dirt and vulgarity. We only see weary working-class people and students at a mahjong parlour, depressed-looking couples at a café, an exhausted cook at a noodle shop, and so forth. While the protagonist of *The Street* is blinded by his hunger for life and enters the street as a 'phantasmagorical' space lit by electric lamps, Akiko in *Tokyo Twilight* is desperate for life and hides in the side street even though it is lit by electric lamps.[10]

In his silent films of the 1930s, which had more synchronic connection to Weimar 'street films', Ozu depicted the street as a perilous but seductive space. In *That Night's Wife*, for instance, white gloves of policemen are conspicuously emphasized with the help of hard electric lighting. As I have discussed elsewhere, the whiteness of the policemen's gloves signifies the arrival of technological modernity, which critically comments on the prevalence of

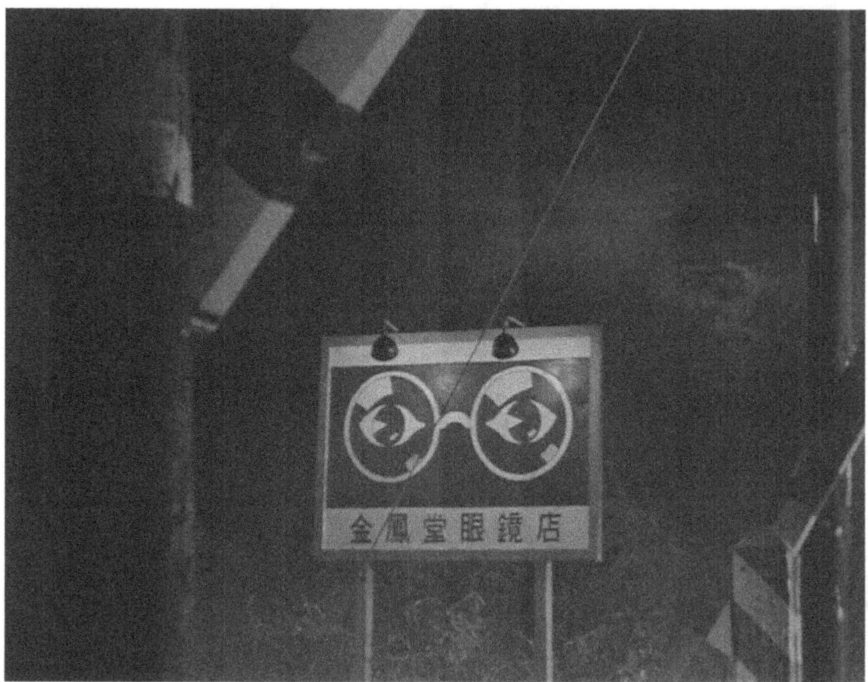

Figure 1.2 In *Tokyo Twilight*, two big eyes gaze at the railroad crossing

the system of surveillance as well as celebrating a spectacle of light in the form of a new visual medium for a mass consumer society.[11] The shining white gloves of the policemen in *That Night's Wife* emphasize the presence in the city streets of the officers from the Sanitary Bureau as the cleansers of society, who police but never leave any physical trace of themselves. The electrical lights are clearly used to articulate a mode of visual surveillance. In *Tokyo Twilight*, even though the detective who takes Akiko to the police station does not wear white gloves, his shiningly white medical mask that emphasizes his sharp gaze surely presents a mode of visual surveillance. Besides, the mask not only indicates the story is set in winter but also implies the notion of sanitation as a preventive method against viruses.

At the same time, through the policemen's outrageously white gloves in particular, *That Night's Wife* presents a technological celebration of cinema's capacity to vibrantly represent urban life, especially the nighttime streets, in the splendour of light and to vividly, or phenomenally, present the materiality of lighting technology in the form of visual attraction. Obsessively displaying white with hard electric light, Ozu's silent films captured anxiety and comfort, dread and confidence, increasing governmental control and flourishing modern culture in Japanese society. On one hand, Japan was in the midst of a political and financial crisis, especially among bureaucrats and political and economic elites. On the other hand, the metropolitan sites were expanding, and enabled Japan to 'dramatize the production of desire inspired by a new life promising new commodities for consumption, new social relationships, identities, and experience'.[12]

The late 1950s shared such conflicting moments between anxiety and comfort, dread and confidence. The famous government white paper, the 1956 Economic White Paper of the Economic Planning Agency, declared, 'The postwar years are no longer'. Thanks to intervention from the US Occupation, Japan had achieved its 'economic miracle'. So-called 'special procurement' from the USA occupied 27 per cent of the total national budget in Japan in 1950, for instance. The export-driven economy was growing rapidly with the support from the USA, but in reality, many Japanese people were not yet able to enjoy the consumer culture.[13]

At the same time, by 1960 Japanese society entered a great political upheaval. Before 1960, when the US–Japan Security Treaty, the renewal of the 1951 Treaty of Peace between Japan and the Allied Nations, strengthened the incorporation of Japan into the Cold War system as a shield against the advancement of Communism in East Asia, opposition movements against the continued US military presence and postwar 'democracy' that actually maintained the wartime bureaucracy occurred. For instance, Nobusuke Kishi, Prime Minister of Japan at that time, became an easy target because he had been imprisoned as a class A war criminal during the Occupation.

Then, in order to prepare for the Olympic Games in Tokyo, in April 1964 the Minister of Health and Welfare announced two plans: purification of the country, and health and physical education. Rapid sanitation of Tokyo's urban area created ambivalence in the big city. Homeless people living in underpasses all over Tokyo were pushed out. The running schedule of 'vacuum cars', tank trucks with a vacuum pump for collecting night soil, became restricted. Garbage cans became standardized. So-called 'ero-guro' – erotic and grotesque magazines – came under control.[14] Many dirty and smelly streams and canals in Tokyo were buried. The law that controls bars and nightclubs was revised and became stricter. Thus in Tokyo, vulgar and filthy things became hidden beneath an apparently clean surface. The high rate of economic growth in Japan starting in the late 1950s fostered this distinction between the clean and developed surface and the hidden and isolated underground.

Despite being produced in such an ambivalent but carnivalesque atmosphere in politics, economics and culture of the late 1950s, there is no excitement for the technology of light in *Tokyo Twilight*. Instead, the last scenes of the film repeatedly display white objects in a mournful manner. First, the scene of Akiko's suicide attempt is followed by two long shots of electric lamps. Noël Burch regards such brief shots as Ozu's typical 'pillow shots' that 'appear rather to serve as *sheer transition*'.[15] Similarly differentiating the styles of Ozu's films from those of classical Hollywood cinema, David Bordwell considers that this 'transition' is based on 'noncausical principles' without any connotative function within the shot of the street lamp.[16] Now that the shot connects devastated Akiko who has no place to go or hide, the policemen with white gloves and masks, and the omnipotent eyes of the advertising board that chase delinquent young adults who try to hide in the dark, those lamps could represent the surveillance system of technological modernity that reveals everything under bright light and leaves nothing to be hidden from policing. These shots have a dramatic function both visually and connotatively.

After Akiko's funeral, Takako receives a bunch of white chrysanthemums, funeral flowers, from their mother (Isuzu Yamada), who had left them years ago for her lover. Takako starts crying, covering her face with her pale hands. Their father (Ryu) prays in front of a photograph of Akiko, who wears a white sweater for most of the film. Next to the photo, a candle flame emits bright white light, which creates a strong contrast between light and shadow on the face of the father. Thus, in *Tokyo Twilight*, the present is connected to the past by way of electrically enhanced whiteness. The lighting scheme for black and white films is fully utilized to comment critically on the socio-political conditions of the late 1950s by referring to the 'street films' of the early 1930s. The end of the monochrome era in Japanese cinema in the late 1950s coincided with the period when the contradictions of modernity became apparent in the political upheaval and in the unprecedented economic boom and technological development. However, this time, Ozu's 'street film' did not celebrate the latter however appeared to mourn the former.

Conflagration: White Past, Black Present

In *Conflagration*, Japan's official entry in the 1959 Venice Film Festival, the director Kon Ichikawa and the cinematographer Kazuo Miyagawa shared with *Tokyo Twilight* the critical stance about the socio-political and economic conditions of late-1950s Japan. *Conflagration* is based on a 1956 psychological crime novel (*Kinkakuji, The Temple of the Golden Pavilion*, by Yukio Mishima), and the film fully utilizes flashbacks to visualize the obsession of a young criminal, Mizoguchi (Raizo Ichikawa), who sets fire to Kinkaku (the temple of the golden pavilion, which becomes Shukaku in the film version). The entire story of *Conflagration* is told from Mizoguchi's perspective as a series of flashbacks. When the film opens, Shukaku is already burned down. Mizoguchi is interrogated at a police station. In the claustrophobic space, he starts to remember what has happened to him during the wartime and postwar period in Japan.

It is understandable that some critics regard this black and white film as a film noir. Yet, the more significant issue about the choice of flashback as the film's major narrational strategy lies in the fact that the strategy makes the film's lighting design more conspicuous. The past and the present are visually contrasted in lighting. Lighting emphasizes how deeply Mizoguchi is obsessed with the past and how strongly he abhors the present. The past is represented in bright whiteness, and the present looks very dark to him. Mizoguchi eventually sets fire to Shukaku in order to bring back the past. The black and white cinematography enhances the whiteness of the fire. No matter how strongly the white past and the black present are contrasted visually by the special lighting design, however, what *Conflagration* emphasizes is the continuity of the ambivalence of Japanese modernity between the pre-war and postwar periods. When Mizoguchi's obsession with the past becomes more and more serious, a question develops on the viewers' end about the relationship between past and present.

In fact, as I have discussed elsewhere, it was not brightness and whiteness but darkness and shadow that pre-war and wartime Japanese cinema widely promoted.[17] There was a shared despair behind the praise of shadow that the Hollywood-style, sophisticated low-key lighting was unapproachable in the limited material conditions of Japanese filmmaking of the 1930s and 1940s. Japanese cinematographers decided to incorporate low-key lighting in a twisted manner. The emphasis was not placed on gorgeous gradation of shadows but on darkness in itself. In order to justify their prioritization of darkness and shadow, Japanese cinematographers resorted to *In Praise of Shadows* ('Inei raisan'), the well-known writing by renowned novelist Jun'ichiro Tanizaki. In a section in which he discusses Japanese architecture, Tanizaki argues that Japanese aesthetics was 'inseparable from darkness', and writes:

> Ultimately, it is the magic of shadows. Were the shadows to be banished from the corners, the alcove [in a Japanese room] would in that instant

> revert to mere void. This was the genius of our [Japanese] ancestors – that by cutting off the light from this empty space they imparted to the world of shadows that formed there a quality of mystery and depth superior to that of any wall painting or ornament.[18]

Harry Harootunian claims, 'In Japan and elsewhere, modernity was seen as a spectacle of ceaseless change (the narrative of historical progress and the law of capitalist expansion) and the specter of unrelieved uncertainty introduced by a dominant historical culture no longer anchored in fixed values but in fantasy and desire'.[19] As a result, Harootunian argues, 'Provoked by a growing sense of homelessness and the search for "shelter"', the concern for 'laying hold of an experience capable of resisting the erosions of change and supplying a stable identity – difference – in a world dominated by increasing homogeneity and sameness' became 'the way discourse recoded the historical problem of the interwar period'.[20] What emerged was:

> an immense effort to recall older cultural practices (religious, aesthetic, literary, linguistic) that derived from a remote past before the establishment of modern, capitalist society, and that were believed to be still capable of communicating an authentic experience of the people [...] race or folk that historical change could not disturb.[21]

Along this line, according to Harootunian, people like Tanizaki 'looked longingly to some moment in the past, or simply the past itself as an indefinite moment, as the place of community or culture, that would serve as the primordial and originary condition of the Japanese folk'.[22] The praise of shadow in Japanese cinema originated in Japanese cinematographers' adoration of Hollywood's low-key lighting, but in order to embrace the limited material conditions, Japanese cinematographers turned to the invented tradition.

It is obvious from his handwritten notes on the script of *Conflagration* that Miyagawa was extremely conscious of how to use lighting. He marks almost all the words in the script that indicate light and change of light – 'Turning off the electric lamp', 'The flickering candlelight', 'In the morning', 'Hot sunny day before rainy season', or 'In May, twilight'.[23] In the climactic scene, in which Shukaku is on fire, Miyagawa did not use real fire but represented it with gold sands blown in the air with numerous fans.[24] He selected this technique not only because sands were more controllable than fire but also because the sands looked much brighter and whiter on the screen, reflecting strong spotlights.

The lighting scheme of *Conflagration* displays wartime in bright high key, while the postwar period is in dark low key. This is a cynical but critical historical choice if we think of the praise of darkness and the condemnation of brightness during wartime, as well as the sense of brightness that the US Occupation tried to bring into postwar Japanese society with colourful and optimistic images of the American way of life. The emphasis on Mizoguchi's obsession with the past in bright light and his despair at the present critically comments on the modern history of Japan.

In *Conflagration*, after the war, Mizoguchi is sent to Soenji temple by his deceased father's last will. The people at the temple notice Mizoguchi's stuttering right away and begin to ridicule him. Some rice that Mizoguchi has brought from home is accidentally spilled on the floor. Feeling ashamed of his stutter and desperate about the spilled white rice, Mizoguchi kneels down onto the floor. The low-angle close-up of Mizoguchi's face captured in the wide frame (using the DaieiScope widescreen process) and highlighted by strong backlight dissolves into another low-angle close-up of him turning his back to his middle school classmates, who ridicule his stuttering. While the former is set on the earth floor of a dark entrance to a house, the latter is set at a schoolyard under bright sunlight. Even though Mizoguchi's face in both shots is in shadow because he is facing the ground, the lighting effects in his backgrounds are completely opposite. In the scene at the schoolyard, a Japanese Navy officer, a graduate of the school, stands behind Mizoguchi in a deep-focus composition. His spotless white uniform, which 'shiningly reflects the flowery sunlight of May', enhances the brightness of the shot.[25] It is as if, at the moment when he felt most ashamed and desperate, the whiteness of spilled rice reminded Mizoguchi of the spotless whiteness of the uniform. It brought his thought to the farther past of wartime. In other words, spotless whiteness triggered Mizoguchi's mind as the thing that represents his ideal beauty, what he adores but cannot achieve. As Dennis Washburn points out, the erotic beauty of the young officer's body in Mishima's original novel is de-emphasized here.[26] Instead, the conspicuous whiteness of the uniform is emphasized along with the close-up of Mizoguchi's sweating face obviously expressing his feeling of shame about his physical disability. In his memory and the film's flashback-within-flashback, and with the use of extremely high-key lighting, whiteness is hyperbolically enhanced as an obsession for Mizoguchi. Miyagawa's handwritten notes in the script confirm the contrastive lighting scheme adopted in this scene. While Miyagawa underlines in blue the sections that should be photographed in low key, he marks 'the sunlight of May' with a red pencil, underlines the

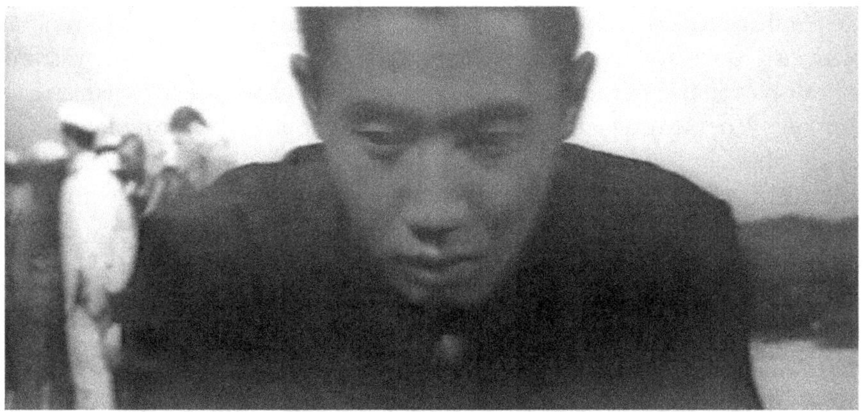

Figure 1.3 In *Conflagration*, the whiteness of spilled rice reminds Mizoguchi (Raizo Ichikawa) of the spotless whiteness of the Navy uniform

whole section set in the schoolyard in red, and in addition, writes special triangle signs in red at the beginning and the ending of the flashback in order to emphasize the lighting difference.

A wartime sequence set in an underground air-raid shelter has a more complicated structure. Mizoguchi blames his mother for selling Kengenji, the temple that his deceased father had owned. Mizoguchi's mother drags him into the extremely dark shelter, where the only light comes from a small open door farther back. The sunlight coming from the door is so bright that the two actors appear in almost complete silhouette, riveting the viewers' eyes to the stark outlines of their faces. The close-up of Mizoguchi in silhouette in the shelter dissolves into that of him in a school uniform standing at the gate of his home. Because the scene in the shelter is already a flashback within a flashback, Mizoguchi in a school uniform exists in a flashback within a flashback within a flashback. This is the farthest past depicted in *Conflagration*. Mizoguchi in a school uniform stares at the far end of his home, Kengenji temple. Mizoguchi's father attempts to shield his son's eyes with his hands and takes him to the backyard. When Mizoguchi's mother, in an untidy dress, comes out of the house with a young man, Mizoguchi and his father stand in front of the Japan Sea 'in dark grey'.[27] Miyagawa underlined in red throughout the flashback-within-flashback sequence in the shelter, which presumably meant being in extremely contrasting lighting. But he added a blue underline to the flashback-within-flashback-within-flashback sequence at Kengenji. Therefore, in the script, the scene at

Kengenji is underlined both in red and blue. On the screen, the scene at Kengenji looks dull and grey, which makes a clear contrast to the wartime past displayed in bright high key and to the postwar period depicted in dark low key. When Mizoguchi runs out of the shelter after the air raid, he looks up at Shukaku under the bright sunlight. The shining roof of Shukaku reflects the strong sunlight. But the temple is depicted in bright white light only when Mizoguchi looks up at Shukaku in the scenes set in wartime – separated from his father. Here, another flashback-within-flashback-within-flashback appears. Looking up at Shukaku, Mizoguchi's father taps him on the shoulder and says to him, 'See, isn't it beautiful?' Miyagawa underlined this flashback-within-flashback-within-flashback in red and blue once again. Interestingly, in this flashback-within-flashback-within-flashback, when Mizoguchi is with his father, Shukaku is displayed in grey – not in bright white light. The major part of the shot is occupied by the silhouette of Mizoguchi and his father, and the sense of darkness and shadow is emphasized instead.

Mizoguchi even tries to clean and polish up Shukaku as much as he can whenever he can find time. Shukaku in its bright whiteness is displayed as a representation of Mizoguchi's ideal aesthetics. In this sense, the bright white flame from the fire he sets does not destroy but enhances the ideal whiteness of the aesthetics, even if momentarily. Thus, in *Conflagration*, three different historical moments – the near past (1947), the wartime past, and the pre-war past – are clearly distinguished in Miyagawa's structured lighting design: low key, high key and grey. In such a strict lighting scheme, while militarism (the Navy uniform) and the traditional Japanese aesthetics (Shukaku) are fetishized in bright whiteness and the postwar society is depicted as discriminating against the weak and disrespectful of traditional aesthetics, Mizoguchi's father, who is apparently a loser in the pre-war Japanese authoritarian patriarchy system, is depicted as an ambivalent figure in grey.

Right in the midst of the transitional period from black and white to colour filmmaking, *Tokyo Twilight* and *Conflagration* utilize black and white cinematography's light and shadow and question Japan's complex history before and after World War II. In these films, the late 1950s were not depicted as the new beginning of reconstructed Japan but as the period when the political and economic problems of Japanese modernity during the pre-war era were maintained and resurfaced. Yet, these two films were nearly their last attempts to use black and white cinematography in such provocative manners. Ozu next directed his first colour film, *Equinox Flower* (*Higanbana*, 1958), and Ichikawa and Miyagawa turned to colour filmmaking in 1959 with *Odd Obsession (Kagi)*. Miyagawa once said that the arrival of colour film was the 'most shocking' incident in his career of filmmaking.[28] Facing the challenge, these filmmakers started to think of how to use colours in critical manners.

Notes

1 Naremore, James, *More Than Night: Film Noir in Its Contexts* (Berkeley: University of California Press, 1998); Nakamura, Hideyuki, 'In the Name of "Film Noir"?: Reconsidering the Noir Discourse', *iichiko: a journal for transdisciplinary studies of pratiques* 102 (Spring 2009), pp. 69–79.

2 O'Brien, Charles, 'Film Noir in France: Before the Liberation', *Iris* 21 (1996), p. 8.

3 Quoted in Abel, Richard, ed., *French Film Theory and Criticism: A History/Anthology 1907–1939, Vol. II 1929–1939* (Princeton: Princeton University Press, 1988), pp. 266–267.

4 Nakamura, 'In the Name of "Film Noir"?', p. 78; Nakamura, Hideyuki, 'Firumu nowaru/Disukuru nowaru: Kokumin eiga to geijutsusei 1938–1949 nen' (Film noir/Discourse noir: National cinema and the artistic, 1938–1949), in Shunya Yoshimi (ed.), *Media sutadisu* (Media Studies) (Tokyo: Serica Shobo, 2000), p. 148.

5 Nakamura, 'In the Name of "Film Noir"?', p. 71.

6 Okada, Hidenori, 'Irodorareta boken: Ozu Yasujiro to Kinoshita Keisuke no shikisai jikken o megutte' (Colourful Adventures: On the colour experiments by Yasujiro Ozu and Keisuke Kinoshita), in Kiyoshi Kurosawa, Inuhiko Yomota, Shunya Yoshimi and Bonu Ri (eds), *Nihon eiga wa ikiteiru dai 2 kan: Eiga-shi o yominaosu* (Japanese Cinema is Alive, Volume 2: Re-reading Film History) (Tokyo: Iwanami shoten, 2010), p. 285.

7 Okada, 'Irodorareta boken', p. 285.

8 Okada, 'Irodorareta boken', p. 287. Kinoshita had already directed his first colour film, *Carmen Goes Home (Carmen kokyo ni kaeru)*, using Fujicolor in 1951, though.

9 See Miyao, Daisuke, *The Aesthetics of Shadow: Lighting and Japanese Cinema* (Durham: Duke University Press, 2013), pp. 141–171; and Miyao, Daisuke, 'Bright Lights, Big City: Lighting, Technological Modernity, and Ozu Yasujiro's *Sono yo no tsuma* (*That Night's Wife*, 1930)', *positions: asia critique* 22.1 (Winter 2014) 161–201, forthcoming in 2014.

10 See Kaes, Anton, 'Sites of Desire: The Weimar Street Films', in Dietrich Neumann and Donald Albrecht (eds), *Film Architecture: Set Designs from* Metropolis *to* Blade Runner (New York: Prestel, 1996), pp. 26–27.

11 Miyao, *The Aesthetics of Shadow*, pp. 141–171; Miyao, 'Bright Lights, Big City'.

12 Harootunian, H. D., *Overcome by Modernity: History, Culture, and Community in Interwar Japan* (Princeton: Princeton University Press, 2000), p. 13.
13 Washburn, Dennis, 'A Story of Cruel Youth: Kon Ichikawa's *Enjo* and the Art of Adapting in 1950s Japan', in James Quandt (ed.), *Kon Ichikawa* (Toronto: Cinematheque Ontario, 2001), p. 156.
14 Sakurai, Tetsuo, *Shiso toshiteno 60 nendai* (The 1960s as thoughts) (Tokyo: Chikuma Shobo, 1993), pp. 36–41.
15 Burch, Noël, *To the Distant Observer: Form and Meaning in the Japanese Cinema* (Berkeley: University of California Press, 1979), p. 155 (italics in original).
16 Bordwell, David, *Ozu and the Poetics of Cinema* (London: BFI, 1988), p. 207.
17 For more detailed historical analysis of the aesthetics of shadow in wartime Japanese filmmaking, see Miyao, *The Aesthetics of Shadow*, pp. 173–254.
18 Tanizaki, Jun'ichiro, *In Praise of Shadows*, trans. Thomas J. Harper and Edward G. Seidensticker (London: Vintage, 2001 [1977]), pp. 17, 32–33.
19 Harootunian, *Overcome by Modernity*, p. xvi, p. xix.
20 Ibid., p. xix.
21 Ibid., p. xxvi.
22 Ibid., p. xxvi.
23 At that point, the title was still 'Kinkakuji', following Mishima's original novel. 'Kinkakuji' Screenplay, pp. c-15–16, p. d-9, pp. d-14–15. Preserved at Kazuo Miyagawa Archive, 3Mast Kyoto.
24 Ota, Yoneo, 'Monokuromu no jidai' (The period of monochrome), in Nobukazu Uekusa (ed.), *Hikari to kage no eiga shi: Satsuei kantoku Miyagawa Kazuo no sekai* (Film history of light and shadow: The world of cinematographer Kazuo Miyagawa) (Tokyo: Kinema Junpo sha, 2000), p. 25.
25 *Enjo* Screenplay for Preparation of Production, pp. a-12–14. Preserved at Kazuo Miyagawa Archive, 3Mast Kyoto.
26 Washburn, 'A Story of Cruel Youth', p. 164.
27 'Kinkakuji' Screenplay, pp. b-5–7. Preserved at Kazuo Miyagawa Archive, 3Mast Kyoto.
28 'Miyagawa Kazuo', in Otake Toru et al. (ed.), *Eizo kenkyu bessatsu: Kojin betsu ryoikibetsu danwa shuroku niyoru eigashi taikei* (Appendix to visual studies: Film history via interviews on individuals and genres) (Tokyo: Nohon daigaku geijutsu gakubu eiga gakka, 1979), p. Miya-17.

Chapter 2

Kurosawa's Noir Quartet: Cinematic Musings on How to Be a Tough Man

Dolores Martinez

'*Otoko wa tsurai yo*' (It's tough being a man).

Can you strip out the urban setting, the hard-boiled detective as protagonist, the convoluted mystery and still make a film noir? This chapter will examine Akira Kurosawa's *Yojimbo* (*Yôjinbô*, or *The Bodyguard* [1961]) in an attempt to answer this question. Although the film is set at the end of the Tokugawa era (1600–1868) when Japan was 'forced' to open to the West and began to modernize, the roots of *Yojimbo* do not lie only in an imagined heroic past but also in the moral dilemmas of the immediate postwar era. Kurosawa's 1961 film was made in the midst of his three modern-day (*gendai geki*) noir films (*Stray Dog* [1949], *The Bad Sleep Well* [1960] and *High and Low* [1963]).[1] In contrast to these three films, *Yojimbo* deconstructed and reinscribed the noir form; so that, although it was based on a Dashiell Hammett novel,[2] it also subverted the *ronin* (masterless samurai) genre in which a wandering loner fights for just causes.

In the immediate postwar era, the unemployed samurai was a significant and symbolic figure. Before the war men could find employment not just within Japan, but also in its colonies, a choice often represented in films as adventurous and romantic.[3] In urban Japan life was cosmopolitan, intellectually liberal, international and exciting.[4] Military service was also a career option. Thus during the first three decades of the twentieth century, there were many lifestyle choices for Japanese men: they could be pioneers, soldiers, left-wing radicals, modern 'boys' or intellectuals, as well as hard-working family men, and the various mass media reflected these options. After the war, every man, woman and child was expected to help rebuild Japan, and new, less adventurous identities were disseminated. Not all of the previous masculine-ideal types disappeared, but they were not necessarily depicted as desirable in the postwar media.

The Japanese film industry, which had been censored from before the war, continued to be monitored during the Occupation (1945–1952) by both American film censors[5] and film studios' own Scenario Review Committees, who looked for 'inappropriate' representations. Pre-war and wartime Japan could not be glorified; the nationalistic protagonists of these eras could not be adulated, and only explorations of ordinary lives or certain 'politically correct' historical dramas escaped censorship. This created a singular problem: how to depict heroic Japanese men? Ironically, as Isolde Standish notes, the Japanese action hero who did not live to fight another day made it past US censors because they assumed that true heroes did not perish; the censors did not realize that the greatest Japanese heroes traditionally tended to die.[6] Despite this loophole, it became so difficult to depict a tough, modern hero who could act violently, a major trope in noir narratives, that the genre essentially failed in Japan, many of its themes shifting into yakuza (gangster) films, where a man could still be a man.[7]

Yet the US and Japanese postwar film industries shared important roots that led to the development of the noir form: an anomie growing out of prewar economic depression;[8] an engagement with German Expressionism; and the traumatic experience of war, a form of suffering frequent in the representation of the hard-boiled hero.[9] However, as a country that had been defeated, Japan could only lay claim to guilt, not to suffering. In the postwar era, Japan had to reinvent itself as a democratic, peaceful nation,[10] and violent men were seen as belonging to the past or to the criminal classes. Given this suppression of certain types of masculine representations, the question arises: what did it mean to be a hero in modern times, under the extraordinary circumstances of postwar Japan?[11] For the Japanese, the everyday had to somehow be remade while burying certain aspects of the past.[12]

The repressed, as Robin Wood noted, always returns.[13] The suppression of war trauma and memories by civilians and soldiers surface in other ways;[14] for example, David Skal argues, following Wood, that horror films are linked to the experiences and terrors of war.[15] The myth of violent masculinity that underpins the depiction of the film noir hero has its roots in war trauma as well. The desire to see men as tough and unflappable, able to face evil villains and yet not be monstrous themselves, requires a shift from ideal to myth in order to be represented, in this case, on screen. This shift creates an evasive myth[16] that associates male uncertainty, fragility and cruelty with certain forms of villainy that are often effete, foreign or mad; while paradoxically it also glorifies these qualities in the noir hero. He can be uncertain at the start of the narrative, fragile in relation to certain others (women, children), and cruel *when necessary*.

In creating this distinction, this evasive myth obscures the fact, while also covertly celebrating it, that all men – all humans – are potential killers. Parker Tyler outlines the dilemma and its narrative solution as offered in postwar crime films: if war is mass murder, then soldiers are murderers, *but if* there is a line between justified and needless killing, the latter often the result of someone's madness, then only this is murder.[17] This sleight of hand permits the depiction of the 'loose cannon' hero, often embodied by the private eye, who operates with a different code than that of the state-sanctioned police officer. It is an elegant, if fictive, solution to the dilemma of how to harness the damaged ex-soldier.

Moreover, if trauma is not even to be acknowledged because the nation and its citizens are not victorious victims but rather conquered enemies, how does this affect the Japanese films we might label as noir? Is everyone guilty? Kurosawa subversively explored this possibility in *Rashomon* (1950), in which three people confess to one murder. Thus the representations of postwar Japanese men concealed a deeper repression than in Hollywood cinema. Although confronted by the same problems that Allied war veterans faced – a changed home environment, women who had coped well without men, as well as physical and psychic injuries[18] – the Japanese man also had to accept the role of the pacified *loser*. If masculine violence is one of the defining characteristics of the noir genre, how did Kurosawa deal with the need for a 'tamer' masculinity in his noir films?

Kurosawa's Modern Noir Trilogy

Kurosawa's modern noir films represent and negotiate the masculine limitations of the 1950s and early 1960s through exploring a variety of the genre's themes. There are elements of blackmail and double-crossing in *The Bad Sleep Well* and *High and Low*; in *Stray Dog* the hero and villain are *doppelgängers*. *The Bad Sleep Well* and *High and Low* critique the ills of modernity: there is corporate and political corruption in *The Bad Sleep Well*, along with drug use and a misguided Marxism in *High and Low*. However, while *Stray*

Dog has one chorus girl and a pickpocket villainess, none of the films has a femme fatale. Most importantly, it is the psychological portrayal of the heroes that unmistakably places all these films within the noir *oeuvre*.

All three films' protagonists are played by Toshiro Mifune: he is young police detective Murakami in *Stray Dog*, the scheming 30-year-old Koichi Nishi in *The Bad Sleep Well*, and the middle-aged Kingo Gondo in *High and Low*. All three represent different facets, at different moments, of the war survivor; although it is only Murakami in *Stray Dog* who is a soldier returned to quasi-civilian life. Nishi (whose name is actually Furuya) discusses with his friend, the real Nishi (Takeshi Kato), who now calls himself Itakura, how they supported the war effort through their factory work, and how they got by afterwards by working in the black market. Gondo, as well, speaks of having worked since the age of 16 in the shoe factory he has inherited from his father-in-law, *except* for his years of national service. Tokyo in *Stray Dog* and *The Bad Sleep Well* is a landscape of ruins and bombed rubble, while the latter film and *High and Low* highlight the disparity between rich and poor in postwar Japan. In none of these films is World War II ever out of mind.

Stray Dog most directly addresses the war. Murakami, whose gun has been stolen, discusses with his mentor, Detective Sato (Takeshi Shimura), how both he and Shinjiro Yusa (Isao Kimura), the petty criminal who has gone on to use his gun to rob and kill others, were soldiers. When demobbed, both had their rucksacks with all their possessions stolen. Yusa is obsessed with this incident and has totally changed after his military service, although his brother-in-law refuses to blame the war for his criminality, articulating

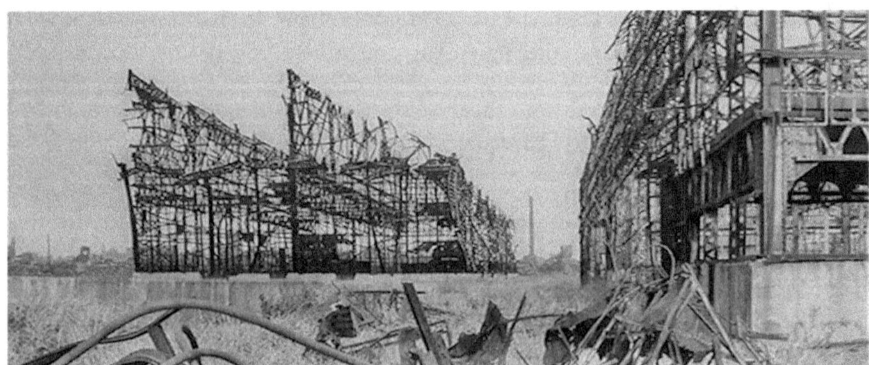

Figure 2.1 In *The Bad Sleep Well*, the bombed-out factory where Nishi and Itakura worked during the war

the sense that there is a difference between soldiers and mentally unstable killers. However, Murakami tells Sato that he saw good men turn bad in the war and that the theft of *his* rucksack was a crossroads for him: one that led him to police work rather than crime. Sato's response to this is: 'You're genuine [*honmono*, literally 'the real thing'], Yusa is a bad sort.' For Sato evil is born, not made by circumstances – an important noir distinction.

This scene hints at what could not be discussed in the postwar era: they are sitting in Sato's house surrounded by his merit awards, won during his 25 years of service.[19] While we might wonder what it means that Murakami is 'genuine', given his service in the Japanese army; we should also wonder how Sato managed to remain 'a good cop' throughout his years of duty to a fascist state and how he has managed to remain a police officer after the war. Whatever his past, Sato sees that distinction necessary to the very stability of the society he says they protect: they are moral men who hunt the men who kill. Noting how obsessed Murakami is becoming in his hunt for Yusa, Sato reminds him of the mad dogs 'who see nothing but their prey'; killers are like those mad dogs. Yet a police officer on the case also 'sees nothing but his prey'. The film makes clear that in order to become a good officer like Sato, Murakami has to overcome Yusa without killing him.

If Murakami has to defeat his alter ego, his worst self, so should Nishi in *The Bad Sleep Well*. Nishi wants to avenge himself on the businessman, Iwabuchi (Masayuki Mori), who ruined his father; but he is inadvertently destroyed by the fact he falls in love with Iwabuchi's daughter, Yoshiko (Kyôko Kagawa), after marrying her. As a corrupt entrepreneur, in cahoots with dishonest politicians and the *yakuza*, Iwabuchi is the very embodiment of modern, capitalistic evil: he has emasculated his son, lies to and drugs his daughter, and ends by having his son-in-law killed. Nishi is little better in his search for retribution: 'Evil can't be fought by lawful means,' he explains when he lists all the crimes he has committed in his quest for vengeance. His most honest impulses seem to be not only his love for Yoshiko, but also his desire simply to expose his father-in-law's dishonest dealings in the press. There is no thought of monetary gain on his part. This is not enough to redeem him, and Nishi must die a tragic hero.

Gondo, the protagonist of *High and Low*, is different.[20] Like Nishi, he has married the boss's daughter, Reiko (Kyôko Kagawa again). She is a virtuous woman, and he is portrayed as a fine man: interested in the quality of his goods, hardworking and deserving of the money and success he, a working-class man, has gained. But when his chauffeur's son is mistakenly kidnapped, Gondo is put to the test: will he sacrifice the boy, because paying the ransom for him will ruin the business deal of a lifetime? Gondo wavers; it is only his wife and son who urge him to do 'the right thing'. Once Gondo chooses to pay the ransom, he becomes involved in chasing down the kidnapper, saves the boy and helps the police capture the villain. Gondo, like Murakami, is a man who has come to a crossroads, and to have chosen the path of not paying the ransom would have led to his becoming as corrupt as Iwabuchi, who prized his business above his family.

All three protagonists are men who have been made by their circumstances: they are of the generation tainted by the situation in which all Japanese found themselves after World War II: guilty by implication. All three have their allies (Detective Sato, the real Nishi and Detective Tokura [Tatsuda Nakadai], respectively) and their alter egos: Yusa, Iwabuchi and the kidnapper, would-be medical student Takeuchi (Tsutomo Yamazaki). All three make moral decisions that reflect the tenor of the era: peaceful, not violent, solutions are seen as the best way forward.

For postwar audiences, these films depicted the conundrums of life in uncertain times. As David Desser notes,[21] Kurosawa's films asked what it meant to be 'good' in a world in which the state's pre-war ideologies were completely repudiated after the war's end. The heroes' dilemmas reveal the contradictions with which everyday Japanese were struggling as they rebuilt the nation-state: how to rise up from the ashes of defeat? Until the success of its hosting of the 1964 Olympic Games, the Japanese state saw itself as being at a moral crossroads;[22] needing to prove itself to the victorious allies in order to gain a place in the new world order.

The struggle to be a good man in uncertain times is central to the Hollywood film noir narrative as well. Both postwar Japan and the USA, despite their different societies, shared this modern predicament, born within the very conditions that would produce a sense of post-modernity. It is significant that Sato in *Stray Dog*, a man born and bred in pre-war Japan, is certain of the delineations between good and bad men, while Murakami is not. Nishi is protean and very much a child of the war itself; Gondo is a survivor, a later version of Murakami, who has made his peace with the postwar discourse in which capitalism and democracy will be the saving of Japan. At the start of the films, all three men seem to fit well into Frank Krutnik's discursive category of the noir hero who is 'both internally divided and alienated from the culturally permissible (or ideal) parameters of masculine identity, desire and achievement'.[23] Given the national drive to rehabilitate, the heroes of these films *must* end as they do – Murakami overcoming Yusa, Nishi dying, Gondo unable to see himself in Takeuchi – for to do more would be to embrace the subversive potentialities of a pre-war, violent masculine identity. Once filmic order is restored, two of these postwar protagonists find stability, having confronted, acknowledged and repressed their potential for monstrosity.

These noir films depict repression as the only possible road to postwar normality, and paradoxically, no film reveals this better than *Yojimbo*. It is this film that best examines the themes of crossroads, choices, instability, possibilities, human monstrosity and the chaos that violence creates. Of all Kurosawa's films it is *Yojimbo* that most neatly fits into the noir category, since it uses and plays with many elements of the category: the first-person narrative, the knight errant, the corruption of elites, the callousness of the authorities, the vulnerability of ordinary folk and the final apocalyptic restoration of the status quo.

The Noir Hero as Trickster

Noir protagonists have been described as morally ambivalent, sexually conflicted, tough, often shabby,[24] fast-talking and generally possessing a weak spot, normally for a 'dame'. The idea of the noir hero as trickster – the comic, cunning and mischievous minor deity, often in an animal incarnation, found in many mythologies – is unusual. The noir hero is more often compared to the valiant knight who offers moral certainty and unwavering loyalty while relying on brute strength and a certain controlled monstrosity. Achilles was such a perfect warrior, while Odysseus was a trickster. Tricksters, in contrast to noble champions, get out of messy situations by stealth, joking and sly intelligence or by changing their shape; yet their actions sometimes bring about cruel results. In many of his incarnations, the noir hero is a combination of the warrior and trickster: clever and tricky, hard and violent, but generally, and often surprisingly, loyal to some cause.

Above I have argued that to be successful, Kurosawa's noir protagonists had to confront their inner monsters and accept that there was a thin line between them and the villain, while holding firmly to that difference. This is a major theme in all of Kurosawa's *oeuvre*,[25] but in *Yojimbo* the line is drawn at its very thinnest by making its protagonist a wily, apparently amoral *ronin* who is willing to work as a bodyguard. This out-of-work warrior, Tsubaki Sanjuro (Thirty Year Old Mulberry Field, a name he makes up on the spot), again played by Mifune, is typical of Kurosawa's heroes who face difficult choices. In contrast to the men described above, however, he is a man with no name, no past and no inner life to which viewers are privy; there is no psychological tension. That he has been left without a master at the end of the Tokugawa era is only implied. We see but the surface: Sanjuro is cynical, shabby and tough, while his wit is dark, sardonic and even malicious at times. He matches the tone of the film itself: the understated humour that occasionally surfaces in other Kurosawa films is allowed full rein here.[26]

This mysterious hero, whose inner life is hidden, is a reference to Hammett's nameless 'continental op', the first-person narrator of *Red Harvest*. While he alternately sells his services to the two factions struggling for control of the corrupt town nicknamed 'Poisonville', the continental operative turns out to be loyal and virtuous, bringing down the gangsters and a corrupt union boss in order to complete his contract. The continental op is, to paraphrase Raymond Chandler, a modern knight errant who will battle to the end to see justice done.[27] The link to the samurai, who were a type of knight, is obvious. Yet *Yojimbo* was Kurosawa's attempt to overturn the stale kabuki-based conventions of most samurai drama,[28] which are not only subverted in this film, but also used in a manner that recalls noir's subversions of Hollywood mainstream films. Another innovative twist to the plot is that Sanjuro is a totally independent agent: in contrast to the continental op, he is not employed by anyone, although he keeps 'considering' offers of paid work. More to the point, *Yojimbo* adds a Japanese twist to Hammett's plot by incorporating 'folkloric elements',[29] the inclusion of which allows Kurosawa to push the anarchic, violent potentials of the antihero even further.

This twist can be inferred by comparing Sanjuro to a further trickster character from Japanese folklore: the wandering deity or *marebito*.[30] The *marebito* is the itinerant who comes to town and, if treated hospitably, will grant a person's desires; if treated badly, he will wreak havoc. Wandering *bodhisattvas* as well as many local Shinto deities are *marebito*: the latter are enshrined, or domesticated, in the local shrine from which their beneficial powers emanate. Sanjuro, apparently blowing into town on a whim, having tossed a stick at a crossroads, fits this description; in fact, Donald Richie refers to him as a *deus ex machina*.[31]

Thus the action in *Yojimbo* is framed in various ways: as a noir narrative, as a western in its visual grammar, while borrowing from and subverting the kabuki conventions long associated with samurai films. As part Japanese folktale, it is a musing on what a traditional deity might do when confronted by the evils of emerging capitalism. In a further inversion of the noir narrative traditionally set in closed urban spaces, *Yojimbo* was filmed outdoors, on location, opening up space and allowing the cameras to follow Sanjuro wherever he goes. The camera does not quite become the first-person narrator, since the protagonist is kept in view, but by peering over his shoulder, it provides us with Sanjuro's point of view. In short, we have a film of savage junctures, a conceptual technique that Kurosawa probably borrowed from his knowledge of Sergei Eisenstein's work.[32] Through such savage junctures Kurosawa widens the noir take on German Expressionism, developing the dark visuals until they become surreal: a dog leaves town with a hand in its muzzle; the villains are literally grotesques; after a beating, Sanjuro emerges looking demonic – these are but a few examples.[33]

An illustration of the complexity of these junctures is the first encounter Sanjuro has on his way into town, with a farming family whose son wants to run away to become a gambler (i.e. a *yakuza*). Leaving aged parents without anyone to care for them is a major dereliction of filial duty in Japan, and the old couple are not only grief stricken at their son's departure, but are being left to almost certain poverty and death: who will till the fields or harvest the rice if they are too feeble to do so? Desperately, the aged mother prays at the family altar; however, in the midst of this consternation, they allow Sanjuro to drink from their well. Such kindness must be repaid, and it is no accident that at the film's end, Sanjuro spares the life of the errant son and instructs him to go home, in answer to his mother's prayer. So much takes place in between that many viewers may have forgotten who this young man is.

Another example is Gonji (Tôno Ejirô), the town barkeeper, who provides Sanjuro with free food and drink and then, after explaining how corrupt the town is, urges him to leave. He has two heartfelt desires: that the town's infighting should end; and (as we learn much later) that the family of the kidnapped woman, Nui (Yôko Tsukasa), be reunited. As a *marebito* repaying Gonji's kindness, Sanjuro's subsequent actions make sense; although not necessarily to the barkeeper himself who recognizes something in his guest, but is not sure what it is. When Sanjuro appears to be manipulating everyone to his own ends, Gonji asks: 'Is this a play that you wrote?' Sanjuro replies: 'Half of it.' He is referring to the fact that the wind has blown in a second 'supernatural' being, Unosuke (Tatsuya Nakadai), named for the year of the rabbit in which he was born: the beautiful, psychotic gambler with a gun.

The story of a crafty *ronin* manipulating two sides to his own ends becomes more violent as he is joined by this truly evil character. While Sanjuro has found much to amuse him in the situations he creates, Unosuke laughs at the bloodshed he wreaks. Once again Kurosawa has given us two characters who are two sides of the same coin. It is no coincidence that in his rough and ready appearance Sanjuro resembles that beloved Japanese trickster the *tanuki* (raccoon dog), who appears in many folktales; and that Unosuke actually means 'rabbit's helper', a possible reference to the even trickier and less liked malevolent fox. And it is worth noting how these animals tend to be portrayed: the *tanuki* is generally depicted as being an incredibly well-endowed male, while the fox tends to be effeminate if not female. Yet, Sanjuro's mastery of the sword appears useless in opposition to the gunslinger who has come to town; it is only Sanjuro's quick reactions and nerves of steel that save him in the end. In Kurosawa's discussions of the film, this was an important point: the older virtues of traditional Japan were losing out to modernity, capitalism and new technologies; he wanted to critique these developments. While set in the 1860s, the film is meant also to be his comment on the rise of the *yakuza* cult of the 1960s, the criminal made hero, who came to dominance in film and on television in this era.

… On Being a Tough Man

The epigraph for this chapter is the title of the film *It's Tough Being a Man* (*Otoko wa tsurai yo*, 1969), which went on to become a popular franchise in Japan, spanning the decades from 1969 to 1997. Its popularity derived from the fact that it spoke to the same problem faced by Japanese film noir: how to depict appropriate moral choices for men living in a rehabilitated Japan. *Otoko wa tsurai yo*'s comic protagonist, Toro-san (Kiyoshi Atsumi), provides an alternative solution to the postwar crisis in masculine identity: he is not part of corporate Japan and its 'samurai' businessman culture because he is a 'traditional' wandering peddler, a throwback to the past. Toro-san solves the dilemmas of modern life without recourse to the violence of the lone warrior, who wanders into town and enacts his own brand of justice. For decades, Toro-san stood in sharp contrast to that other postwar version of a Japanese hard or tough masculinity, the *yakuza*, who got to act violently but often died for his efforts. What the analyses of this popular film series often fail to discuss is that the evolution of the easygoing comic protagonist should be seen as one post-1960s response to the problem of how to represent good men in Japan and marks a narrowing of the appropriate mainstream masculinities available to ordinary men – violence is definitely out.

The intertextual play among *Yojimbo* and Kurosawa's modern noir films,[34] particularly *Stray Dog*, reveals how Kurosawa explored the contrast between past and present masculine ideals; this exploration is his final subversion of the noir genre. *Yojimbo* is a response to all that had been, and would continue to be, repressed by the heroes of the postwar films set in the contemporary era. Sanjuro is the super-heroic version of Kurosawa's modern, more moderate characters, doing more than they ever could. *Stray Dog* is a first version of the story of the out-of-work warrior who, at the end of an era, must find a new role for himself. The dog leaving town with a hand in its mouth in *Yojimbo* is a reference to the panting stray dog at the beginning of the earlier film. Like Detective Murakami, Sanjuro beats the man with the gun, but it is in a deadly draw against his sword rather than in fisticuffs. Craftier than Nishi, Sanjuro manipulates the two sides of the town so that *they* end up dead rather than he. More proactive than Gondo, he rescues the kidnapped woman, redeems the runaway son, and does not require any help from the police to do so. Finally, Sanjuro takes over as bodyguard from another samurai, played by Fujita Susumu, the actor who played the hero in Kurosawa's earlier popular films about a martial-arts student (*Sanshiro Sugata* parts 1 and 2, 1943 and 1945). Upon seeing Sanjuro's sword work, this man, Homma, hightails it out of a window and across the mulberry fields that surround the village. He turns and waves goodbye to Sanjuro, who is watching him. Stephen Prince sees this as a farewell to Kurosawa's earlier, clean-cut heroes;[35] but this moment also recalls the generational contrast between Sato and Murakami in *Stray Dog*: the virtues of the past seem to be dissipating in the morally complex present.

How were the post-*Yojimbo* protagonists different? The dualism found in Kurosawa's earlier films does not disappear, but the thin line between the main characters becomes even more blurred, and the moral choices become part of heroes' *internal* struggles. Kurosawa avoids psychologizing Sanjuro,

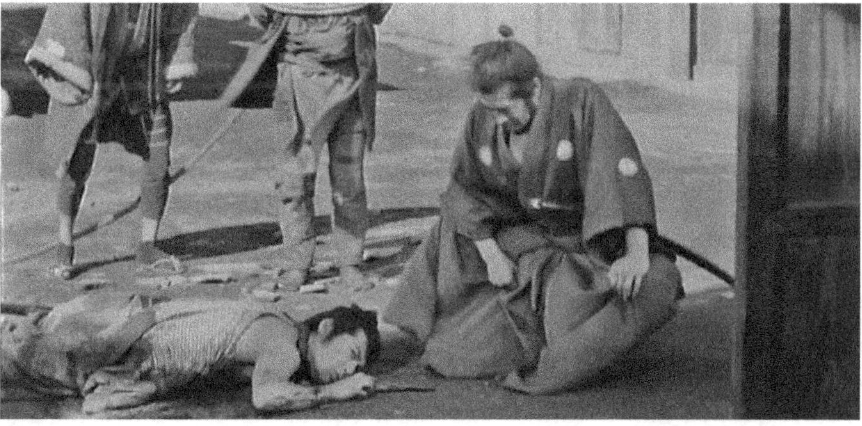

Figure 2.2 'I will be waiting at the entrance to hell' (*Jigoku no iriguchi de matteruze*). *Yojimbo*

instead giving the character superhuman aspects: he is pure action hero.[36] In fact the sequel to *Yojimbo*, *Sanjuro* (*Tsubaki Sanjûrô*, 1962), begins with a further revelation of Sanjuro's supernatural nature by having him mysteriously appear from the back of a shrine. In contradistinction to *Yojimbo*, in *Sanjuro* the hero is implored *not* to draw his sword, and he resolves most of the plot's dilemmas without resorting to violence. *Sanjuro*'s origins in a romantic work of fiction are revealed by this alteration,[37] which allows Sanjuro to be purely heroic: unlike *Yojimbo*, this is not a noir film. In *Yojimbo*, Kurosawa undermines Sanjuro's heroism by having the dying Unosuke say to him: 'I will be waiting at the entrance to hell.' There is nothing optimistic about him here; both he and the villain are doomed. Their brand of cathartic violence is but a fantasy that ultimately leads to sterile solutions.

Postwar films could not depict triumphant yet morally ambivalent and violent heroes as veterans of Japan's recent war. The anarchic, chaotic form of aggressive heroics that characterizes the 'damaged' noir hero, often depicted by Hollywood as a veteran of World War II or the Korean, Vietnam or Iraq wars, was not permissible in 1950s Japan. Such men could only be tragic heroes and die. That has changed in the decades since the end of the war, but was still a limitation in the Japan of the 1950s and 1960s. Given these social constraints in the postwar period, a fully noir film set in the modern era was impossible. The contemporary heroes of Kurosawa's noir work had to end by becoming stable, conventional and moral – or die trying. Only Hollywood heroes had the prerogative of brooding over their injuries in psychological, but never fully explicit, detail; and only they were allowed to purge their doubts through representations of brutal and thus liberating action. Yet I agree with Daisuke Miyao,[38] who notes the looseness of the noir form, and argues that today noir elements can be found in other Japanese media that might not be identified with the genre: samurai dramas, manga, anime and even children's programmes. All of these frequently depict a damaged hero resorting to a liberating violence that is not sanctioned in mainstream Japan. In the post-censorship era, it was *Yojimbo* that helped establish these tropes, and it is telling that it became Kurosawa's most successful film in Japan, spawning endless variations on the theme in the samurai genre.

Given the complexity of Kurosawa's work, no single explanation can sufficiently unpack all of his films' meanings. However, in transporting *Red Harvest*'s plot to the past, he was able to explore all the contradictions embodied within a noir protagonist. Adding the *marebito* and trickster themes allowed him to satirize extreme masculinities, all while critiquing the rise of modern political corruption and capitalist culture. Through these savage junctures, *Yojimbo* is as close to the sentiments of Western noir films as it was possible to be in a Japan that was recreating itself as a society that prized harmony, hard work and conformity over anarchy, violence and individualism. *Yojimbo* pitted an honourable albeit violent veteran against a psychopathic *yakuza* and, in conjunction with the three modern noir films Kurosawa made, imagined a heroic role for Japan's silenced war veterans,[39] who had come to know only too well that it was tough being a man.

Acknowledgements

I am grateful to Chi-Yun Shin and Mark Gallagher for their patience; to Richard Fardon who asked me what 'evasive myths' actually meant; to Kit Davis for listening to my theories on the animal symbolism in *Yojimbo*; to Isolde Standish and Laura Treglia, who know so much more about Japanese heroes; and to David Gellner, my ever patient proofreader. All the views expressed and any errors are entirely my own.

Notes

1 In Japanese the respective titles are: *Nora Inu*, *Warui yatsu hodo Yoko Nemuru* (lit. 'The worse you are the better you sleep', although here 'sleep' could be slang for 'die') and *Tengoku to Jigoku* (lit. 'Heaven and Hell').

2 There is a debate about which Hammett novel is the basis of *Yojimbo*; see Barra, Allen, 'From "Red Harvest" to "Deadwood"', *Salon.com*, 28 February 2005, <http://dir.salon.com/story/books/feature/2005/02/28/hammett/index.htm>, accessed 14 April 2013. I remain convinced that Dashiell Hammett's *Red Harvest* (New York: Vintage Books, 2003 [1929]) is the source for the film.

3 See Baskett, Michael, *The Attractive Empire: Transnational Film Culture in Imperial Japan* (Honolulu: University of Hawaii Press, 2008).

4 See Silverberg, Miriam, *Erotic Grotesque Nonsense: The Mass Culture of Japanese Modern Times* (Berkeley: University of California Press, 2009).

5 See Sorensen, Lars-Martin, *Censorship of Japanese Films During the U.S. Occupation of Japan: The Cases of Yasujiro Ozu and Akira Kurosawa* (London: Edwin Mellen Press, 2009).

6 Standish, Isolde, *Myth and Masculinity in the Japanese Cinema: Towards a Political Reading of the Tragic Hero* (London: Curzon, 2000).

7 See Naremore, James, *More Than Night: Film Noir in Its Contexts* (Berkeley: University of California Press, 1998), p. 227.

8 See Biesen, Sheri Chinen, *Blackout: World War II and the Origins of Film Noir* (Baltimore: Johns Hopkins University Press, 2005).

9 See Schrader, Paul, 'Notes on *Film Noir*', in Alain Silver and James Ursini (eds), *Film Noir Reader* (Pompton Plains, NJ: Limelight Editions, 1996), pp. 54–56.
10 See Gluck, Carol, 'The Past in the Present', in Andrew Gordon (ed.), *Postwar Japan as History* (Berkeley: University of California Press: 1993), pp. 64–95.
11 See Desser, David, '*Ikiru*: Narration as Moral Act', in Arthur Nolletti Jr and David Desser (eds), *Reframing Japanese Cinema: Authorship, Genre, History* (Bloomington: Indiana University Press, 1992), pp. 56–68.
12 The consequences of Japan not being allowed a discourse of suffering, despite it being the only nation to have suffered an atomic bomb attack, is examined in Igarashi, Yoshikuni, *Bodies of Memory: Narratives of War in Postwar Japanese Culture, 1945–1970* (Princeton: Princeton University Press, 2000).
13 Wood, Robin, 'Return of the Repressed', *Film Comment* 14.4 (1978), pp. 25–32.
14 See Grossman, Dave, *On Killing* (New York: Back Bay Books, 1996).
15 Skal, David J., 'I Used to Know Your Daddy: The Horrors of War, Part 2', in Skal, *The Monster Show: A Cultural History of Horror* (New York: Faber & Faber, 1993), pp. 211–228.
16 To coin the concept of evasive myth, I have reworked the term 'mythic evasions' from Borde, Raymond and Étienne Chaumeton, 'Towards a Definition of *Film Noir*', in Alain Silver and James Ursini (eds), *Film Noir Reader* (Pompton Plains, NJ: Limelight Editions, 1996), p. 18. I define evasive myth as escapism masquerading as unflinching realism; see Martinez, Dolores, 'Politics and the Olympic Film Documentary', *Sport in Society* 12.6 (2009), p. 820.
17 Tyler, Parker, *Magic and Myth of the Movies* (London: Secker & Warburg, 1971), see pp. 167–168, 233–234.
18 See Shay, Jonathan, *Achilles in Vietnam: Combat Trauma and the Undoing of Character* (New York: Simon & Schuster, 1995).
19 See Yoshimoto, Mitsuhiro, *Kurosawa: Film Studies and Japanese Cinema* (Durham: Duke University Press, 2000), pp. 171–172.
20 *High and Low* is based on Ed McBain's *King's Ransom* (New York: Signet, 1975 [1959]).
21 Desser, '*Ikiru*', p. 59.
22 See Cazdyn, Eric, 'The Ends of Adaptation', in James Quandt (ed.), *Kon Ichikawa* (Toronto: Toronto Film Festival Group, 2001), pp. 221–235.
23 Krutnik, Frank, *In a Lonely Street: Film Noir Genre, Masculinity* (London: Routledge, 1991), p. xiii.
24 Houseman, John, 'Today's Hero: A Review', in *Hollywood Quarterly* 2.2 (1947), pp. 161–163.
25 See Yoshimoto, *Kurosawa*, p. 314.
26 See Karatsu, Rie, 'Between Comedy and Kitsch: Kitano's *Zatoichi* and Kurosawa's Traditions of "Jidaigeki" Comedies', *Scope: An Online Journal of*

Film and Television Studies 6 (October 2006), <http://www.scope.nottingham.ac.uk/article.php?id=185&issue=6>, accessed 14 April 2013.

27 Chandler, Raymond. 'The Simple Art of Murder', in *The Atlantic Monthly* (November 1944), pp. 53–59.

28 See Yoshimoto, *Kurosawa*, p. 289.

29 Galbraith, Stuart, *The Emperor and the Wolf* (New York: Faber & Faber, 2000), p. 313.

30 See Martinez, Dolores, *Remaking Kurosawa: Translations and Permutations in Global Cinema* (New York: Palgrave Macmillan, 2009), pp. 143–147.

31 Richie, Donald, *The Films of Akira Kurosawa*, with additional material by Joan Mellen, 3rd ed. (Berkeley: University of California Press 1996), pp. 149–150. In traditional Japan, anyone could be a *kami* (deity), albeit briefly; thus strangers might be just as human as you or me, but also could possess the qualities of a deity, see Yoshida, Tiego, 'The Stranger as God', in *Ethnography* 20 (1981), pp. 87–89.

32 Anne Nesbet defines this concept by noting that Eisenstein 'mined Hegel, Engels, Lenin, Freud (and Stalin's speeches, too) for their figures, their images, which he then threw into sometimes blasphemous conjunction with images borrowed from literature, folklore, popular culture and myth'; Nesbet, *Savage Junctures: Sergei Eisenstein and the Shape of Thinking* (New York: Palgrave Macmillan, 2003), p. 2. In the case of *Yojimbo*, it is not the world of Marxist ideology that is being mined for Kurosawa's conjunctions, but rather the discourses of capitalism and of modern forms of Japanese masculinity.

33 Surrealism is an aspect of the noir genre not normally discussed, although James Naremore points out that it was the French surrealists who often critiqued and discussed early film noir; Naremore, *More Than Night*, pp. 17–18.

34 For an analysis of Kurosawa's intertexuality see Goodwin, James, *Akira Kurosawa and Intertextual Cinema* (Baltimore: Johns Hopkins University Press, 1994).

35 Prince, Stephen, *The Warrior's Camera* (Princeton: Princeton University Press, 1991), p. 62.

36 Stephen Prince quotes Kurosawa on this point: Prince, *The Warrior's Camera*, p. 224. *Yojimbo* also highlights an aspect of film noir that is not generally noted: the hero often survives situations that most human beings would not. Noir protagonists anticipate the action hero of the 1970s onwards, but no one more so than Sanjuro, whose wry sense of humour resonated with Hammett's and Chandler's own work, as well as inspiring an entire career for Clint Eastwood.

37 Donald Richie quotes Kurosawa on this subject: 'Originally this was a story by Shugoto Yamamoto', entitled '*Nichinichi Hei-an*' (Peaceful Days); Richie, *The Films of Akira Kurosawa*, p. 156. Kurosawa had begun an adaptation of the story before making *Yojimbo*, and then dramatically altered the

screenplay to cash in on the success of the first film and to bring back the character Sanjuro.

38 Miyao, Daisuke, 'Dark Visions of Japanese Film Noir: Suzuki Seijin's *Branded to Kill*', in Alastair Philips and Julian Stringer (eds), *Japanese Cinema: Texts and Contexts* (Abingdon: Routledge, 2007), p. 194.

39 See Frühstück, Sabine, *Uneasy Warriors: Gender, Memory, and Popular Culture in the Japanese Army* (Berkeley: University of California Press, 2007) and Seaton, Philip A., *Japan's Contested War Memories: The 'Memory Rifts' in Historical Consciousness of World War II* (London: Routledge, 2007) for a discussion of these issues.

Chapter 3

The Japanese Los Angeles of *The Crimson Kimono* and *Brother*

Suzanne Arakawa

Samuel Fuller's *The Crimson Kimono* (1959) and Takeshi Kitano's *Brother* (2000) place protagonists of Japanese descent in the quintessential film noir city of Los Angeles. These films challenge depictions of the traditionally aestheticized and racialized Asian urban enclave in Hollywood noir mysteries. Fuller's post-Korean War film and Kitano's post-1990s Japanese bubble-economy film feature downtown Los Angeles' Little Tokyo district as a community space. Both films depict Little Tokyo as a locale where American and Japanese criminality meet. These locations draw attention to both Japanese-American and Japanese cultural traditions while exploiting the popular American narrative opposition of official and outlaw bodies. As a result, the male bodies framed in these films affect and are affected by the *mise-en-scène* of the Little Tokyo space; they are deployed in shots that rely on crime and gangster-film genre and cinematic noir conventions to increase audiences' attention while they ingest the levelled critique against racism in the United States. Although released over 40 years apart, both films resist the Hollywood trope of inscrutability by not representing Japanese and Japanese-American male bodies as objects for pleasure and consumption. The films instead use these bodies to illustrate each filmmaker's vision of multiculturalism, to combat social injustice, and ultimately, to facilitate apt critique of each film's particular socio-economic moment.

At first glance, *Brother* demonstrates what some critics, most notably Vivian Sobchack, have termed an empty strategy of 'aestheticization of violence'.[1] *Brother* highlights explosive violence enacted against Japanese men wounded or killed in gang battles. *The Crimson Kimono* uses violence less for aesthetic appeal than for critical commentary; however, both films stress the symbolic meanings of violence waged against Japanese male bodies. Moreover, in traditional noir-style shots in *The Crimson Kimono*, Japanese and American male bodies are contrastingly shown as either chaotic or purposeful as they traverse the Little Tokyo district. Both films highlight violence against the official and criminal bodies in Little Tokyo spaces, while also using or referencing film noir and gangster-film conventions. The films position Japanese and American official and outlaw heroes in strategic relation to the Little Tokyo space, resulting in the resuscitation of a Little Tokyo site – ordinarily associated with mysteriousness and connected to unspeakable crimes – as a place that suggests more nuanced associations. By destabilizing this trope of inscrutability, the two works challenge traditional Hollywood cinematic strategies.

In both films, the Japanese-American and Japanese national male bodies are empowered through noir and neo-noir filmic turns. *The Crimson Kimono*'s noir-style cinematography showcases downtown LA's Little Tokyo space, reflecting the main character's interiority and dramatizing his anxieties. *Brother*, on the other hand, does not employ traditional noir shots and lighting. It refigures the 'inscrutable Asian' stereotype by revamping noir's manner and mode. *Brother* can be framed as a neo-noir, a contemporary reworking of classical noir elements often directed toward social critique. Tom Conley explains the difference between noir and neo-noir, hypothesizing that classical noir is '[d]ark in tone (if not always chiaroscuro in lighting), twisted in vision (if not always in framing), urban in sensibility (if not always in location), impotently angry and disillusioned in spirit (if not always in execution)'.[2] Following the 1940s–1950s heyday of film noir, a revised neo-noir emerged in the 1960s and 1970s, gaining visibility particularly in 1990s films that, continues Conley, revived this 'rubric' of 'defining traits of film noir' but included a much 'stronger critical dimension'.[3] Fittingly, across historical periods, noir and neo-noir both offer filmmakers resources to address social and political inequities. Although *The Crimson Kimono* and *Brother* are both anti-racist projects that beneficially challenge the inscrutability stereotype, each film engages with noir differently. *The Crimson Kimono*'s location shots render a complex Japanese-American character's interiority. *Brother*, on the other hand, subverts traditional noir expectations, diminishes the depictions of its own traditional film noir location choices, and instead highlights wounded Japanese male bodies to call attention to themes of gang fealty over self-serving greed.

This chapter focuses on how an American and a Japanese filmmaker have utilized the crime genre to deploy Japanese-American and Japanese national male bodies in order to address US racism. However, *The Crimson Kimono* exhorts the American dream as an untainted, almost salvific solution. In contrast, *Brother* indirectly critiques effects of post-1971 capitalism on the erosion of gang loyalty. I consider how the male Japanese-American characters wrestle with the intoxicating myth of the American dream after the Korean War and after an economic collapse in Japan. I address how these crime-genre films deploy downtown Los Angeles and Little Tokyo spaces but veer from traditional Hollywood conventions through strategically connecting Japanese and Japanese-American male characters with these spaces. Ultimately, this chapter examines how outlaw and official Japanese-American and Japanese national male bodies, framed within non-touristic shots of the Little Tokyo district and downtown Los Angeles spaces, not only help to highlight character development but also undergird each film's anti-racist themes.

The Trope of Inscrutability in Hollywood Noir: Urban Asians in Ethnic Enclaves

David Bordwell and Kristin Thompson explain that one of the tenets of the Hollywood studio style is to promote 'a fundamental emotional appeal that transcends class and nation' while striving 'to conceal its artifice through techniques of continuity and "invisible" storytelling';[4] this style tries to create a 'realistic' and seamless product for audience consumption. This dominant style tends to encourage the creation of universalized products that appeal to mainstream audiences because they transcend class and nation, while at the same time promoting a white-centred, patriarchal fantasy.[5] The 1930s Mr Moto and 1920s–1940s Charlie Chan film series legitimized so-called 'yellowface' acting (i.e. white actors playing Asian roles, as with Peter Lorre in the former series, and Warner Oland and Sidney Toler in the latter) as well as normalizing the inscrutable Asian as exotic background figure or wily antagonist. Further, once Asian bodies and sites become essentialized as inscrutable, identity becomes hardened and fixed, stripped of its history and subjectivity.

In the classical era of the 1930s to 1950s, the dominant Hollywood style for the most part created monolithic identities in the name of entertaining the masses, and at the expense of history and of progressive cultural and race relations.[6] By the 1960s and 1970s, as films broke away from the strictures of the Production Code, we see even more sophisticated renderings of the detective; however, these renderings still often come at the expense of the racial 'Other'. For example, Asian male 'heroes' continued to be played by white actors in yellowface and were shown as containable and highly assimilable. Given this situation, whenever Oriental themes are invoked in classical-era films, the trope of Chinatown's inscrutable spectacle again emerges. Though some minor films, including silent-era works such as *The House Without a Key* (1926) and *The Chinese Parrot* (1927), avoid yellowface and use Japanese actors as detectives, the casting of Asians in these lead roles was not subsequently reproduced with any urgency.

In post-classical Hollywood, numerous notable films continue to promote the trope of the inscrutable, racialized 'Other'. One is the critically acclaimed *Chinatown* (1974). Although Roman Polanski's neo-noir deconstructs the myth of the detective who can solve all mysteries and restore order in the end, the film problematically furthers the myth of Oriental inscrutability. Despite the film's title, Chinatown itself is mainly referred to in the film metaphorically and shown only once, rather enigmatically, in the end. Race is invoked but is neither narratively nor visually foregrounded. Chinatown as a place is almost erased from the film; it exists predominantly merely as a trope or metaphor for irresolvable mystery. The following decade, Ridley Scott's *Blade Runner* (1982) depicts a claustrophobic downtown Los Angeles, divided into hierarchical vertical spaces, the lowest sector a grimy, gritty, Orientalized spectacle. A number of critics, Robin Wood in particular, argue that the film explicitly critiques capitalistic greed, for those who suffer are those without economic power – the Asians, the skin-jobs, the squalid ethnicized masses. Even as *Blade Runner* critiques commercialism and exploitation, its representation strategies undermine this critique; as Lisa Lowe points out, its 'aesthetic display erases the awareness of the material condition'.[7] The film's representation does not probe, in Lowe's terms, 'the material differentiations of heterogeneous and unequal racial, ethnic, and immigrant communities in Los Angeles'.[8] Thus, while *Blade Runner* offers an economic critique of sorts, its iconography of neon lights, billboards and quaint dragon-noodle bar elides connection to any socio-historical conditions in which these objects can be contextually grounded.

Norman Klein argues that *Blade Runner*'s aesthetics represent nostalgia in architecture, particularly nostalgia for a fantasy tourist downtown. Klein explains the popularity of the film's noodle-bar scene as a result of this desire to:

> aestheticize poverty; not to look like a safe white boulevard, but rather like an explosive Lower East Side from the twenties, elbow to elbow. Americans, or at least Angelinos, want that old community sensation back, now that the density in L.A. must grow, particularly given that the immigrant population is expanding massively.[9]

Klein calls into question this aesthetic, identifying it as 'primarily a nostalgia machine, even when the subject is the future'.[10] Although Klein admits a fondness for noir, he exposes the limitations of noir conventions in films:

> it pits the white, usually Protestant, shamus against a world that is utterly transient, as if no poor communities exist except as a hangout for crooks and addicts. What results is a pose really; it distracts the memory away from community life as it existed inside the city. It is the dark side of tourism, a roller-coaster ride through 'mean' streets (often poor neighborhoods).[11]

Blade Runner exposes the corruption of capitalism, but this impulse is also undercut by the emphasis on the aestheticized, ethnicized noir settings. The dystopic future of *Blade Runner* becomes merely a tourist attraction. While *Blade Runner* incorporates a social critique of exploitative capitalist practices, it also does little to revise Hollywood detective films' depiction of Asian enclaves as unknowable. In contrast, both *The Crimson Kimono* and *Brother* revise past cinematic depictions of these enclaves. Using noir-inspired cinematography, they destabilize the trope of inscrutability. Strategically placed in these mysterious enclaves, the Japanese and Japanese-American male body normally depicted as inscrutable makes these spaces intelligible.

The Contextualization of *The Crimson Kimono*'s Little Tokyo

The Crimson Kimono combines a murder investigation with an interracial romance, a brave move for its time. Police detective partners (and best friends since shared combat duty during the Korean War) Nisei Detective Joe Kojaku (James Shigeta) and Detective Sergeant Charlie Bancroft

(Glenn Corbett) fall in love with the same woman, a Caucasian artist named Christine (or Chris) Downs (Victoria Shaw), who becomes an integral witness in their current murder case. The police detectives are investigating the murder of a red-light-district stripper with the stage name of Sugar Torch who had plans to exploit aspects of Japanese geisha, samurai and judo subcultures in an onstage burlesque routine. The film's premise is that this audacity, as well as Sugar's consultations with experts in Japanese culture, gets her killed. The detectives must investigate the Little Tokyo cultural community (which in the film includes depictions of decorative arts, martial arts and performance arts) as well as Skid Row to find clues. *The Crimson Kimono*, at first glance, appears to catalogue an actual LA Asian enclave: downtown LA's Little Tokyo or Japantown. Little Tokyo receives a number of establishing shots, shots that exist not only for aesthetic and expository purposes but also to map the area's historical and cross-cultural architectural monuments, storefronts and signs. These images show that Little Tokyo contains a unique blend of Japanese and American influences.[12] Before the film's late-1950s production, 'Little Tokyo's shrinking population was reduced further in the early 1950s when construction of the police administration building (Parker Center) destroyed housing for nearly 1000 people and one-fourth of the district's commercial frontage.'[13] The shots of Parker Center in the film highlight a benign panoptic authority of the civic centre in relation to this district enclave. *The Crimson Kimono*'s Little Tokyo does not show evidence of civic battles over the space. Instead, the shots of Little Tokyo depict a robust community space bordered by the Los Angeles Police Department and City Hall.

Within Little Tokyo, Buddhist priests and Catholic nuns are shown as well as Japanese cultural rituals, including judo and *ningyo* (Japanese doll) demonstrations. These mapping shots of historically and culturally iconographic Japanese-American places visually underscore Joe Kojaku's legitimate place as a US citizen, police detective and Korean War veteran rightfully pursuing the American dream. Furthermore, strategic shots of this Little Tokyo district also avoid presenting this enclave as only an exotic tourist space. As the investigation heats up, Joe Kojaku seeks out the help of George Yoshinaga and finds him in the nearby Boyle Heights' Evergreen Cemetery visiting the grave of his son, a casualty of the Korean War. Here a crane shot displays the breadth and height of the World War II Nisei Veterans' Memorial, which is shown as a sizeable monument. The next sequence of shots provides close-ups of the memorial inscriptions that flank each side of the monument. These inscriptions are material reminders of the Nisei soldiers who fought in the European campaign. The camera then slowly pulls back and upward. The crane shot ends with a medium-long shot of the graves surrounding the memorial, indicating the number of loyal Nisei soldiers who died fighting for a country that had stripped them of their constitutional rights. A few frames later, we see a two-shot of Yoshinaga at the headstone of his son, who died a Private First Class during the Korean War and was posthumously awarded the Congressional Medal of Honor. These establishing and mobile shots document the cemetery, long known to the Japanese-American community as generations of LA-area Japanese-Americans are buried there, and they place the sacrifices of Japanese-American soldiers in the wider context of American history.

With just these few mapping scenes of monuments and spaces, *The Crimson Kimono* links Japanese America and the Little Tokyo district to US patriotism and sacrifice, reinforcing post-World War II national myths along with an anti-racist message of inclusion. Inscrutability in space, place and body becomes dismantled. A subsequent scene further demonstrates the breadth of Little Tokyo and its spatial relationship with City Hall. The scene employs extensive following, tracking and panning shots of Joe and Yoshinaga as they traverse the streets of Little Tokyo in search of a suspect. The film moves from medium shots of the Koyasan Buddhist Temple front, where earlier Yoshinaga attends a Buddhist service for his son, to long shots including the Los Angeles Police Department's Administrative Headquarters, Parker Center, City Hall, and even the LA Cathedral in the distant background. That these buildings share the same panning and tracking shots with the Little Tokyo buildings shows Little Tokyo's connection to the larger city, bordered by the LAPD and city-government buildings. Many of the shots with Joe and Yoshinaga in Little Tokyo also include storefront-window mirror shots where the City Hall or Parker Center buildings appear as backdrops. In subsequent shots, signs for the Japanese-American Koyasan Boy Scouts troop and military recruitment as well as posters advertising the joint Kendo match involving the LAPD are placed adjacent to banners advertising the Nisei Week Festival and the fictional Koga Rice Cake Factory. The juxtaposition of these elements emphasizes the Japanese-American community's patriotism. These sequences indicate the film's effort to counter any lingering negative post-World War II public opinion of Japanese-Americans and their ability to be assimilated into the dominant culture.

In *The Crimson Kimono*, touches of noir visual motifs punctuate certain frames, most notably to reveal the main character, Joe Kojaku. This linkage of the Japanese-American male character with a culturally resonant space dismantles the Hollywood inscrutability trope. Joe's closeness to the

Japanese-American community allows the crime to be solved and offers the remarkable representation in a Hollywood detective or crime film of a well-rounded Japanese-American male character with agency. *The Crimson Kimono*'s handful of night-for-night shots in Little Tokyo symbolizes not only when crimes happen but also the emotional darkness associated with these transgressions. J. A. Place and L. S. Peterson explain that most non-noir night scenes were shot 'day-for-night'.[14] Accordingly, night-for-night scenes were 'night scenes actually shot at night' and required:

> that artificial light sources be brought in to illuminate each area of light seen in the frame. The effect produced is one of the highest contrast, the sky rendered jet black, as opposed to the grey sky of day-for-night. Although night-for-night becomes quite a bit more costly and time-consuming to shoot than day-for-night, nearly every *film noir*, even of the cheapest 'B' variety, used night-for-night extensively as an integral component of the *noir* look.[15]

Many of the true exterior shots in *The Crimson Kimono*, mainly day shots but a number at night, with the exception of the murder on Main Street, are of the Little Tokyo area. In addition, while cinematographer Sam Leavitt makes use of the inky blackness of the sky, the way he lights the characters,

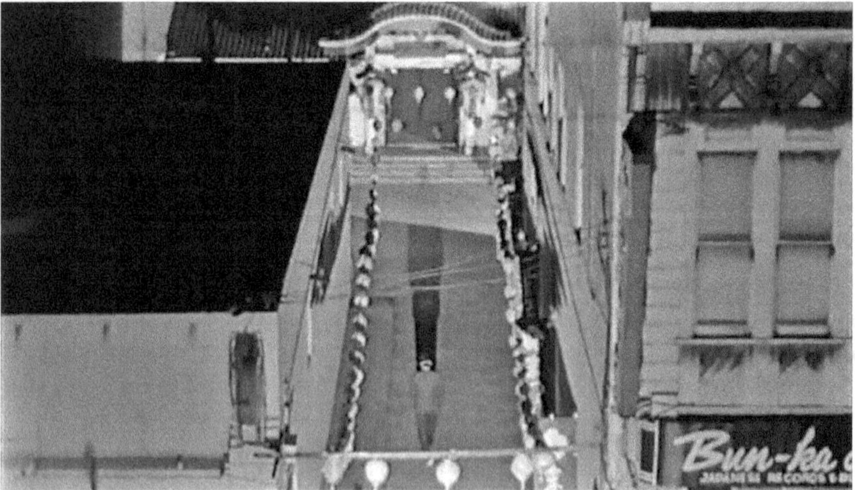

Figure 3.1 In *The Crimson Kimono*, a stylized nighttime shot of Joe Kojaku and his extended shadow

especially Joe Kojaku, speaks to a strategic deployment of light and shadows to emphasize angst. As the mystery deepens, the shots showing Joe in relation to the Little Tokyo space become more distorted, at times claustrophobic, all in keeping with a noir sensibility. For example, about midway through the film, one scene employs a stylized nighttime shot of a lone figure, apparently Joe Kojaku. His lengthy shadow stretches in exaggerated fashion across a short corridor as he walks toward the Koyasan temple, presumably to receive some relief from his emotional burdens.

In the scenes where Joe's partner, Charlie Bancroft, visits his city domain, the lower-class mission district, we see a nondescript, economically depressed area. In fact, many of the shots outside the actual Little Tokyo district that highlight the seedier parts of town are studio shots. In these, the film utilizes unnerving 'choker' close-ups to indicate the desperate and depressed nature of the lower-class environment, thus managing to represent the space negatively without actually showing it.[16] In showing Charlie interacting with lower-class people in his investigations, *The Crimson Kimono* uses these types of shots to jar audiences. During these quests, Charlie does not receive the same noir-style spatial treatment as Joe and thus appears less connected and integral to his surroundings. The key, as I will argue further, is for the Japanese-American male character to appear more integrated into this Little Tokyo space. Charlie does not have to appear as connected to place, since he is already 'marked' as a white American male. In addition to showing his skills as a pianist in one scene he shares with Chris, the Japanese-American Joe must also appear assimilable yet simultaneously emotionally complex to appeal to the white female artist love interest in the film. While the noirish, stylized shots in *The Crimson Kimono* deepen Joe's characterization, aspects of noir technique also further the film's pro-interracial romance theme. At this point, we may question whether Fuller merely decided to create a genre film and plugged in the character's feelings of angst over his perceived guilt and racial inferiority because angst served the requirements of genre. Conversely, we could argue that the film includes genre elements to make palatable an anti-racist theme, male-bonding discourse and diatribes about the nature of women and art. According to David Cochran, Joe fruitfully experiences this absurdity and, I would argue, becomes one of the most complex Japanese-American male characters developed in Hollywood film to date.[17]

The combination of noir shots in the closing scene creates a satisfying conclusion to Joe Kojaku's arc and story. His realization at the end of the film that his darker side, the side that allowed him to think that his white best friend and war buddy had looked at him with abject racist hatred rather than with a 'normal red-blooded American male jealousy', is explained away by the solving of the external mystery. The murderer confesses in the end that her motive for killing, her extreme jealousy, was all in her 'mind'. Upon hearing her confession, Joe experiences an epiphany about his own irrational emotions. He had attributed his detective partner's comments to racism rather than normal male jealousy over a woman. The chase after Roma, the killer, while she races through the Nisei Week parade in full swing, involves tracking shots and periodic close-ups of those from the parade wearing traditional Japanese masks, pushing into the frame. The film's strategic uses of these noir shots and camera movements depict the mind-set of a paranoid killer as well as the stultifying claustrophobia Joe feels as a Nisei who is not attracted to a more culturally traditional Japanese-American beauty queen from Gardena but to a lovely Caucasian artist. According to Place and Peterson, while classical noir films tend to use elaborate tracking shots sparingly due to costs,

> What moving shots that were made seem to have been carefully considered and often tied very directly to the emotions of the characters. Typical is the shot in which the camera tracks backward before a running man, at once involving the audience in the movement and excitement of the chase, recording the terror on the character's face; and looking over his shoulder at the forces, visible or not, which are pursuing him.[18]

In this climactic chase scene, it is Joe who closely follows the female killer, Roma, her anxiety and fear made obvious by means of shots that emphasize her facial expressions and contorted body as she runs through the ongoing Nisei Week parade to get away. When Roma is felled by a shot from Joe's gun, she then concedes to him that she was wrong to think that stripper Sugar Torch was trying to steal her 'boyfriend'. This sweating, mentally unseated woman represents the illogic in Joe's mind about his racially paranoid feelings. The cutaway shot to his expression when he arrives at this understanding deflates the suspenseful build-up of noir shots from earlier, indicating his descent into the darkness of his own tortured mind-set. In the end, Joe recognizes that as a Japanese-American man in a post-Korean War moment, he has every right to his definition of the American Dream: a successful career in the Los Angeles Police Department and the girl of his dreams, a beautiful, educated, artistic white woman.

Altogether, the film reserves use of highly expressive noir shots mainly to complicate the narrative and Joe's character development, and the mobile shots create another character working with and against Joe. Unlike Mr Moto of the 1930s, who is depicted as an accented Japanese 'American', where particular lighting and shots depict him as having a dark and wily side to counter his polite, passive, gentlemanly side, Joe Kojaku instead represents a complex Asian ethnic male. As a result, the Japanese-American male image does not circulate here merely for consumption. Shigeta's Joe Kojaku is represented as a good citizen who is at war with himself, not just depicted as a stereotypically inscrutable Asian.

Seeing Los Angeles through *Yakuza* Eyes in *Brother*

Brother, Japanese director Takeshi Kitano's first international co-production (a joint Japanese/British/American project), entwines the life of an exiled Japanese *yakuza*, Aniki (Kitano), with young US would-be gangsters who enter into an ultimately doomed turf war against other ethnically segregated US gangs in and around downtown Los Angeles. This cross-cultural gang's success at grabbing territories eventually pits them against the established juggernaut power, the Mafia, which wants half of Aniki's gang's resources and profits. *Brother* draws attention to the late twentieth-century incarnation of US racism through the deployment of Japanese criminal bodies, and posits that the bodies that have the most authenticity are shown in death as loyal to a masculine code. Customary noir locations, lighting and editing need not be utilized to rework an entrenched Asian inscrutability trope in Hollywood noirs, especially as linked to an Asian enclave. *Brother* instead connects its Asian enclave to a nuanced Japanese criminal masculinity.

In *Brother*, Aniki and his gang's embodied relationships to the geographical space of downtown Los Angeles' Little Tokyo area are differentiated from the pre- and post-World War II depiction of downtown LA spaces in Hollywood noir films. The film's use of the downtown Los Angeles backdrop subverts the old Hollywood fantasy trope of inscrutability. In one scene, a subtle homage is paid to the Japanese-American National History Museum (a project for which Japanese-Americans fought hard and that came to fruition in the late 1990s) with both interior and exterior shots of the older church side of the museum. That the film pays homage to this building is telling. In a few key scenes, Aniki critiques the Japanese-American and naturalized Japanese business owners as having fully bought into the capitalist myth of the American Dream. In *Brother*, this geographic location and the Japanese-American National Museum's historic building serve as sites that harbour transplanted *yakuza*, a 'natural' place for Aniki's Japanese criminal rivals to use as their headquarters. The film highlights one wide crane shot of Aniki's limousine exiting Little Tokyo on historic First Street, the main thoroughfare that reveals the mixture of Japanese-American and Japanese national businesses bordering Parker Center and City Hall. This shot comes after viewers have witnessed Kato (Aniki's *yakuza* lieutenant in Japan who has followed his beloved Aniki to the United States, played by Susumu Terajima) shooting himself in the head, sacrificing his life so that rival *yakuza* Shirase's promise to merge his gang with Aniki's can be fulfilled. In this pivotal Little Tokyo scene, Kato's loyalty to Aniki and the greater establishment of Aniki's power due to Kato's sacrifice complicate the film's thematic emphasis on Aniki's inscrutability and his explosive rage whenever rival gang members use the word 'Jap'.

Earlier in the film, we see Aniki has set up his own Los Angeles headquarters, not in Little Tokyo, but in a building near the Hotel Cecil and Nishiki Sushi Restaurant, close to downtown Los Angeles, residing in an area also known for its own 1920s Art Deco history. One notable scene romantically accentuates the loftiness of Aniki's goal and foreshadows the gang's eventual downfall. A shock cut occurs from the previous interior scene, with a close-up of the silent and 'inscrutable' Aniki wearing sunglasses cutting to a daytime long shot of Japanese gangsters on the roof of the building in which they plan to set up their criminal headquarters, above the fray of the business streets below. This scene's shots alternate between overhead crane shots of the men on the roof and shots with the camera positioned in the opposite office building, the camera lens canted slightly upwards at the men; the majority of the shots are medium-full ones of Kato and Aniki. The film cuts to a medium close-up shot of Kato about to fly a paper aeroplane off the roof. As soon as Kato releases the aeroplane, the camera maintains a medium tight shot on it as it slowly descends, spiralling downward. This continuous tracking shot foreshadows the doomed fate of this group and its leaders, and the non-diegetic strains of string and wind instruments romanticize their warrior-criminal masculinity. This elaborately shot scene symbolizes this group's particular strength, a combination of inclusiveness and a fealty code that bests any racist underworld gang's. A mono-ethnic gang's entrenched power is no match for Aniki's new multicultural brood of Japanese, African-American, Hispanic and white gangsters in the United States, unless the entrenched power's roots are as insidious as the Italian-American Mafia's. *Brother*'s multicultural statement appears both transgressive and yet simplistic, but the film's additional declarations about race in the United States become further complicated by its depictions of both criminal and working-class Japanese-Americans.

Brother's revision of noir's blackness or darkness motifs additionally reflects neo-noir stylistic choices. In 'Noir by Noirs: Toward a New Realism in Black Cinema', Manthia Diawara observes that, in classical noir films, blackness is symbolically associated with questionable moral behaviour.[19] These corrupt or tainted individuals, who are usually 'women, bad guys, and detectives' in film noir, become 'black' as a result of their unethical behaviour, having occupied 'indeterminate and monstrous spaces such as whiteness traditionally reserves for blackness in our culture'.[20] In *Brother*, 'blackness' is profitably grafted onto the Japanese *yakuza* body. This noir sensibility does not come from the traditional shadowing effects, as most of the exterior scenes are brightly lit. The *yakuza* clan members all wear dark shirts and suits. This costume choice emphasizes the darkness that punishes the light. The bodies clothed in black represent the ritualized and at times aestheticized violence. Also, the *yakuza* darkness contrasts with the lightness of the daytime *mise-en-scène*. For example, the Italian-American Mafia characters are often depicted in well-lit scenes, wearing light-coloured clothing. The Mafia, who the film depict as racist, want either to destroy or steal from the Japanese *yakuza* and its own US dual-nationality, insider-outsider, multiethnic gangster crew. After Aniki's crew incurs the wrath of the Italian-American Mafia because they refuse to give over half of their operations, they also retaliate against some Mafia killings, and Aniki's men are all eventually gunned down, sacrificed in the gang war.

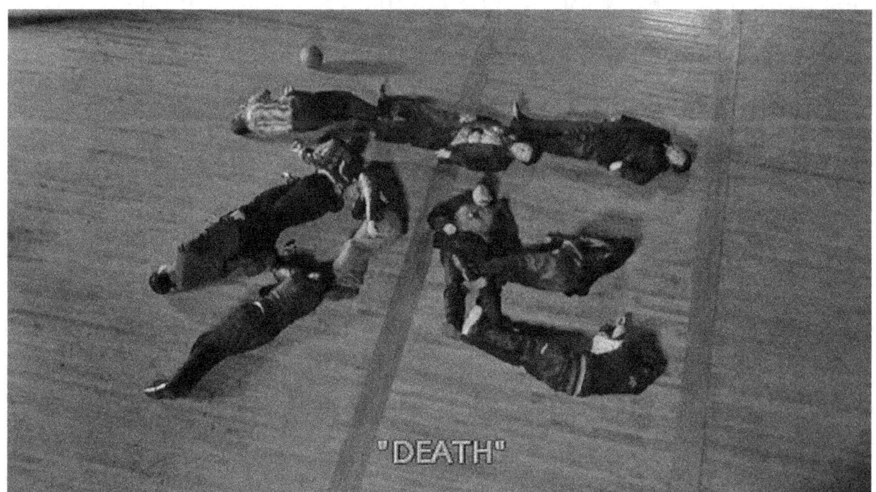

Figure 3.2 In *Brother*, Aniki's dead gang members' bodies forming the Kanji 'Death'

Though shown as defeated, they are ennobled in their deaths. Their deaths not only represent loss, thus critiquing racist Mafia actions, but also give them legitimacy as criminals who defy the law. In the second half of the film, Kitano shows the dead Japanese *yakuza* bodies alongside their dead US compatriots after each battle against the Mafia has been fought. In one scene in the loft toward the end of the film, Kitano uses an overhead shot of dead *yakuza* on the headquarters floor, their bodies forming the Kanji character meaning 'death'. Hence, their dark-clothed corpses convey meaning both iconically and in a calligraphic fashion. Framed in this repose, these bodies depict a truth, as well as writer-director Kitano's playfulness, even when in narrative terms, all is lost.

Brother uses Japanese male bodies in ways that defy Hollywood genre conventions and provide the foundation for Kitano's social critique. This sacrifice of *yakuza* bodies confers validity onto them, and they are marked in violence and in death as having proven a code of loyalty. The most extreme example of this loyalty is shown when Aniki's lieutenant, Kato, wagers his own life to obtain for Aniki a merger with another established Japanese *yakuza*, Shirase, and his gang based in Little Tokyo. The fate of these *yakuza* leads to Aniki's tragic downfall. Although he redeems himself in the end, Aniki's tribe has been wiped out, and the dark masculine shadow they cast over the encroaching Mafia is eclipsed. The 'war' Aniki fights is in the East as well as the West, and Aniki and his gang for the time being are the antidote to ruthless greed.

The ending employs a twist on the chaotic, psychopathic gangster being killed by greater forces. The film punctuates its critique of racism and greed with the concluding scenes involving Aniki's demise outside Los Angeles, in the Inland Empire's Palmdale desert at an off-Route 66 café and motel advertising 'Homestyle Cooking', an establishment owned by an elderly Japanese-American man who appears not to have left the desert since the internment. At one point, while waiting inside the café, Aniki smiles at the elderly owner, who then asks Aniki in Japanese, 'Are you Japanese?' and 'Are you here on business?' When Aniki does not reply but merely smiles, the proprietor frowns and comments: 'You Japanese sure are inscrutable.' The owner, assimilated into American culture and living his desert 'dream' of being a small-business owner, shows, with his 'inscrutable' comment, his own displaced identity within the system. Having learned his lesson from the internment, the owner has assimilated into American culture, and his attitude toward Aniki reflects a slightly disparaging, out-of-touch understanding of Aniki's brand of Japanese masculinity. Aniki apologizes before giving the owner cash for the damages Aniki knows will be inflicted on the space from the automatic machine guns the Mafia will fire on him once he exits the café. Aniki waits for the Mafia to arrive at the roadside diner, because he wants to face death squarely and refuses to be caught running away like a coward. Aniki sacrifices himself, but not to engineer a glorious, sensationalized death. He wants to save his African-American protégé, Denny (Omar Epps), the last man standing from Aniki's US tribe, who will be left to tell the tale. Aniki sacrifices himself to the Mafia after having made them believe that he has killed Denny nearby in the desert, thus giving Denny enough time to flee LA via Route 66 and start again with the case filled with cash that Aniki has passed on to him. Aniki's apparent killing of one of his own without provocation makes him appear monstrous, but in actuality, Aniki as the 'Oyabun' sacrifices his own life for Denny. Aniki is satisfied waiting for the Italian-American Mafia to gun him down in the desert, because he knows he has saved Denny's life, paid back a debt, and financially provided for his young protégé's future. The sacrifice of the *yakuza* brethren and Aniki himself becomes a romantically noble rather than futile gesture. In this film, the criminal Japanese male and the bodies of the American cohort in their brutalized and violated states signify their self-determination in their battle against the Mafia's deep-rooted, racist power structures. Thus, while shown lying face down in a pool of his own blood, Aniki sacrifices himself to atone for his transgressions; he has redeemed himself and his 'brothers' in their battle royal against destructive greed.

Brother does not take a United States multiculturalist agenda as its sole, entrenched ideology. Rather, a set of criminal Japanese male bodies is positioned to give them a depth usually not shown in Hollywood films with Japanese and Japanese-American characters. In some small measure, these bodies refuse to remain 'invisible'. The film subverts Japanese inscrutability to reveal the seams of entrenched power. That is, the Japanese masculine codes, although criminal and violent, make visible a usually 'invisible' racist capitalist system. *Brother*'s use of noir and crime-genre elements destabilizes the Hollywood production of Asian inscrutability, as tied to downtown Los Angeles' Little Tokyo space, ultimately creating a nuanced anti-racist project. Templates of genre and of the noir sensibility allow the film to comment on race, class, space and the body, filtering that commentary through an anti-capitalist lens while also critiquing the problematic myth of the multicultural model minority. *Brother* critiques the desire for economic advancement without connection to any code or tradition, whether it is a racist criminal's grab for power or territory, or a Japanese-American café owner's belief that by achieving the American dream of owning a business, he is seen as less 'inscrutable' to the status quo than is Aniki. The two competing masculinist narratives in the film force an apocalyptic end for the outlaw hero, Aniki, who is positioned as being both radically inside and outside the boundaries of *yakuza* conventions that have eroded over time due to Western influences. Ultimately, Aniki uses his power as Oyabun, or head of his own ethnically diverse brood of Japanese and American ethnic criminals in Los Angeles, to sacrifice himself and others in his gang for the benefit of one male character, Denny. This African-American character's presence affirms that xenophobia can be challenged.

Bringing the two works together, we can see that *The Crimson Kimono*'s depiction of Little Tokyo reconstitutes, although it does not wholly contextualize, a site flattened over the years in Hollywood film. Traditionally, this filmic tourist space existed merely as entertainment to arouse desires for consumption and 'adaptability' to modern change without need to acknowledge social inequality and unjust labour practices. Emerging from a different production and cultural context, *Brother* illuminates the corruption, racism and classism of late twentieth-century US capitalism. Rather than employ noir motifs in a traditional manner, *Brother* offers Hollywood neo-noir but without reconstituting the inscrutable Asian enclave as in *Chinatown* and *Blade Runner*. Together, *The Crimson Kimono* and *Brother* demonstrate how films in a broadly constituted East Asian noir category can use particular generic devices and stylistic templates not only for aesthetic satisfaction but to draw attention to persistent power imbalances involving race, place and culture.

Notes

1 Sobchack, Vivian, 'The Postmorbid Condition', in Sonia Maasik and Jack Solomon (eds), *Signs of Life in the USA: Readings on Popular Culture for Writers* (New York: Bedford/St. Martin's, 2000), pp. 414–419.

2 Conley, Tom, 'Noir in the Red and the Nineties in the Black', in Wheeler Winston Dixon (ed.), *Film Genre 2000: New Critical Essays* (Albany: State University of New York Press, 2000), p. 194.

3 Ibid., p. 194.

4 Bordwell, David and Kristin Thompson, *The Classical Hollywood Cinema: Film Style and Mode of Production to 1960* (New York: McGraw-Hill, 1992), p. 3.

5 Ibid.

6 Lowe, Lisa, *Immigrant Acts: On Asian American Cultural Politics* (Durham: Duke University Press, 1996), p. 64.

7 Ibid., p. 86.
8 Ibid., p. 85.
9 Klein, Norman M., *The History of Forgetting: Los Angeles and the Erasure of Memory* (London: Verso, 1997), p. 96.
10 Ibid., p. 97.
11 Ibid., p. 80.
12 Toji, Dean S. and Karen Umemoto, 'The Paradox of Dispersal: Ethnic Continuity and Community Development Among Japanese Americans in Little Tokyo', *AAPI Nexus*, 1.1 (2003), p. 22. According to Toji and Umemoto:

> Los Angeles' Little Tokyo, situated adjacent to the downtown civic center, was one of the first and largest Japanese-American urban communities to form in the U.S. Over the last 100 years, its physical boundaries and land uses, as well as the human activities within the space, have drastically changed. While it once was a bustling center of civic, economic, political and cultural life for Japanese immigrants and their second-generation offspring from the early 1900s to World War II, the community underwent wholesale change following wartime mass internment and mid-century urban renewal.

13 Several, Michael, 'Little Tokyo: Historical Background', *Public Art in Los Angeles*, January 1998, http://www.publicartinla.com/Downtown/Little_Tokyo/little_tokyo.html, accessed 25 March 2013.
14 Place, J. A. and L. S. Peterson, 'Some Visual Motifs of *Film Noir*', in Bill Nichols (ed.), *Movies and Methods, Volume I* (Berkeley: University of California Press, 1976), p. 330.
15 Ibid., p. 330.
16 Ibid., p. 334; for Place and Peterson, 'Choker close-ups, framing the head or chin, are obtrusive and disturbing.'
17 Cochran, David, *American Noir: Underground Writers and Filmmakers of the Postwar Era* (Washington, DC: Smithsonian Institution Press, 2000), p. 148. Cochran states:

> The world of Fuller's films is, like the noir world, marked by chaos, violence, and paranoia. It also, as Porfirio has said of film noir, features a strong sense of the absurd. As Farber remarked, Fuller's iconoclasm frequently turned his movies into 'black comedies' filled with absurdities, such as dialogue which often consisting of strings of bad clichés, the attack of the nymphomaniacs in *Shock Corridor* (1963), and a Japanese fan dance performed by a white stripper in *The Crimson Kimono* (1959) as a symbol of interracial understanding.

18 Place and Peterson, 'Some Visual Motifs of *Film Noir*', pp. 337–338.
19 Diawara, Manthia, 'Noir by Noirs: Toward a New Realism in Black Cinema', in Joan Copjec (ed.), *Shades of Noir* (London: Verso, 1993), p. 262.
20 Ibid.

Chapter 4

Ghost in the Shell: The Noir Instinct

Dan North

Mamoru Oshii's animated feature *Ghost in the Shell* (1995) has attracted extensive scholarly attention for its prescient explorations of subjectivity in a predicted posthuman age and for its visions of the eroticized female cyborg. This legitimate emphasis on what the film anticipates often neglects what the film memorializes. Across its sequels and ancillary texts, the *Ghost in the Shell* franchise draws upon a number of historical and cultural reference points, including film noir. I will argue that the effect of 'noirness' here is to temper the sense of contemporaneity or futurity with reminders of the past, puncturing the rhetoric of progress and modernity with the insoluble corruptions, criminal pathologies and alienating environments that always drag the present into repetitions of traumatic pasts.

The Trouble With Noir

The difficulty of studying noir is in the capaciousness of its definitions, the heterogeneity of an object of study that is supposed to describe a generic unity. Steve Neale has described the peculiar tenacity of 'noir' as a *word* rather than as a recognizable genre, calling it 'a phenomenon whose unity and coherence are presumed in the single term used to label them rather than demonstrated through any systematic, empirical analysis'.[1] The invocation of the word therefore operates *talismanically*: once it is uttered in reference to a particular film, noir becomes a constructing force that grafts its interpretive codes onto the film text. Marc Vernet has referred to noir as 'a cinephilic ready-made', a self-fulfilling critical construct, since 'speaking about *film noir* consists, from the beginning, in being installed in repetition'.[2] We assemble our own definition of noir from a loosely linked set of components (detectives, doomed protagonists, femmes fatales, low-key lighting), all of which can be mapped just as easily onto other genres, and its subjective construction means, for Vernet, that noir remains 'a collector's idea that, for the moment, can only be found in books'.[3] James Naremore warns readers of his *More Than Night* from the outset that the object of study is not a solid or fixed one. Although film noir can be described as 'one of the dominant intellectual categories of the late twentieth century, operating across the entire cultural arena of art, popular memory, and criticism', it is also 'a kind of mythology', viewable in terms of 'noirness' rather than a concrete canon of texts and characteristics.[4] Paradoxically, he argues, 'film noir is both an important cinematic legacy and an idea we have projected onto the past'.[5]

Despite the failings of genre designations to definitively categorize and tame the chaotic diversity of film, we persist in applying them. We are prompted into a kind of *apophenic* approach to genre, where we search for (and invariably find) connections, semblances and patterns in random phenomena, in disconnected lists of films that may or may not exhibit signs of influence, reproduction, mirroring, homage or repetition. As a result, when films come to us labelled – either by critics, advertisers or word-of-mouth – as noir, we instinctively read them *as* noir by seeking out the characteristics implied to us by the generic 'brand'. Reciprocally, the same impetus is built into the systems of production, where conformity to a successful template can be a guarantor of success or a filtration system for projects that will be put into production. Finally, it arises in the interpretive schema of spectators, who are pushed toward reading diverse media products as exhibitors of noir-like traits.

Film noir offers up, in Noël Carroll's phrase, an 'approved cinematic iconography' through which a new film can indicate to the informed spectator that the present film is to be contemplated in relation to an existing hermeneutic framework.[6] *Allusion* became, according to Carroll, one of the key expressive devices through which filmmakers came 'to make comments on the fictional worlds of their films'.[7] Interpretive schema based on allusion can be highly ambiguous, so it should not be a surprise to find apophenic pattern recognition assisting the spread of noir as a widely perceived cultural category.

Jennifer Fay and Justus Nieland remark that 'noir lends itself to domestication in different national contexts, in part because it is concerned with the local and for this reason travels well and endures historically'.[8] For them, noir is a 'fully international phenomenon', so we still find its traces decades after the classical noir era, in a country such as Japan, thousands of miles from the birthplace of the genre. Noir also expresses 'disquiet with the conditions of a modern, globalized age'.[9] Noir narratives, they tell us, 'have functioned for critics and scholars as celluloid clocks telling the time of national life (its rootedness in tradition, or its movement into the future, or its traumatic upheavals, displacements, and confusions) and keeping pace with global movements that may render that life a phenomenon of the past'.[10] This will be an instructive line of thinking when explaining how noir influences commingle with *Ghost in the Shell*'s iconographic responses to globalized environments (both urban/architectural and informational/virtual). However, it tells us nothing that is exclusive to noir, and I suspect that the opposite is true: rather than using a rigid noir template to take the pulse of a nation's responses to globalization, we are driven instead to single out those crime films that perform just such a diagnostic social function. We then brand them as noir, thus validating the category and 'proving' the value of the term by reconstituting it as a perpetually useful tool.

What I have described is something akin to a 'noir instinct'. One might think of 'the noir genre' as a set of aesthetic choices made in order to convey a particular mood or a response to postwar US society, the foundational myth of noir. The noir instinct, on the other hand, points to the way stories are selectively interpreted so they accord with the expected traits of the genre. The end product is an increasingly notional definition of noir lingering around a number of disparate crime films. If the task of genre is to sort and shape films, increasing their intertextual legibility, then this body of work is too diverse to constitute anything like a usable genre.

The noir instinct is a reflex in artists and spectators that compels them almost automatically to situate film texts within the terminological frameworks of noir. For the various authors of the *Ghost in the Shell* franchise, the reflex takes the form of a memorialization of noir in the depictions of cityscapes, detective stories and existential crises played out as criminal investigations. An instinctive recourse to the iconography, thematics and interpretive schema of noir is one of the primary links between the limbs of the *Ghost in the Shell* narrational networks. Noir thus provides the various shows with aesthetic continuities and invites viewers to consider their depiction of a future world through a particular lens.

A Palimpsestic Franchise

The *Ghost in the Shell* franchise originated in Masamune Shirow's manga series (1989–1997), but also comprises two theatrical feature films, *Ghost in the Shell* (1995) and *Ghost in the Shell 2: Innocence* (2002); two television series, *Ghost in the Shell: Standalone Complex* (52 episodes in total, 2002–2005); one television film, or OVA (original video animation), *Ghost in the Shell: Standalone Complex: Solid State Society* (2006, re-released in 3D in 2011); three Playstation videogames (1997, 2004, 2005); and four novels.[11] In 2008 Oshii produced *Ghost in the Shell 2.0*, a remastered version of the original film with parts of the original animation reconstructed, including extensive CGI and a re-recorded soundtrack. The characters have also been extensively merchandised. The components of the series come from multiple authors across various media, and the chronologies, character traits and backstories inevitably contain variances or inconsistencies. Such attributes correspond to what Clare Parody defines as 'franchise storytelling', an 'aggregate text' (after Arnett), 'a palimpsest of a storyworld and its inhabitants built-up over time from repeated remakes, reimaginings, and remediations'.[12]

Ghost in the Shell's various plotlines are too complex to delineate in detail here, and much has already been written about individual franchise components, but the overarching master narrative concerns Section 9, a team of special operatives who investigate cybercrime. They are usually faced with cases that hinge upon transgressions of the border between humans and machines: artificial intelligences running amok or behaving too much like humans, black-market cybernetic prostheses and malfunctioning androids are just some of the subjects of their investigations. In Oshii's first film, for instance, the team tracks the Puppet Master, an artificial intelligence that has escaped from its government-run military programme and seeks asylum in a host body. Even though the components do not quite fit into a single, cohesive narrative, the palimpsestic franchise explores consistent conceptual terrain, revisiting questions of electronic identities and machine consciousness. While Oshii's two feature films each follow a single case to its conclusion, *Standalone Complex* covers the history of Section 9 before the events of those films, opening a casebook of stories and investigations: each series has both a continuous plotline (these were also compiled into two continuous television films, *The Laughing Man* [2005] and *The Individual Eleven* [2006], stripped of the other episodes) and a number of 'standalone' stories that focus on cases unrelated to the ongoing story, or give minor characters their own branching narratives. The franchise is built, then, around narratives of crime and its detection, the most noticeable manifestation of a noir structure at work.

Whatever crimes Section 9 investigates, the identity of Major Motoko Kusanagi is the central, ongoing enigma of *Ghost in the Shell* and all of its satellite stories. The series confirms that she is almost entirely prosthetic, and that she is haunted by remnants of her ghost (in the storyworld of *GITS*, this word is used in a manner similar to 'soul', to describe the defining elements of persona or living essence that can inhabit organic or synthetic bodies) that shape her personality. However, even she does not know how much of her persona is a synthetic byproduct of the cyberbody she inhabits, and how much is the accumulation of 'real-world' memories. This secreted backstory is never used as a structuring prop for the narrative, and only rarely does the series provide additional insights into her subjectivity, mood, origins or private life. Instead, our knowledge of her inner life accretes slowly, in fragments stashed in obscure corners of the franchise rather than being used as cliffhanger bait for its main attractions.

Kusanagi thus polices the transgressive crimes of machines stepping out of their programmed functions and stable identities, but embodies exactly those ambiguities herself. By using an ontological problem as the connective membrane of a series of investigative narratives, *Ghost in the Shell* conforms to Patricia Merivale and Susan Elizabeth Sweeney's delineation of the 'metaphysical detective story', which poses 'questions about mysteries of being and knowing which transcend the mere machinations of the mystery plot'. Within these self-reflexive narrative structures, the detective might also end up 'confronting the insoluble mysteries of his own interpretation and his own identity'.[13]

As well as being a complex of detection narratives, *Ghost in the Shell* is often cited as a prime example of cyberpunk cinema. As Stephen Connor puts it, in terms directly relevant to this discussion, cyberpunk 'blends the evocation of extravagant technological possibilities with the most hard-bitten and unillusioned of narrative styles, borrowed from the historical forms of the detective story and the *film noir*, which choke off the exhilaration of futurity'.[14] *Ghost in the Shell* accordingly gives its futurescapes a lived-in, worn-out look and a wistfully retrospective tone that signals a hesitant attitude toward its diegetic technologies.

Brian McHale has distinguished 'epistemologically oriented fiction' such as detective stories from the ontologically preoccupied cyberpunk genre, which itself breaks from other iterations of science fiction in its depictions of the technologized city. Instead of a perfectly ordered urban future, whether dystopian or utopian, cyberpunk stories are more likely to propose what

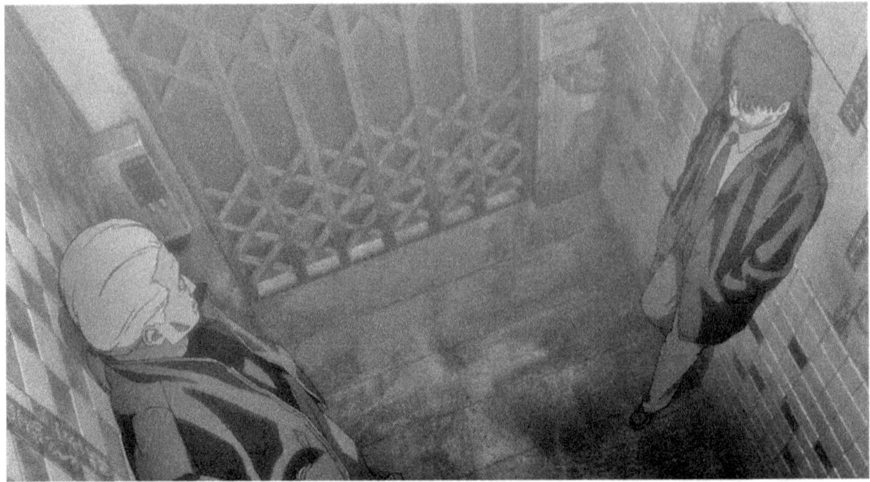

Figure 4.1 Agents Batou (left) and Togusa (right) in a noirish scene from *Ghost in the Shell 2: Innocence*

McHale dubs 'the Sprawl', a vision of the city as a 'maximally intimate juxtaposition of maximally diverse and heterogeneous culture materials (Japanese, Western, and Third World, high-tech and low-tech, elite and popular, mainstream "official" culture and youth or criminal subcultures').[15] The labyrinthine Sprawl collapses distinctions between peoples, even as the authorities try to segregate them into manageable, legible zones.

The permeability of categories is visible throughout *GITS*, where the members of Section 9 are privileged in their powers of movement and surveillance throughout the city, but still need to pursue the Puppet Master through a course of streets and networks that blend physical and virtual spaces into a nest of hiding places where a person can disappear, faceless, into the crowd. *GITS SAC 2nd Gig* (2004–2005) builds an elaborate plot around conflicts (almost escalating to the status of a civil war) between Section 9, the corrupt Cabinet Intelligence Service and a population of refugees settling on the Japanese island of Dejima, a former colonial trading post. Dejima is an artificial island, built by merchants in 1634 in the Bay of Nagasaki so traders visiting the country during the Edo period could be kept in isolation from the mainland. The reverberations of this history carry into *GITS SAC* to show postwar Japan (following the two fictional world wars that precede the start of the story) as a repository of historical memory: the futuristic and the high-tech are constantly held in check by sobering reminders of the ancient and the analogue.

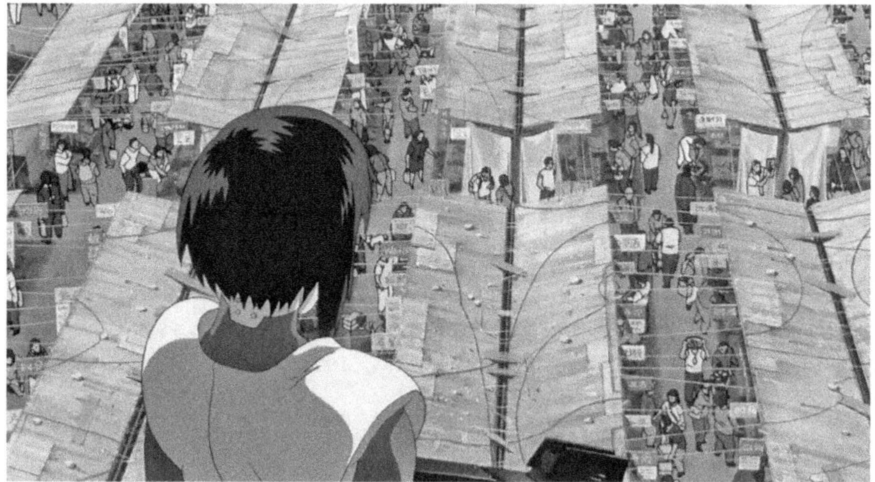

Figure 4.2 Major Motoko Kusanagi searches for a suspect in the 'sprawl' of the city in 1995's *Ghost in the Shell*

Considering noir's relationship to history, Naremore notes the backward-looking nature of noir discourse, since 'most contemporary writing and film-making associated with noir provokes a mourning and melancholy for the past'.[16] The essential motifs of noir have been transformed, by years of inter-textual correspondence, into 'a vehicle for nostalgia and parody, available to anyone who wants to engage self-consciously with the traditions of American cinema'.[17] One meaning of the title '*Stand Alone Complex*' relates to the phenomenon of copycat crimes where no one recalls the originating incident. Something similar has happened with film noir, whereby generic traits are endlessly replicated, despite the nebulous nature of the source.

Noir, then, has become a touchstone for films seeking to explore ambivalent relationships between past and present, shorthand for metaphysical discomfort inflicted on the protagonists by their situation and environment. *Ghost in the Shell* translates the diffuse, nested evils of noir to a vision of the tentacular spread of global information, its capacity for abuse, and the ambiguities of the beings who inhabit it. This is globalization as informational creep. The hiding places for evil are neither the shadows of a back alley nor the concrete shelter of an ornate office, but the malleable cyberspaces of the internet. Fay and Nieland give us the idea of 'noir-humanism', which 'offers a specific vision of human agency as increasingly governed by forces beyond reason or rational control, not only within the human (passion, madness, paranoia, trauma and the like), but beyond and abstracted from human capacity in the very modernity of the modern world'.[18] The fatalism of noir and its powerful, invisible moral forces find expression in *GITS*'s depictions of a world ordered by flows of information that can confer demagogic status on some users and grant them control over others.

The franchise features numerous border crossings and transgressions in terms of subjectivity and location, but not to the extent of erasing all categories of identity. The opening title of *Ghost in the Shell* declares that computerization has not yet wiped out nations and ethnicities, as if a tension still exists between the technological drive to eradicate boundaries and the inertial human allegiance to the past. Eric Cazdyn interprets *GITS*' 'focus on the breakup of the individual as a desire to express the breakup of the nation'.[19] He continues:

> If we think about [...] Motoko's body in *Ghost* as representing the national body, then we can understand the cyberpunk genre as symptomatic of a greater desire to map the global system. The problematic of the 'I' and its instability, the realization that we are irrevocably cyborgian and that this is nothing to regret, prefigures the problematic of the 'nation' and its instability.[20]

The metaphysical detectives of *Ghost in the Shell* conduct their investigations into the nature of the machine, the self and the body by specializing in tracking criminals who transgress the boundaries between those zones, even as such boundaries become increasingly blurred.

Animated Ontologies

In visualizing the *GITS* series' dramas of ontological ambivalence, the processes of animation are, more than technical tools, structural and thematic contributors. Toshiya Ueno suggests that Mamoru Oshii, arguably the most significant authorial influence on the franchise after manga writer Masamune Shirow, sees the world in terms of animation storyboards: 'To Oshii, animation is not necessarily just a reflection or copy of reality; it is in itself an independent reality. For him, the world and reality itself are structured and schematized as animation'.[21] Referring to Oshii as a 'puppet master', Ueno claims that he draws few distinctions between animation and 'live action', and instead directs his actors in the same way he treats cartoon characters. Oshii organizes an 'exchange' between animation and film; he 'uses actors' bodies like animation in his live-action films and brings the blur, distortion, and devices of the camera into his animated films like *Patlabor* and *Ghost in the Shell*'.[22] Animation, then, represents 'an intermediary space between film and reality' rather than being at the far end of a sliding scale between representation and the Real.[23]

For Dani Cavallaro, animated images exhibit an 'uncompromising madeness', and Japanese anime in particular 'wears its madeness on its sleeve by overtly shunning the aesthetic and ideological precepts of classic realism'.[24] This 'madeness' (a reference to animation's composition out of ink, paint, plastic cels and frame-by-frame photography) confers on the films' characters a crucial remove from the requirements of naturalistic representation. They can embody fictional subjectivities uninflected by the personae of human actors, even as their self-evident artifice allows them to represent the ambiguities of figures whose own composition is uncertain, hybrid. Whatever the specific attributes of animation, however, important vestigial traces of 'live-action' cinema remain in much of the visual syntax of *Ghost in the Shell*. Susan Napier has argued that animation is unsettling for viewers because it is under no obligation to adhere to conventions of form, but *Ghost in the Shell* deploys many realist techniques in its simulations of bodies in motion, and in general mimics cinematic aesthetics.[25] In both its film and TV incarnations, *Ghost in the Shell* uses numerous techniques that render the imagery cinematic, including extremes of depth of field and lighting simulations that emphasize areas of light and shadow. In *Innocence* and *Ghost in the Shell 2.0*, digital animation is used to create machines, bodies, sets and other effects that lend a kind of precise shape and motion to parts of the *mise-en-scène*. Rather than the formal unpredictability noted by Napier, it is these contests of ontology, where disparately sourced animated content shares the same frame, that are discomforting. They offer a visual embodiment of the franchise's connecting theme of border crossings between organic and electronic identities, 'a fitting technical correlative for the film's thematic emphasis on the nebulousness of the boundaries putatively separating "natural" human organisms from cyborgs, automata, clones, holograms – or indeed dreams'.[26]

The blend of digital and traditional animation methods in *GITS 2.0* and *Innocence* constitutes a metanarrative of artificial bodies and the continually contested ontologies of their various organic/synthetic components. That is, animation is not just a convenient technical means to a representational end, but a foundational part of the way the films set about their thematic, conceptual and philosophical labour. For the remastered re-release *GITS 2.0*, Oshii oversaw hundreds of adjustments to the film's lighting, sound and special effects, inserting digital animations to replace the earlier onscreen computer graphics, replacing their green hue with a glowing amber aesthetic that more closely matched the look of the sequel, *Innocence*. This process also involved adjusting the contrast for most of the film's imagery, adding saturation to some colours and deepening shadows. For key sequences, the Major's body was replaced with a digital double, as were many external shots of aircraft and road vehicles. The intention may have been to make *Ghost in the Shell* more contemporary, and to update its aesthetic template in line with the rest of the franchise components, but the result is a true palimpsest: an overwritten copy beneath which the original is still visible, where the old speaks from beneath the façade of the new. Often in *Innocence* the 3D digital backgrounds are intensely coloured, leaving the foreground character action muted by comparison, giving the city a forcible presence and shoring up the distinct subjectivity of the detectives as estranged from their environment. At other times, lighting effects create the kinds of extremes of shadow and illumination that have come to be seen as defining characteristics of noir aesthetics. It is in the fabrication of its animated people and places that *Ghost in the Shell* evokes noir's disquiet in the face of modernity. These disjunctures between old and new elements speak to the franchise's ambivalent articulation of the relationship between past and present, between bodies and technology.

The Major's Memory

Linking the city and the Major is the signature image of her body diving serenely from a tall building, alone in free-fall. This action appears at the start of *Ghost in the Shell*, in the title sequences of both series of *Stand Alone Complex*, and at the opening of *Solid State Society*. The image of the Major's isolation, the discrepancy between her calm interiority and the dizzying spatiality of her external movement, is fetishistically replayed across the franchise, accentuating each time the relationship between body and space through the accelerated dance between foreground figure and background scenery. Periodically, then, the series presents a heroine who is fundamentally separate, other.

In many ways, the Major fits the template of the femme fatale beloved of followers of films noirs, but this may be more of an 'instinctual' categorization (she is inscrutably dangerous, and the only recurring female character) than a perfect match. As established by Mary Ann Doane, the femme fatale is 'the figure of a certain discursive unease, a potential epistemological trauma [...] She harbours a threat which is not entirely legible, predictable, or manageable'.[27] Moreover, 'if the female fatale overrepresents the body it is because she is attributed with a body which is itself given agency independently of consciousness'.[28] Kusanagi maintains a balance between her body and her consciousness in the way she assimilates herself with the world of information and demonstrates physical dominance, agility and strategic intelligence in combat. But this tentative equilibrium comes at the expense of full understanding of her self, and with the loss of a full remembrance of her childhood, upbringing and formative experiences. Like the femme fatale, she is made sexually alluring, but emotionally distant and sexually unavailable: she has a male romantic partner in the original graphic novel, and there are brief allusions to lesbian relationships in SAC, but for the most part she is solitary and uninterested in companionship. Contrastingly, she is not coded as evil or manipulative.

According to Helen Hanson and Catherine O'Rawe, the femme fatale is 'read simultaneously as both entrenched cultural stereotype and yet never quite fully known: she is always beyond definition'.[29] The Major's unknowability is not the product of restricted narration, but an accurate description of a character whose very being is contested. Key to the mystery of Kusanagi's nature is her memory – what does she recall of her childhood, her upbringing, for instance? The questioning begins in *Ghost in the Shell*, when Kusanagi observes in a conversation with Batou that her 'self' is composed of a unique physical body, memories of childhood *and* a sense of the future, plus the mass of data contained in the Net, which her cyberbrain can access. This statement of being is undermined by the Puppet Master, who implants false memories in the minds of his physical hosts and claims that the memory he has acquired through the Net make him fully conscious, 'a life-form born in the sea of information'.

The TV series take place before the events shown in the films, but refuses to perform the prequel's expected function of fleshing out the Major's backstory. Episode 11 (2004) of *SAC 2nd Gig* reveals more about her past than any other episode, but even here, the evidence is not confirmed. During her visit to the 'Memory Store', a pawnshop where people leave their cherished belongings for safekeeping (the shelves can be seen lined with VHS cassettes, associating personal memory with media storage), she finds two child cyberbodies, one of which may or may not have once been her own before she transferred to her current form. Instead of confirming the Major's origins, we are granted only allusions to another corporeal shell that could have housed an earlier version of the Major, as if her mind has been repeatedly transplanted to a new storage medium. By the time of Oshii's *Innocence*, the Major is only a spectral presence, completely disembodied and operating within the Net following her merger with the Puppet Master. At every turn, then, *GITS* refuses to solve the case of the Major's subjectivity. Never are we allowed to locate the entirety of her being in a single stable body or persona.

Instead, the Major's complex, dispersed identity becomes part of a broader metaphor about the information society. In *Innocence*, agents Togusa and Batou fly over the city, which is depicted as a mix of futurity and cathedralic classicism. Surveying the view below, Batou observes: 'Society and culture are just enormous memory storage systems. Cities are huge external memory devices.' The observation that communal memory finds concrete manifestation in human construction, art and architecture sets the stage for how the cinematic city and its inhabitants are to be interpreted.

The Net, as depicted throughout *GITS*, is not a Gibsonian cyberspace where data exists in a parallel cityscape. Rather, it infiltrates bodies and minds, even at the level of perception, where eyes and thoughts can record or transmit data. Steven Shaviro, examining Marshall McLuhan's claim that 'electronic circuitry [is] an extension of the central nervous system',[30] argues instead that:

> every individual brain is a miniaturized replica of the global communications network. The network is the great Outside that always surrounds and envelops me. But it is also the Inside: its alien circuitry is what I find when I look deeply within myself. The network is impersonal, universal, without a center, but it is also perturbingly intimate, uncannily close at hand.[31]

Shaviro's construction parallels the way *GITS* depicts identity as simultaneously isolated (the subject is individuated by the control granted by the technology) and networked (the subject is always linked and available to communications systems beyond her control).

Memory connects *Ghost in the Shell* to noir in another way – through the use of cinema history as a kind of surrogate memory bank, just like those VHS tapes in the Memory Store. For Naremore, noir, 'a concept that was generated ex post facto has become part of a worldwide mass memory; a dream image of bygone glamour, it represses as much history as it recalls, usually in the service of cinephilia and commodification'.[32] *Ghost in the Shell* expresses this through adherence to many of the codes and conventions of classical cinema, but more directly through references to individual films.

Each episode of *Stand Alone Complex* includes an additional revelation about the inner workings of androids and cyborgs, or the parameters of posthuman identity. In episode three (2002), Section 9 investigates a spate of

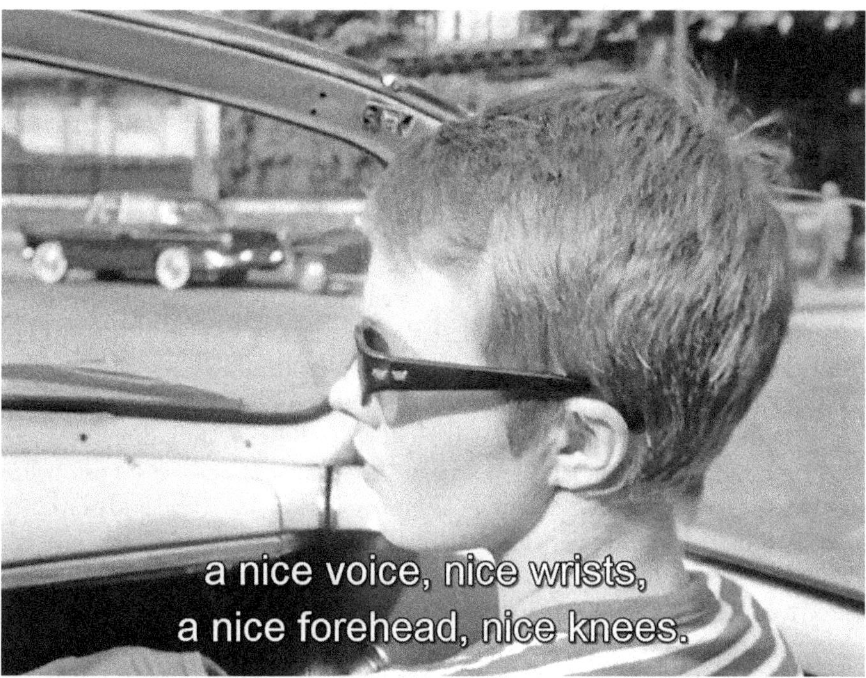

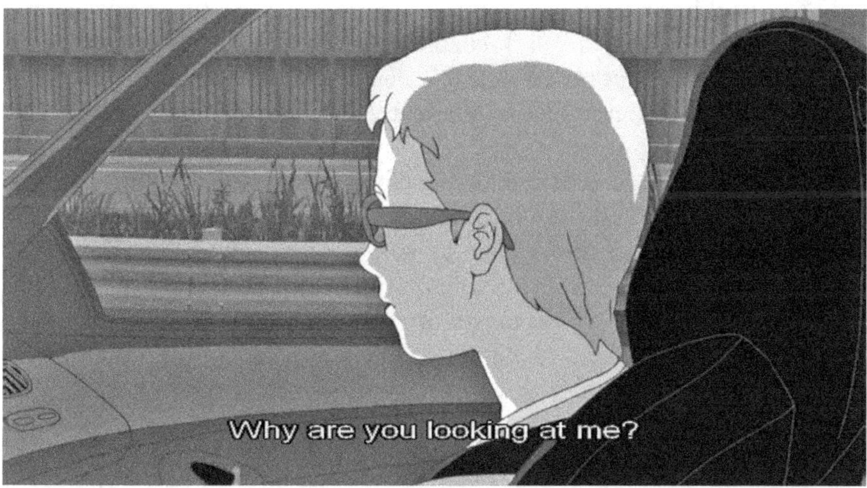

Figures 4.3/4.4 Jean Seberg in *À bout de souffle* (top) and the Jeri android in *Standalone Complex* (bottom)

suicides by the 'Jeri', a female android series that has recently been superseded. Raiding a suspect's house, Batou finds a stack of old films, anachronistically stored on reels in cans. Two titles can clearly be seen, Jean-Luc Godard's *À bout de souffle* (1960) and *Alphaville* (1965), both films with nostalgic, revisionist positions on the American crime or detective movie. As the story develops, it emerges that the Canadian ambassador's son is attempting to elope with a Jeri with whom he has fallen in love. He believes she is capable of feeling love for him in return. The Jeri strongly resembles Jean Seberg in *À bout de souffle*, and he describes her appearance in the same inventoried manner as Belmondo describes Seberg's in Godard's film, noting the beauty of her face, neck, arms. The episode ultimately reveals that the words of love pronounced by the Jeri to demonstrate her willingness to elope are actually rote-learned from French New Wave movies, including Godard's science-fiction noir homage, *Alphaville*. In *Alphaville*, Eddie Constantine reprises the role of grizzled detective Lemmy Caution, a part he had played in a series of French B movies beginning in 1953. While on the trail of a missing secret agent, Caution rescues a woman (Anna Karina) who has been rendered robotically servile in a bureaucratized futurescape, by teaching her how to love. At the end of the *GITS* episode that seems to mirror this plotline, the Major notes that some of the words spoken by Jeri were *not* in any of the movies' scripts, leaving behind a trace of uncertainty about the android's level of sentience: the emotional capacities of machines represent the franchise's central insoluble mystery. If the rhetoric of digital technology is that it gives us ever more stable and reliable access to archived information and imagery, *Ghost in the Shell* offers an ambivalent reply by depicting the increased capacity for deception, and the attenuated sense of presence, fostered by visual media.

The theme of images and memory is elaborated at various points throughout the series. In episode seven (2003), a revolutionary leader has a 'ghost-dubbing device' that allows him to perpetuate copies of himself, thus continuing as an image of revolutionary strength even after the original has died; in episode 12 (2003), a movie director captures people in his virtual cinema and subjects them to a film they are powerless to stop watching; in *2nd Gig* episode two (2004), a war veteran, now a helicopter pilot, wrestles with fantasies of assassination when he is assigned to transport a high-level official. The pilot sermonizes about the state of the nation and the degradation of the media and society, and he becomes obsessed with a beautiful woman he sees on his regular trips to a late-night cinema. The references to *Taxi Driver* (1976), itself a film suffused with pastness and that updates noir tropes, are so pronounced that they need to be seen not as supplementary homages that add value to the narrative, but as a mnemonic framework for the interpretation of the episode as an act of nostalgia, the inscription of the past onto the present. The intertextual citations of *Taxi Driver* and *À bout de souffle* are so blatant that they ask the spectator not merely to notice and catalogue a series of homages, but to engage with these moments *as* borrowings, as iconic units of memory dropped wholesale into the intertextual flow of the palimpsestic franchise.

Some years before he wrote the screenplay for *Taxi Driver*, Paul Schrader offered his 'Notes on Film Noir',[33] which Naremore in turn maps onto a reading of that film. *Taxi Driver* follows a sexually repressed Vietnam veteran ('analogous to all those returning World War II soldiers in Hollywood thrillers of the 1940s')[34] who projects his fantasies of justice, retribution and apocalypse onto his environment and the people in it. Naremore puts it in the same category as *The Long Goodbye* (1973), *Chinatown* (1974) and *Body Heat* (1981) as films of the period that 'were made with a nostalgic idea of noir in mind'.[35] It makes sense that *Ghost in the Shell*, a network of stories about the commingling of humans and machines, the blending of digital file-storage and human memory, should draw upon cinema in this way; cinema *is* machine memory. Characters in the franchise are constantly hooked up to the Net, which can serve as a kind of prosthetic memory: they can access historical documents, personal records, even sensory data from others' cyberbrains. We see this happen several times in *SAC*, as when Section 9's agents look up the history of the assassination of Prime Minister Tsuyoshi Inukai by eleven naval officers on 15 May 1932. That incident provides inspiration for the revolutionary group The Individual Eleven, whose activities occupy much of *GITS SAC 2nd Gig*. Just as the Eleven are able to leave clues as to their motives and demands by citing past events, so Section 9 is able to decode those messages through immediate access to audiovisual databanks of historical records. In the final, 26th episode (2003) of *SAC 1st Gig*, Motoko debates with the Laughing Man, a hacker who has blown the whistle on a massive governmental cover-up in the pharmaceutical industry. Meeting in a virtual library, the two draw upon a range of critical theories and quotations from Robert Doisneau, Dziga Vertov, Fredric Jameson and Richard Dawkins, apparently rote-learned. However, their conversation is not a display of studied erudition, but a demonstration of how well they can navigate the ideational databases to which their cyberbrains are permanently connected. Each of them searches the collective cultural memory store for the most apt conceptualization of the state of the nation and the nature of being. These remembered lines could just as easily be part of a broader 'culture of quotation' where memory has been externalized, made readily accessible but located outside the body and attenuated from lived experience. Bodies and information, past and present, have become indivisibly interwoven, but *Ghost in the Shell* never succumbs to a wholly dystopian view of human bodies and brains under technological sway. Instead, it considers the place of human memory and affect in a technologized, cyborg-dominated future.

Noir influences complement the nostalgic view of the pre-cybernetic past that suffuses the franchise. The stable family life of Agent Togusa, who refuses most prosthetic alterations to his body, provides a benchmark for non-cyborg life. In *Ghost in the Shell*, Kusanagi tells him that his 'natural' body is an advantage to Section 9, since it differentiates him from the other members and 'no matter how powerful we may be fighting-wise, a system where all parts react the same way is a system with a fatal flaw'. In *Innocence*, Batou's beloved Basset Hound, lovingly animated, is a symbol of organic goodness, of simple needs and affections (and, modelled on Oshii's own pet, it appears as a recurrent motif in many of his films). Pastness, contained in references to collective and personal memory, and in the iconography and allusion seen in the visual style across the franchise, gives the *Ghost in the Shell* series its distinctively melancholic flavour. Its noirness provides the substance of a culturally legible, shared memory that makes the films' vision of the future a continually backward-facing, reflective one. *Ghost in the Shell* is often analysed for its science fictional content, for the way it might be seen to predict questions of subjectivity prompted by the spread of digital technologies. But it is also, even when taken as a whole, an old-fashioned crime thriller, mining the tropes of noir across its franchise components to tell stories of a detective whose very nature is interrogated in the process. It takes place in an environment where knowledge of the labyrinths of both the city and cyberspace, *and* the interrelationships between them, is vital to an understanding of how criminals are to be pursued and thwarted.

Notes

1 Neale, Steve, *Genre and Hollywood* (London: Routledge, 2000), p. 144.
2 Vernet, Marc, '*Film Noir* on the Edge of Doom', trans. J. Swenson, in Joan Copjec (ed.), *Shades of Noir: A Reader* (London: Verso, 1993), p. 2.
3 Ibid., p. 26.
4 Naremore, James, *More Than Night: Film Noir in Its Contexts* (Berkeley: University of California Press, 1998), p. 2.

5 Ibid., p. 11.
6 Carroll, Noël, 'The Future of an Allusion: Hollywood in the Seventies (and Beyond)', *October* 20 (Spring 1982), p. 51.
7 Ibid., p. 52.
8 Fay, Jennifer and Justus Nieland, *Film Noir: Hard-Boiled Modernity and the Cultures of Globalization* (London: Routledge, 2010), p. x.
9 Ibid., p. xi.
10 Ibid., p. xiii.
11 Fujisaku, Junichi, *The Lost Memory*, *Revenge of the Cold Machines* and *White Maze* (Dark Horse Comics, 2006); Yamada, Masaki, *Innocence: After the Long Goodbye* (Viz Media, 2007).
12 Parody, Clare, 'Franchising/Adaptation', *Adaptation* 4.2 (2011), p. 211; Arnett, Robert P., '*Casino Royale* and Franchise Remix: James Bond as Superhero', *Film Criticism* 33 (2009): 1–16.
13 Merivale, Patricia and Susan Elizabeth Sweeney, 'The Game's Afoot: On the Trail of the Metaphysical Detective Story', in Merivale and Sweeney (eds), *Detecting Texts: The Metaphysical Detective Story from Poe to Postmodernism* (Philadelphia: University of Pennsylvania Press, 1999), p. 2.
14 Connor, Stephen, *Postmodernist Culture: An Introduction to Theories of the Contemporary* (Oxford: Blackwell, 1997), p. 135.
15 McHale, Brian, 'Elements of a Poetics of Cyberpunk', *Critique* 33.3 (Spring 1992), p. 154.
16 Naremore, *More Than Night*, p. 4.
17 Ibid., p. 168.
18 Fay and Nieland, *Film Noir*, p. 8.
19 Cazdyn, Eric, *The Flash of Capital: Film and Geopolitics in Japan* (Durham: Duke University Press, 2002), p. 250.
20 Ibid., p. 251.
21 Ueno, Toshiya, 'Kurenai no metalsuits, "Anime to wa nani ka/What is animation"', *Mechademia* 1 (2006), p. 111.
22 Ibid., p. 116.
23 Ibid., p. 117.
24 Cavallaro, Dani, *Anime Intersections: Tradition and Innovation in Theme and Technique* (Jefferson, NC: McFarland, 2007), p. 1.
25 Napier, Susan J., 'The Problem of Existence in Japanese Animation', *Proceedings of the American Philosophical Society* 149.1 (March 2005): 72–79.
26 Cavallaro, *Anime Intersections*, p. 104.
27 Doane, Mary Ann, *Femmes Fatales: Feminism, Film Theory, Psychoanalysis* (London: Routledge, 1991), p. 1.
28 Ibid., p. 2.
29 Hanson, Helen and Catherine O'Rawe, 'Introduction: Cherchez La *Femme*' in Hanson and O'Rawe (eds), *The Femme Fatale: Images, Histories, Contexts* (Basingstoke: Palgrave Macmillan, 2010), p. 1.

30 McLuhan, Marshall, *The Medium is the Massage: An Inventory of Effects* (Corte Madera, CA: Gingko Press, 2001 [1967]), p. 40.
31 Shaviro, Steven, *Connected, or What it Means to Live in the Network Society* (Minneapolis: University of Minnesota Press, 2003), p. 12.
32 Naremore, *More Than Night*, p. 39.
33 Schrader, Paul, 'Notes on Film Noir', *Film Comment* 8.1 (Spring 1972): 8–13.
34 Naremore, *More Than Night*, p. 34.
35 Ibid., p. 36.

PART II

SOUTH KOREA: FROM POSTWAR MODERNITY TO CRIME AND DETECTION ON A GLOBAL STAGE

Chapter 5

Allegorizing Noir: Violence, Body and Space in the Postwar Korean Film Noir

Hyun S. Park

Introduction

The noir sensibility has been a vital force driving the global success of contemporary Korean cinema. The acclaimed gangster film *A Bittersweet Life* (*Dalkomhan insaeng*, 2005), Tartan Films' UK distribution of Chan-wook Park's *Vengeance* trilogy (2002–2005), and the planned US remake of the Korean box office hit *The Man From Nowhere* (*Ajeossi*, 2010) are just a small sample of releases that have made recent Korean films smash hits overseas. Abundant with the noir mode of violence, revenge and crimes, these post-millennium Korean films have lured the international audience to explore the looming darkness of the world system. However, this chapter proposes that this peculiar mode of noir is less a new phenomenon than part of historical discourse regarding the global process of modernization in Korea. To examine the genealogy of the noir sensibility, I return to the 1960s, one of the historical periods that witnessed the most vigorous and violent shapings of modern Korean society. By the term noir sensibility, what I mean is the possibility of reclaiming the lived experience and aesthetic immediacy of the tumultuous, violent time. Korea's 1960s film noirs are historically significant for two reasons. First, even though film noir did not thrive as a dominant genre of the era like melodrama or war films, which were utilized as a means to frame the boundaries of national identity and national cinema, it was this noir sensibility that paradoxically flourished in the course of economy-driven policies in the postwar era. Second, in spite of the generic formation of noir since the 1960s, it became 'virtually taboo' to make noirish crime films under the worsened military dictatorship of the 1970s and 1980s.[1] Thus, it was in the early and mid-1960s that noir films had the chance to address the geopolitical circumstances of postwar Korea society. In particular, *Black Hair (Geomeun meori)* and *The Devil's Stairway (Maeui gyedan)*, both made by director Man-hee Lee in 1964, are remarkable postwar film noirs that deserve close illumination. Building on the notions of allegory and violence articulated by Walter Benjamin, who so shrewdly critiqued the dubious project of modernity and enlightenment, this chapter will address the way these 1960s Korean noir films can be envisioned as the allegorizing critique of the compressed, totalitarian process of modernity. The comparative reading of two films will provide a critical thread to detect the hidden relationship between law and violence, which was embedded in the urban space and the gendered body of the emerging post-colonial nation state.

The Emergence of the Noir Sensibility in Postwar Korean Cinema

Conjuring up a series of thematic and technical characteristics from Hollywood films of the 1940s and 1950s, the term 'film noir' is used to designate some definitive traits of a genre, generally speaking, a film genre based on moral ambiguity and low-key lighting. However, it is also notable that film noir belongs to 'one of the most amorphous categories in film history',[2] always raising definitional questions in regard to its periods, styles or origins. For instance, Paul Schrader writes that film noir 'is not defined, as are the western and gangster genres, by conventions of setting and conflict, but rather by the more subtle qualities of tone and mood'.[3] Also, emphasizing that the meaning of noir has changed over time and space, James Naremore argues that noir is 'not merely a descriptive term, but a name for a critical tendency within the popular cinema' to renovate the theme of violence.[4] Interestingly enough, I think the very difficulty imbedded in the definition of noir can be considered as a critical lever to shift the hegemonic paradigm of the centre and the periphery within global cultures. In other words, to expand the critical territory of noir to non-Western experiences could be a way of challenging cultural imperialism that has sustained the discourse of noir's canonization and Western origins. Even if it is an established fact that Hollywood has produced the pantheon of film genres, it is worthwhile to recalibrate the generic geopolitics by examining the cultural production of noir in Asia. Thus, rather than taking up a generic approach to the noirish styles and themes of Korean films in relation to the Hollywood tradition, my approach to Korean film noir engages a historical understanding of noir as a 'discursive construct' (James Naremore and Andrew Spicer) or a cultural or critical 'sensibility' (Paul Schrader and Mark Conard) *vis-à-vis* the violent imposition of postwar modernity in Korea.

In the history of Korean film, film noir became a regular part of the film scene in the early 1960s. 'It was so popular that it became the main trend and stream of filmmaking of that period',[5] writes prominent Korean film historian Young-il Lee. The emergence of new genres such as crime films and action films was particularly visible in the period from 1963 to 1967. Mostly made in this short period of time, thrillers and action films were combined with noir style to the extent that terms such as 'action', 'thrill' and 'suspense' were also used together so often they became idioms. The popularity of these genres is attributed to the sensibility and aesthetic for which these new genres: '*a faster tempo*'.[6] Directors of the old generation could not produce films with such rapid pacing, and so younger directors, who could cater to the sensibilities of the contemporary audience, came to the fore. Beside this trendy characteristic of speed, crime films provided a cultural space that could deal with the social issues that filled newspapers at the time, such as kidnapping, smuggling, sexual trafficking, murder and organized crime. In the course of delivering these stories, 'there was also a noticeable improvement in the sophistication of gunfight and car chase scenes'.[7] And, compared to the previous versions of investigation films which showed 'just policemen chasing after criminals', these crime films in the 1960s were 'more complicated and more polished'.[8] For instance, 'psychological thrillers' such as *A Murder Without Passion* (*Jeong-yeol-eobneun sal-in*, 1960) and *The Housemaid* (*Hanyeo*, 1960) were produced, focusing more on criminal psychology than on the description of crime itself.

It was Man-hee Lee who vigorously inspired postwar Korean cinema with a noir sensibility. Lee was a passionate pioneer in filmmaking. He made 50 films over 15 years and has been acclaimed by many Korean film critics as 'one of the rare directors who displayed the auteurist consciousness and enhanced the quality of 1960s Korean cinema'.[9] From his debut film, *Kaleidoscope* (*Jumadeung*, 1961), to his posthumously edited film, *The Road to Sampo* (*Sampoganeun gil*, 1975), he experimented with various modernist aesthetics of dislocated time and space. In fact, Lee gained critical and popular recognition with his sophisticated war films such as *The Marines Who Never Returned* (*Doraoji aneun haebyeong*, 1963) and *7 Women P.O.W's* (*7inui yeoporo*, 1965). However, he also regularly made criminal thriller films, and his genuine passion for noir genres earned him the title of 'a poet of the night' from his friends and film critics. His first noir film is the 1962 thriller *Dial 112* (*112reul dollyeora*), based on the popular novel *The Beautiful Woman on the Night Train* (*Yagan yeolcha-ui minyeo*) that was serialized in the monthly magazine *Arirang*. Lee also made two other films based on this original story, in 1969 and in 1975.[10] Conveying a tale of murder and conspiracy centring on an inheritance, *Dial 112* was deemed 'almost the first Korean thriller of quality' and won critical acclaim with its cinematography and montage techniques. Lee also amalgamated noir with other genres such as action, thriller, mystery and melodrama, as shown in works such as *Never Look Back* (*Doraboji mara*, 1963), *The Devil's Stairway*, *Black Hair*, *Intimidator* (*Hyeopbakja*, 1964), *Train Whistle* (*Gijeok*, 1967) and *Assassin* (*Amsalja*, 1969). According to Korean film scholar So-yong Kim, these thriller films provided a refreshing mood for the Korean film industry, which was excessively saturated with melodramas, and fostered less a story-driven world than an atmosphere-driven one in relation to the turbulent history of modern Korea.[11] In other words, Lee's experimentation with the noir sensibility gave contemporary Korean cinema a tactile and allegorical alternative to the widespread appeal of narrative development and progressive modernity.

Among many intriguing films by Man-hee Lee, two 1964 films – a gangster noir, *Black Hair*, and a psychological thriller, *The Devil's Stairway* – draw critical attention in the sense that they address the peculiar aesthetic regime of body and space in relation to global modernization. The spatial allegories in these films, whether they are architectural sites or characters' own bodies, make an environmental inquiry surrounding modernity, aesthetics and power. Through the comparative reading of *Black Hair* and *The Devil's Stairway*, this chapter investigates their noir approach to urban space, modern architecture and the gendered body. It also probes Korean film noir's fragmenting of the totalitarian vision of modernized and institutionalized space and body. The following discussion inquires into the problematic implementation of violence upon gendered bodies and moves onto the environmental sites of streets and buildings. The allegorical portrayal of the city and its dwellers in these films provides us with an opportunity to address the entangled realm of violence, power and modern subjects in Korean film noir.

Noir and the Critique of Violence

What does violence mean in noir films? In general, this question leads us to the discussion of their cinematic representations of violence and the body, such as the grotesque portrayal of scarred faces, bleeding hands, burning bodies and buried corpses. As one of the fiercest film genres, film noir sets up violence as a centrepiece of landscape and a narrative force. Murder, gunfights, car chases and smuggling are pervasive motifs that drive noir narratives to their fatal destinations and give the audience a cathartic sensation. However, what is more significant is that violence in film noir appears in tandem with the critique of violence. For instance, during the years 1941 to 1958, generally agreed as the boundaries of film noir's classic period, cinematic violence encompasses the traumatic experience of war as well as a sense of loss due to urban developments.[12] The violence found in film noir has an interesting relationship to the social and political climate after the war and parallels this period's passion for aesthetic toughness, revealing 'the dark side of savage capitalism'.[13] Naremore insightfully points out that with violence, 'noir produces a psychological and moral disorientation, an inversion of capitalist and puritan values, as if it were pushing the American system toward revolutionary destruction'.[14] Likewise, the noir sensibility of postwar Korea delineates the intertwined relationship between the political violence of 'militarized modernity' and the aesthetic violence of urban noir films.[15]

In Lee's films, violence plays a vital role. In an interview conducted by the Korean Film Archive, screenwriter Gyeol Baek, a close friend of Lee's, recollects that Lee always wanted to express the conflicts between violence and non-violence and had a repulsion and resistance to violence. Baek says that in Lee's films, 'there is always the aesthetic of violence within violence, which director Lee wanted to discover and finally found'.[16] Regarding the two films, even a brief glance at their narratives can show how they are saturated with the violent mood of noir. In the case of *Black Hair*, a female protagonist, Yeon-sil (played by Jeong-suk Mun, who was director Lee's female persona at the time), is the mistress of a crime boss but gets trapped by the blackmailing of one of the boss's henchmen, who had raped her. After being falsely accused of having a love affair, Yeon-sil is punished by the gangsters, who disfigure the right side of her face and expel her from the group. With this series of violent acts, she is forced to descend from a secure position as the boss's mistress to the shabby alleys of prostitution. Her fall down to the street alludes to the social and political degeneracy that was rampant in 1960s Korean society. It shows not only the gangster's

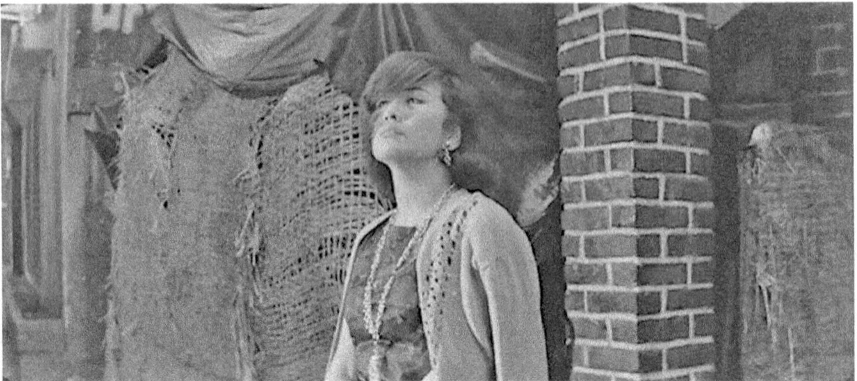

Figure 5.1 The female protagonist, Yeon-sil (Jeong-suk Mun), on the street in *Black Hair*

domination of urban culture but also the state of torpor in the socially outcast peoples' daily experience.

Starring the same actress, *The Devil's Stairway* depicts another journey of a woman, who is a female nurse and implicitly North Korean refugee. This time, the violence is implemented by her own lover: a medical doctor who plots the murder of his clandestine lover, Nurse Nam, when he has an opportunity to marry the daughter of the hospital director and receive a promotion. One stormy night, he seems to commit the perfect crime; he dumps Nurse Nam's narcotized body into a pond in the front yard of the hospital, and the murder is successfully disguised as a missing-person case, until the film reveals the haunting return of the repressed. The two films show the multiple layers of violence, including the sexual, the corporeal, the social and the political. And, more importantly, they address the problematic principle of violence that has paradoxically thrived in the formation of sovereign power.

I want to go further in addressing the haunting relationship between violence and sovereign power, as profoundly articulated in Walter Benjamin's influential essay 'Critique of Violence'. Written in the aftermath of World War I, it opens with the poignant statement 'The task of a critique of violence can be summarized as that of expounding its relation to law and justice.'[17] Regardless of any attempts to justify the implementation of violence, the problem of violence lies not in its unjust utilization and presentation but in the very principle of violence within the system of law and sovereign governance. Benjamin observes how a modern nation-state endorses the dual activities of law-making violence and law-preserving violence. The sovereign power established by the foundation of law threatens any attempt to break the law with law-preserving violence. In this sense, unlike the maxim that law sees violence in the hands of individuals as a danger undermining the legal system, violence by principle resides within the sovereign territory of law. Benjamin astutely observes, 'When the consciousness of the latent presence of violence in a legal institution disappears, the institution falls into decay.'[18] The invisible connection between violence and law is what Benjamin critically designates in the heart of the modern nation-state.

This Benjaminian notion of violence provides a radical understanding of the noir sensibility since it is different from the conventional accounts of violence that focus on the representation of violence in cinema. In this vein, what I pay attention to is less the graphic visual representation of violence than its multilayered meanings in relation to law and justice. Even though the violent visuality in film noir needs to be considered in relation to the effect of violence at the level of spectatorship and narrative, what is significant in this study of Korean film noir is the principle of violence foregrounded in the motif of a vanished or disfigured corporeality and spatiality. For instance, let's take a look at the sequence in *Black Hair* that shows the organization's punishment of Yeon-sil for her adultery, adultery that is in fact her initial victimization by rape. However, the gang members do not allow her to explain the truth to their boss and enforce their rule through particular punishment. While two men seize her arms and another keeps watch at the door, a man with a grotesque face, revealing three blade scars and a disfigured eye, approaches her. The camera foregrounds his back in a dark shadow and depicts Yeon-sil caught by the men on her bed in light. As he steps forward to Yeon-sil holding a broken bottle, the camera likewise moves forward toward her. This corresponding movement accelerates the tension between the violator and the oppressed and deepens the fear experienced by the victim by showing how the violent force steadily approaches the body of the victim. And more significantly, the rules of the organization are cited as the executor is about to carry out his punishment on the betrayer: first, betrayers get their faces cut up; second, anyone who helps her get rid of the scars will get it worse; third, under no circumstances can she leave her affair partner. What draws my attention in this sequence is the verbal citation of law in the moment of punishment. In line with Benjamin's argument, this story addresses the process of conserving the law in the form of violence and its way of justifying the punishment. Likewise, the body of Yeon-sil becomes a site of law-preserving violence that Benjamin discussed as one form of violence.

Without knowing expiation, law is exercised to manifest only guilt and sins. And, as this violent event takes place in Yeon-sil's boudoir at night, the sequence shows the way that the oppressiveness of law enactment intrudes into private life.

The critical notion of violence is quite relevant to the context of Korea's modern nation building in the 1960s. The 1960s marks one of the formative eras in South Korean politics and economic development. After the Korean War, Korean society experienced significant social and political turmoil in the process of building a new, modern nation. In his book *Transformations in Twentieth Century Korea*, Steven Hugh Lee points out, 'During these years, policy-makers and bureaucrats in the republic also established some of the foundations for the longer term accelerated integration of the peninsula into the capitalist world system, a process that has been described as Korea's "globalization".'[19] In a way, the path to globalization was something prosperous. It has often been described as 'one of the few success stories of the developing world', and rhetoric such as that surrounding the 'Miracle of the Han River' has epitomized the development of South Korea in the postwar period.[20] However, as many Korean-studies scholars point out, it was also the site of violence and military disciplines.[21] As the Chung Hee Park military regime implemented the ambitious project of industrial modernization (*San-eop geundaehwa*) and skyscrapers decorated the urban sky, the major problems of political corruption and an unequal distribution of wealth were reflected by the high rates of crime, violence and injustice in Korean metropolises. Also, the economic policies based on export markets aggravated the regional imbalance between the major centralized urban area and the rest of the country. In particular, Seoul, holding 40 per cent of the urban population, became the overly concentrated industrial site of violent class exploitation and gender discrimination. Visualizing the dark side of urban spaces in these historical circumstances, 1960s Korean film noir reveals the long shadow rapid national development casts upon the lives of marginalized and unrepresented social bodies.

Concerning the issue of gender, it is notable that the military government's nation-building project designated national subjectivity as exclusively masculine and located female subjectivities at the margin in a doubling structure, sexually and economically. Likewise, the two films show how violence emerges from the patriarchal, socio-economically determined structure of the world. Similarly caught in the cold grid of masculine power, the female protagonists in the films endure the exploitation of their bodies and sexualities by the law of hyper-masculine society or the ambitious desire of the male characters. While the boss and his gangsters in *Black Hair* engage in biopolitics concerning the enactment of law and rules through torturing and disfiguring the 'sexual' body, *The Devil's Stairway*'s Dr Hyun, Jin-suk's lover as well as father of her unborn baby, uses his knowledge of medical discourse, a rather familiar form of modern biopolitics, for his own criminal act of violence.

The following section maintains that the allegorical impulse of film noir has unremittingly condensed the entangled relationship between body, space and modernity in the form of urban ruins and uncanny architecture. The way the urban city was implemented in the creation of modernized Seoul draws a parallel with the way women's bodies were employed as a site of masculine identity construction. The allegorizing linkage between urban space, architecture and female bodies takes place whenever instrumental violence is implemented.

Urban Ruins and Uncanny Architecture

The allegorical reading of global modernity through the noir sensibility brings up the faculty of decoding the cultural, historical mythology behind the curtain of modern nation-building. Recognizing allegory as a mode of contemplation on ruins and fragments, Benjamin writes in *The Origin of German Tragic Drama*: 'Allegory is in the realm of thought what ruins are in the realm of things'.[22] His inquiry into allegory is none other than the aesthetic recognition of the crisis and rupture in the modern episteme: 'In the field of allegorical intuition, the image is a fragment, a rune. Its beauty as a symbol evaporates when the light of divine learning falls upon it. The false appearance of totality is extinguished.'[23] The spatial dimension of allegory allows us to understand the intermingled problems of city-space and body-space, which are the very symptoms in the discourse of modernity. For instance, demystifying the urban miracle of Seoul and stripping away the national and economic symbolism of the developmental leap, the opening sequence of *Black Hair* sets up its cinematic environment in the imagery of ruins and mazes. Desolate backstreets and architectural interiors foreground the allegorical aesthetics based on fragments and debris. And in this space, there is no escape, which is also what Jean-Paul Sartre captures in the existential condition of modern life. Sartre sees modern life as 'fantastic', made up of 'a labyrinth of hallways, doors, and stairways that lead nowhere, innumerable signposts that dot routes and signify nothing'.[24] In Korean noir films, the allegorical image of Seoul is also represented as a giant labyrinth in which characters appear lost, melancholic or horrified. No individual heroes are allowed to escape from this maze.

Allegorical space in *Black Hair* includes images of ruins and mazes. From the beginning, the film establishes the urban setting and modern architecture in the image of fragments and destruction. In the opening, the gangster mob fights against each other in an abandoned building and a dark alley of the city. In particular, the cinematography emphasizes the geometrical significance of the interior corridors and the exterior walls when it shows the gangsters shooting or escaping. The vertical lines of pillars and stairs convey, ironically enough, less the sense of supporting the total entity than of a crisis of structure and integration.

The distinctive urban geography of *Black Hair* has an interesting point of contrast to another 1960s Korean film, *The Coachman* (*Mabu*, 1961), which deals with the harsh life of an urban, lower-class family. In this film, the ending sequence shows the coachman's eldest son passing the bar exam. The family members embrace each other with joy and tears as they walk on a snow-covered Gwang-hwa-mun Street. This sequence functions as a metaphor that represents 'the reaffirmation of patriarchy' and the 'construction of a modern masculine national subject'.[25] In particular, the familial union and the nation-building project are united in the direction of their movement, which is toward the centre of the Seoul Jung-ang-cheong. This Seoul-centred image in *The Coachman* is very centripetal and progressive. However, cities in Korean films noirs such as *Black Hair* and *The Devil's Stairway* completely negate any kind of central movement for the symbols of urbanity. Rather, they present the urban city as a ruin or fragment in which characters are lost in an exit-less maze. In a distinctive way, the allegorical maze in *Black Hair* introduces the female's experience of the city. Unlike the private detective's or the male hero's journey in the major hard-boiled films noirs, *Black Hair* foregrounds the experience of Yeon-sil, who is expelled from the gangster organization and becomes a prostitute. What is at stake is this anti-centripetal mode of a city space in postwar Korean film noir. In his study of American noirs, *Film Noir and Spaces of Modernity*, Edward Dimendberg writes,

> The period from 1940 to 1959, within which the Hollywood film noir can be conveniently located, adumbrates the height of late modernity and its distinctive spatiality. The historical coincidence of film noir with the eclipse of the concentrated 'centripetal' urban space in the American metropolis constitutes one key strand of this dynamic. New modalities of dispersed 'centrifugal space' constitute the other.[26]

This historical coincidence in Hollywood not only reveals that film noir expresses the experience of modernity in a spatial configuration, but also indicates the different strategies of modernist aesthetics that drift from the centre, and thus the symbolic representation and social transcendence.

In *The Devil's Stairway*, the spatial allegories have a significant parallel with those of *Black Hair*. Whereas *Black Hair* reveals the environmental problems of entrapping urban settings through the form of labyrinth, *The Devil's Stairway* asks questions of the interior spaces and their critical relationship to the corporeal sensation by stirring up the spectral significance of architectural allegories. The haunting figure of the hospital in *The Devil's Stairway* shows what Anthony Vidler calls 'the architectural uncanny' by addressing 'the role of architecture in staging the sensation (of the uncanny) and in acting as an instrument for its narrative and spatial manifestations'.[27] In *The Devil's Stairway*, the problematic relationship between body and architecture is set up through the linkage between the female protagonist and the hospital. As if it is a living character, the hospital corresponds to Jin-suk's physical, emotional and spectral status, through its flickering lights, rattling windows and doors, and aural elements. And, in this fashion, 'the complex and shifting relations between buildings and bodies, structures and sites'[28] serve as an analytical diagram that embodies the allegorical paradigm of spatial violence in relation to class and gender anxiety.

As the title of *The Devil's Stairway* shows, one of the most significant allegories throughout the film is the stairway. In film noir, stairs, as dynamic and spatially fragmented structures, often lead to catastrophe. As symptomatically shown in American noir films such as *The Naked City* (1948) and *Sudden Fear* (1952), violence awaits at the top of the stairs.[29] Also, as shown by the term 'staircase complex' applied to Hitchcock's thrillers in reference to one of Hitchcock's favourite architectural motifs, staircases are often places of crisis, and their perspectival effects isolate and confine characters. The central spine of domestic space, the staircase presents itself as an arena for psychological tensions.[30] In *The Devil's Stairway*, the stairways represent the male protagonist's ambition to step up the social ladder by marrying the hospital chief's daughter. The visual allegory of stairs as a social ladder is shown in one sequence in which Dr Hyun and the hospital chief's daughter go out on a date. As the two arrive at a hillside observatory, the camera focuses on the giant spiral stairways, and makes the characters visually miniaturized. The meaning of the staircase as a social ladder has been also addressed and problematized in Ki-young Kim's *The Housemaid*. As Kyung Hyun Kim points out, 'The staircase in *The Housemaid* is where the desire for class mobility is both imagined and thwarted – becoming finally the

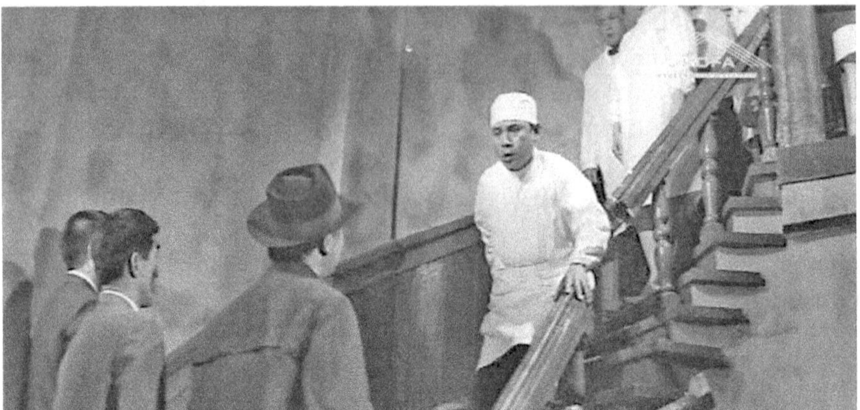

Figure 5.2 The stairway as an allegorizing predicament in *The Devil's Stairway*

setting for despair and death'.[31] In a similar fashion, the significance of stairways does not remain at the symbolic level but moves onto the allegorical level, in that stairs turn out to be the uncanny space of violence, where falls and death occur repeatedly. As Nurse Nam, Dr Hyun's wife, and finally Dr Hyun fall from the stairway, the film shows the haunting failure of the upward movement.

Also in the allegorical reading of *The Devil's Stairway*, a seemingly peripheral site from a narrative perspective takes on a crucial role in relation to space, violence and the body. This site, the morgue outside the hospital building, generates a feeling of the uncanny. Like an invisible but substantial figure of a ghost, the exteriority of the morgue is highly expressed. The morgue, built of grey cement, is represented as an exterior space with closed walls and isolated locality; that is, an absolute space of death. The camera often stays outside the building and conveys a sense of uncanny gazing usually reserved for something invisible. Even on the two occasions that the film shows the characters inside the morgue – first, when the male interns carry a young girl's dead body to the morgue, and second, when her father visits to claim his daughter's body – the interior space of the morgue is not revealed. The camera remains outside the building, blocked by the closed door, or directs its gaze toward the outside when situated inside of the building. With this intricate dialectic between the location and a camera gaze, the film creates the architectural uncanny. In particular, in the latter case, the cinematography brings about an absolute dislocation and invisibility since the camera remains inside the morgue to the close of the scene. Here, the claustrophobic sense of being confined in the space of death is conveyed as the door is closed and the light disappears.

Similar to the space of death, women's dead bodies become haunting objects toward the end of *The Devil's Stairway*. On the one hand, the disappearance of a body has a synchronic relationship with the emergence of modern architecture. The living experiences of space and body have become invisible and are excluded from the architectural boom of modern urbanization. On the other hand, the body does not disappear completely, but leaves its traces and transforms the architectural space into an uncanny site, a haunting space. The complex and shifting relations between buildings and bodies, structures and sites serve not only as a vehicle of narrative dramaturgy, but also as an analytical diagram that embodies the modernist paradigm of spatial violence and anxiety.

The Face and Body as a Counter-Space

In his book *The Architectural Uncanny*, Anthony Vidler points to the disappearance of the face as a characteristic of the modern city and architecture. Here, the architectural face implies the particularity, the specific landmarks, or names of objects. Architecture in the modern metropolis effaces indexicality and presents a faceless space by erasing appearance and interior. Then, the multiple proliferations of the face and the return of the body can be considered as a counter-aesthetic to the effacement that has been propagated in architectural high modernism. The last section of this chapter focuses on the image of the face and the return of the body and illuminates them as Korean noir's allegorizing critique of violence.

In *Black Hair*, anxious that she may weaken their boss and ruin their organization, the gangsters target Yeon-sil and conspire to get rid of her. Even though their murderous chase fails thanks to the interruption of a taxi driver who once met Yeon-sil on the street, other gangsters instructed by the former henchman maliciously move to find her. In one sequence, they search for her with her photo, which shows her face before its disfigurement. From a high angle, the camera shows copies of her image being displayed on a table and distributed to each of the gangsters. This sequence is followed by a montage sequence in which the gangsters show her picture to cosmetic surgeons, hoping to catch her disguised by plastic surgery. This sequence is interestingly composed as if the gangsters are conducting the detectives' job of searching for a missing or lost person. The sequence ends with another scene in which a doctor, the taxi driver's old acquaintance, examines Yeon-sil's face after the surgery. She gets her face back in spite of a residual trace, which the doctor says will be completely removed by the second surgery. In the end, the film never shows Yeon-sil's fully recovered face. In this sense, the photographic image of her face is something that is not possible to be recovered, something lost for ever. Even after the recovery of her status as a social and political being, her face remains in between the disfigured, banned status and the completely forgotten status. The mark of violence lingers; the trace of exclusion remains.

The face is a profoundly intriguing object in several respects. As an allegory of a bodily fragment, the face lets us speculate on its aesthetical status. Georg Simmel regards the aesthetic significance of the face as being in relation to spirituality and individuality, in other words, to the personality.[32]

> Aesthetically, there is no other part of the body whose wholeness can as easily be destroyed by the disfigurement of only one of its elements. For this is what unity out of and above diversity means: that face cannot strike any one part without striking every other part at the same time – as if through the root that binds the whole together.[33]

But, paradoxically, a face in *Black Hair* is rather anti-aesthetical and anti-humanistic. The abjection that men on the street used to show on sight of her scarred face is similar to Simmel's reluctance toward the distorted bodies. However, Simmel's understanding of the face as an expression of spiritual wholeness has a paradox, because the face can also have the power of subverting the relationship between spirituality and the aesthetic. The noir face especially, as a trace of spectacular/spectral violence, disturbs 'the most remarkable aesthetic synthesis of the formal principles of symmetry and of individuality'.[34] It becomes the trace of violence, the veiling and unveiling of violence.

Regarding *The Devil's Stairway*, what is at stake is a woman's body itself. In her book *Vanishing Women*, in which she discusses the divergent traditions of women's disappearance by magicians, surgeons and filmmakers, Karen Beckman deals with the figure of the vanishing woman and its cultural and political significance. Her questioning includes 'not only why it is a woman who vanishes but what kind of woman in this period is most in danger of vanishing into thin air'.[35] Even though it is a brief moment, the film discloses Nurse Nam's background as a North Korean refugee during the Korean War – a so-called woman without any roots. With this information, her disappearance reveals the critical significance of vanishing women in a certain cultural and political environment. But, it is also true that the film catches the rare moment of subversion within the history of the vanishing woman. The denouement of *The Devil's Stairway* shows how her ghostly apparitions haunt the disciplinary, masculine space of the hospital. The male protagonist's interior mind is completely occupied by hysterical anxiety. In an exemplary sequence, the place of secret love turns out to be a horrific space. One sequence shows that Dr Hyun tries to catch her – in fact, her ghostly image – in the examination room where he first seduced her. Likewise, he loses his power to see and examine objects, and is disturbed by illusory images and sounds. Vision and visual representation are interrupted by sounds and invisible presences. The psychological dimension of horror creates the optical misunderstanding. The limit of vision unsettles the boundary between dead objects and the living being, creating the ghostly feeling of the uncanny. Her haunting presence is amplified by the multitude of her faces in the surgery room. Dr Hyun is horrified by these faces and falls from the stairway as he runs from her ghostly presence. At the very end, it turns out that Nurse Nam has not died and has actually enacted her own disappearance.

The Devil's Stairway and *Black Hair* are allegorical films that address the entangled relationship between aesthetical problems of corporeality and political problems of violence in postwar, globally modernizing South Korea. In these two films, the de-aestheticization of the face and the de-materialization of the body pose critical questions about the violent nature within the structure of sovereign power and law. Disclosing a hidden geopolitical topos in the ongoing construction of global economics, the films foreground the Möbius strip – like entanglement between the architectural impasse of the urban city and the uncanny aesthetics of the disfigured body. In the dark shadow of the urban city, noir bodies become part of the architectural form of an urban life, an allegorical site of violence.

Notes

1 Lee, Hyangjin, 'The Shadow of Outlaws in Asian Noir: Hiroshima, Hong Kong, and Seoul', in Mark Bould, Kathrina Glitre and Greg Tuck (eds), *Neo-Noir* (London: Wallflower Press, 2009), p. 119.
2 Conard, Mark T., 'Nietzsche and the Meaning and Definition of Noir', in Conard (ed.), *The Philosophy of Film Noir* (Lexington: University Press of Kentucky, 2006), p. 11.
3 Schrader, Paul, 'Notes on Film Noir' in Barry Keith Grant (ed.), *Film Genre Reader III* (Austin: University of Texas Press, 2003), p. 230.

4 Naremore, James, *More than Night: Film Noir in Its Contexts* (Berkeley: University of California Press, 1998), p. 22.
5 Lee, Young-il, *History of Korean Cinema* (Seoul: Jimoondang Pub. Co.), p. 153.
6 Ibid.
7 Ibid., p. 188.
8 Ibid., p. 153.
9 Shin, Kang-ho, 'Research on the Style of Director Lee Man-hee' ('Lee Man-hee Gamdok seutail yeongu'), *Yeonghwa Yeongu* 22 (Seoul: Hanguk yeonghwa hakhoe, 2003), p. 145.
10 They are *Six Shadows* (*Yeoseotgae-ui geurimja*, 1969) and *A Triangular Trap* (*Samgak-ui hamjeong*, 1975).
11 Kim, So-yong, 'The Effect of the Moods and Modes of Lee Man-hee' ('Lee Man-hee mudeuwa modeu hyogwa'), *The Best 10 of Korean Cinema* (*Hankuk yeonghwa choigo ui 10 kyung*) (Seoul: Hyunsil munwha, 2010), p. 107.
12 Silver, Alain and James Ursini (eds), *The Film Noir Reader* (New York: Proscenium Publishers, 1996), p. 11.
13 Naremore, *More Than Night*, p. 22.
14 Ibid., p. 2.
15 Seungsook Mun coined the term 'military modernity' for the Chung-hee Park regime's interpretation of modernity as a nation-building project during the postwar era. See Mun, Seungsook, *Militarized Modernity and Gendered Citizenship in South Korea* (Durham: Duke University Press, 2005).
16 See the interview with Baek in *Filmography of Lee Man-hee: Film Genius Lee Man-hee* (*Lee Man-hee gamdok jeonjakjeon: youngwha cheonjae Lee Man-hee*) (Seoul: Hanguk Younghwa Jaryowon, 2006), p. 245.
17 Benjamin, Walter, 'Critique of Violence', *Reflections* (New York: Harcourt Brace Jovanovich, 1978), p. 277.
18 Benjamin, Walter, 'The Author as Producer', *Reflections*, p. 234.
19 Lee, Steven Hugh, 'Development Without Democracy', in Yun-Shik Chang and Steven Hugh Lee (eds), *Transformations in Twentieth Century Korea* (New York: Routledge, 2006), p. 155.
20 Brinton, Mary C. and Moonkyung Choi, 'Women's Incorporation into the Urban Economy of South Korea', in Yun-Shik Chang and Steven Hugh Lee (eds), *Transformations in Twentieth Century Korea* (New York: Routledge, 2006), p. 312.
21 Mun, *Militarized Modernity and Gendered Citizenship in South Korea*, pp. 7–18.
22 Benjamin, Walter, *The Origin of German Tragic Drama* (London: NLB, 1977), p. 178.
23 Ibid., p. 176.
24 Quoted in Naremore, *More Than Night*, p. 24.
25 Jeong, Kelly, *Crisis of Gender and the Nation in Korean Literature and Cinema* (Lanham, MD: Lexington Books, 2011), p. 78.

26 Dimendberg, Edward, *Film Noir and Spaces of Modernity* (Cambridge, MA: Harvard University Press, 2004), p. 6.
27 Vidler, Anthony, *The Architectural Uncanny* (Cambridge, MA: MIT Press, 1992), p. 14.
28 Ibid., p. xi.
29 Hirsch, Foster, *The Dark Side of the Screen: Film Noir* (New York: Da Capo Press, 1983), p. 95.
30 Jacobs, Steven, *Wrong House: The Architecture of Alfred Hitchcock* (Rotterdam: 010 Publishers, 2007), pp. 27–28.
31 Kim, Kyung Hyun, *The Remasculinization of Korean Cinema* (Durham: Duke University Press, 2004), p. 247.
32 What is intriguing about Simmel's argument of the face is that he grasps the opposing principles of the face in relation to the aesthetical problem of pure perception. See Simmel, Georg, 'The Aesthetic Significance of the Face', in Kurt H. Wolff (ed.), *Georg Simmel, 1858–1918: A Collection of Essays* (Columbus: Ohio State University Press, 1959).
33 Ibid., p. 276.
34 Ibid., p. 279.
35 Beckman, Karen, *Vanishing Women: Magic, Film and Feminism* (Durham: Duke University Press, 2003), p. 15.

Chapter 6

The True Colours of the 'Action Kid': Seung-wan Ryoo's Urban Film Noir

Kyu Hyun Kim

Introduction: Film Noir, New Korean Cinema and Seung-wan Ryoo

Seung-wan Ryoo, born in 1973 and one of the youngest driving forces behind the 'New Korean Cinema', is often grouped into a cohort with other celebrated filmmakers of a slightly older generation, including Chan-wook Park, Je-woon Kim and Joon-ho Bong, known for their distinct aesthetics and creative approaches to cinematic genres.[1] His works, however, have received relatively little critical attention in English-language scholarship. My objective is to briefly examine his urban crime thrillers in light of critical discourses on film noir. I concede at the outset that Seung-wan Ryoo's crime thrillers may not be the obvious choices for discussing film noir in the Korean context, compared to such films as *Sorum* (2001), *Oldboy* (2003) and *A Bittersweet Life* (2005). Nonetheless, I will make a case below for his films as a form of Asian neo-noir, distinct from the so-called 'Hong Kong noir'. I will also argue that they have gone through a process of evolution that intriguingly parallels the development of the American film noir genre from the late-1930s prototype based on (tragic) gangster heroes to the more complex form of sociological noir of later periods.

The present chapter expands on Young-jin Kim's insight that Ryoo's films are radical hybrids not only of seemingly incompatible genre elements but also of genre conventions and realistic representations of everyday lives.[2] Kim and other journalists and critics often refer to Ryoo as 'Action Kid' (Ryoo himself has conceded many times to this *imprimatur*) and highlight the representation and rehabilitation of masculinity in his cinema. However, my analysis below will downplay this aspect of the director's films, instead focusing on their unique patterns of engagement with postwar Korean modernity. This, I argue, is the nodal point at which his works evince the characteristics of films noirs most clearly.

In this chapter, following James Naremore, film noir is construed as a discursive construct rather than a terminology assigned to a concrete set of films. For our purpose, we can accept the streamlined definition of a film noir offered by William Park: a cinematic story of 'crime' unfolding and accounted for in 'a contemporary setting', involving fallible and 'tarnished' man and woman, and following an 'investigation' ensued by the said crime.[3] Naremore, among others, has shown that 'noir qualities' can be decoupled from classical canons and adapted into cinematic products from radically different histories, cultural backgrounds and even political agendas.[4] In fact, film noir can be construed as a part of the broader cultural response to modernity in the context of the twentieth-century history of global social change.

In the Korean context, Mi-na Sin and Han-seok Jeong have used the category of film noir to analyse Korean cinema.[5] They identify Chang-dong Lee's *Green Fish* (1997) as the prototypical 'Korean-style noir'. Jeong argues that, before the early 2000s, Korean media and viewers had associated 'noir' qualities with the hyper-masculinity of Hong Kong action films, dubbed by the news media as 'Hong Kong noir'. The marketing agents used the designation 'noir' to confer a sense of sophistication and class to what they in substance saw as masculine action films with criminal elements. Echoing Jin-soo An, Jeong argues that the films constituted as Korean noir in the late 1990s are in fact male melodramas that, by destroying their protagonists, evoke the nostalgia of the past and thereby solidify the patriarchal order centred on the masculine hero.[6] Criticizing these films as regressive and conservative, Jeong proposes as counter-examples *Tell Me Something* (1999) and *Sorum*, which examine the wounds and scars left by patriarchal dictatorship and, by inference, take to task (developmental) capitalism.[7]

Curiously, Jeong ignores Seung-wan Ryoo's *Die Bad* (2000) and *No Blood No Tears* (2002) in his discussion, perhaps because he sees the latter as engaging in the ('Hong Kong noir'-style) celebration of hyper-masculinity. In my view, Ryoo's films, while at least partially indulging in the kind of male melodrama that Jeong criticizes, present acute critiques of the modernized (and modernizing) hyper-masculinity, in the manner perhaps akin to how Clint Eastwood in his latter-day career has problematized and undermined his own masculine persona to create powerfully critical gazes toward American history and identity and to destabilize the conventions of westerns, prizefighting films, detective mysteries and other Hollywood film genres.[8] Let us then take a close look at Ryoo's two films.

Did He Really Want to Be Another Jackie Chan?: *Die Bad*

Die Bad (Juggeona hoggeun nappeugeona), in retrospect, was one of the astonishing debut films of the new millennium, and its release was one of the events that signalled the arrival of New Korean Cinema. When it opened theatrically on 15 July 2000, the media acknowledged its newness, portraying it as an example of the 'non-mainstream' *(bijuryu)* culture. Ryoo, too, identified himself as a member of the 'non-mainstream' filmmaking community, referring to the feature's unusual structure, comprised of four shorts with overlapping characters and story arcs, filmed under extremely low-budget conditions over more than three years.[9] Intriguingly, these short films, edited together, form a coherent whole that tells a story that would not be out of place in 1930s or 1940s Hollywood.

The film opens with 'Rumble', set entirely in a billiard room, introducing protagonists Seok-hwan (played by the director) and Seong-bin (Seong-bin Park). In the midst of a nasty run-in with kids from an art school, Seong-bin accidentally commits a murder. In the next segment, 'Nightmare', we meet him after seven years in prison. Haunted by the ghostly vision of the murder victim, Seong-bin finds himself drifting into the underworld, when he inadvertently saves the life of a local boss, Tae-hoon Kim. The third episode, 'Modern Man', is a mock documentary, in which Tae-hoon and Seok-hwan, now a cop, are interviewed at length. Interspersed among the interviews is a harrowing, utterly unglamorous fistfight between two men. In the final episode, 'Die Bad', shot in black and white, the two protagonists clash over Seok-hwan's brother, Sang-hwan (the director's real-life younger brother, Seung-beom Ryoo), who wants to join Seong-bin's gang. The climax again shows intercut scenes of carnage, as Sang-hwan is beaten to death during a suicide mission that Seok-hwan is too late to prevent.

Despite Ryoo's own professed love for Jackie Chan and Bruce Lee (and to a certain degree Hong Kong genre cinema of the 1980s and early 1990s),

Die Bad is in fact a strikingly different species, devoid of the acrobatic grace and kinetic romanticism of major Hong Kong genre films made between the 1970s and 1990s.[10] *Die Bad* directly comments on this fact. In 'Rumble', when Seok-hwan imagines launching himself at his nemesis Hyun-soo (Su-hyeon Kim), he sees video-clip flashes of Bruce Lee in *Fist of Fury* (*Jing wu men*, 1972; aka *The Chinese Connection*). However, the fight in the film does not unfold at all like the graceful but lethal duels orchestrated by the Hong Kong star. Instead it gets messy, awkward and ultimately out of control. Later in 'Die Bad', one of Sang-hwan's friends watches *A Better Tomorrow* (*Yingxiong bense*, 1986) on VHS, while waiting for an assignment from the gang boss. Here too, the climactic carnage that overwhelms Sang-hwan and his friends is as far removed as one can think from the romantic heroism displayed by Yun-Fat Chow and Leslie Cheung in the quoted film.

Die Bad, rather than being a loving pastiche of these Hong Kong 'noirs', evinces the qualities associated with the American crime thrillers in transition from the gangster films of classical Hollywood, such as *Little Caesar* (1931) and *Scarface: The Shame of the Nation* (1932), to the films noirs with a certain tragic dignity to their criminal characters, such as *They Live By Night* (1948) and *White Heat* (1949). As Foster Hirsch, among others, has pointed out, the difference between a classical Hollywood gangster-action film and a film noir can be seen in the way the former predominantly presents its (ultimately bound-to-fail) hero as a 'celebration of self-assertiveness', whereas the latter focuses on the internal psychology of its characters and 'stories of doom and withdrawal'.[11] In Hirsch's view, the classical gangster figure was a product of the Prohibition and Great Depression eras, and the classical axis composed of 'the kingpin mobster and the cop who is intent on capturing him' became no longer interesting or believable in the postwar period, as investigation of crime was increasingly taken over by surveillance technology and the criminal characters moved farther into the territory of psychosis and moral murkiness.[12]

Film scholars have recognized the romanticization of gangster heroes in 1980s and 1990s Hong Kong action film and that cinema's relationships to neo-noir.[13] Jin-soo An, in discussing the cult status of John Woo's *The Killer* (1989), argues that its 'unique' quality in the eyes of foreign consumers and critics was partly derived from a mismatching of the film's sophisticated, highly stylised *mise-en-scène* and its overt positing of the male protagonist as a melodramatic, 'suffering' figure. The 'balletic' violence in the film, in this view, is a transferred figuration of the melodramatic intent to articulate that cannot be represented in a realistic mode.[14]

At first glance, Seung-wan Ryoo seems to be doing a grungier, South Korean version of the same: making a male melodrama that uses criminal violence as a tool for expressing emotional affect. There are indeed passages in *Die Bad* characterized by their quasi-melodramatic excess, especially in the climactic sequences (e.g. the blinded Seok-hwan's blood-curdling scream). Conceding this point, however, Ryoo's personages are overall resolutely de-romanticized, disaffected and morally ambivalent, rather than models of righteous suffering or societal victimization. The 'ghost' of the dead student in 'Nightmare' is not presented as a supernatural being but as an Expressionistic device to probe the depth of Seong-bin's guilt and alienation. The 'established' gangster Tae-hoon is also de-glamourized, partly through the device of making him appear as an interviewee in 'Modern Man', where he makes observations about his criminal life in a tersely ironic manner. His comments are infused with deadpan humour, but are neither romantic/existential reflections nor political criticism: they are instead starkly mundane, and their curious sense of authenticity is derived from their non-generic and non-affective qualities. Indeed, these 'interviews', as well as the filmed 'comments' made by supporting characters such as the owner of the billiard parlour, are like variants of the voice-over narration found in a classical film noir, purposefully flattening affective qualities of the actions on screen. Moreover, the documentary realism in these passages is utilized ironically to create distrust in the depiction of the events presented. This strategy is something a 'Hong Kong noir' film with which Ryoo grew up would never consider.[15]

These ironically deployed realist elements co-exist in *Die Bad* with the openly Expressionist techniques and styles, probing the psychological depths of the characters, de-romanticizing their motivations and the characters overall. All these characteristics point to a film noir. In fact, Ryoo's film appears to give a strong voice to the seemingly contradictory impulse in film noir that J. P. Telotte identifies, 'to talk [...] toward community' and at the same time to lean 'toward the isolation of a universal otherness [...] along with widespread feelings of disillusionment and alienation'.[16] This contradictory pull, and the creative synergy that fuels the film generated by this very contradiction, is identifiable in the 1970s urban crime thrillers of certain American directors such as Martin Scorsese, Paul Schrader and Walter Hill. Ryoo's true brethren are these American filmmakers, not John Woo, Woo-ping Yuen or Siu-tung Ching.

He's No Tarantino, and That's Good News: *No Blood No Tears*

Seung-wan Ryoo's sophomore film, *No Blood No Tears (Pido nunmuldo eopsi)*, was released amidst high expectations, only to underperform commercially. It is on the surface a story of two women. Kyung-seon (Hye-young Lee) is a taxicab driver violently manhandled by the Seven Star gang for a sizable debt she owes to them. Su-jin (Do-yeon Jeon) is a gun moll of former boxer turned two-bit gangster Dokbul (Jae-young Jung). Su-jin hatches a plot to filch the pot money for the illegal dogfight gambling trade that Dokbul is put in charge of by a senior crime boss, KGB (Gu Shin), and she ropes Kyung-seon in as a partner. When the unlikely heist succeeds, all hell breaks loose, as the canvas bag full of the stolen cash ends up being pursued by a range of characters, including KGB's frightening enforcer Silent Man (martial arts director Doo-hong Jung).

Both marketing agents and journalists, noticing similarities between Ryoo's film and the works of Quentin Tarantino, especially *Reservoir Dogs* (1992) and *Pulp Fiction* (1994), both well received in Korea, made an active association between the two filmmakers. *No Blood No Tears* was thus marketed as a 'pulp noir'. This designation unfortunately has since become a cliché that has dogged all Ryoo's films to this day. Young-jin Kim, one of the few interpreters of Ryoo's works who has resisted such pat labelling, interprets *No Blood No Tears* as a variant of male melodrama (even though he never uses the term), a film of pathos filled with sympathetic gazes toward the downtrodden and under-privileged members of society. Ryoo engages with them to such an extent that, Kim argues, he often sacrifices the smooth flow of the narrative to dwell on colourful supporting characters, such as the old gangsters played by Yeong-in Kim and Chan-ki Baek, veteran actors of 1960s and 1970s potboilers.[17] Even though Kim is one of the most insightful critics (and supporters) of Ryoo's films, he again regards the filmmaker's agenda as rehabilitation of the masculinity in Korean cinema via reconstruction of the (male-centred) action genre.

My interpretation departs from Young-jin Kim's. Seung-wan Ryoo time and again refutes the melodramatic affect and denies tragico-heroic restoration of the male protagonists. A notorious sequence, in which Silent Man, embodying the 'unreasonable' violence of a film noir through his absolute refusal to explain or even comment on his behaviour, punishes Dokbul in a dogfight ring, encapsulates this seeming contradiction at the film's heart. Defying audience expectations, Silent Man and Dokbul do not engage in a duel between two fighting styles, the *taekwondo*-based acrobatic martial arts and boxing. Instead, Silent Man mercilessly brutalizes the ex-boxer, until the latter is profusely bleeding and barely alive. Dokbul, whose name is an anagram of sorts of 'Bulldog' and also could mean 'Lone Wolf' in Korean, is presented metaphorically as a whipped dog. His sudden revival and equally brutal but utterly graceless killing of Silent Man that follows, therefore, may both surprise and discomfit us. We would ordinarily expect them to engage in a violent but kinetically beautiful and exciting (in the manner of a Hong Kong action film) fight sequence that provides the sheer pleasure of seeing bodies in motion, or, conversely, one in which Dokbul recovers or (tragically) fails to recover his masculine self through the 'suffering' of the body in a melodramatic form, generating catharsis or pathos. Both expectations are completely dashed in the sequence. We are left unsure if we were supposed to cheer Dokbul on, or be utterly repelled by his coarse, animal-like curses of triumph bellowed at the broken body of Silent Man.

Frank Krutnik analyses masculinity found in the classical noir films and concludes that heroic masculinity is either undercut or destabilized in them, despite the signs of 'toughness', that is, 'overt masculinisation of both language (the "hard-boiled" banter) and action (the acts of violence)'. He argues that 'the conventionalised figuration of "tough", unified and controlled masculinity is invoked not so much as a model of worthwhile or realistic achievement but more as a worrying mark of what is precisely lacking'.[18] In *No Blood No Tears*, the 'worrisome' signs of failed masculinity return with brutality and violence to more or less destroy Dokbul, a victim/villain who fails to become an 'investigating' hero. *Die Bad* pays little attention to the desire for sexual transgression, which Krutnik identifies as one of the signature motivations of a film noir hero. Even compared to other Asian gangster-action movies that express covert and overt homoeroticism, often substituting sexual acts with acts of physical violence, *Die Bad* is not particularly sexually charged. However, male sexuality becomes one of the central problems in *No Blood No Tears*, because Ryoo has chosen to reconfigure gender dynamics of a classical film noir by shifting the genders and character traits of his protagonists.

Today we know that even from a feminist perspective, the femme fatale remains a complex figure. E. Ann Kaplan acknowledges in her new preface to the 1998 edition of *Women in Film Noir* that it is no longer possible to simply categorize the femme fatale as a 'male fantasy', and that '*film noir* offers a space for the playing out of *various* gender fantasies'.[19] Unlike the relationships among main characters in a typical classical film noir, Dokbul in *No Blood No Tears* is displaced from the central position of the 'suffering' or 'tough' male hero, and rendered as both the victim of the femme fatale

Su-jin and the villain who must be overcome by the combined efforts of the heroines, Kyung-seon and Su-jin. Indeed, it becomes gradually evident as we see the film that Su-jin is the real instigator of the movie's sometimes maddeningly complex plot: she is the femme fatale and 'good girl' (with the muted homoerotic attraction working in a lesbian direction toward Kyung-seon) all in one. As such, despite *No Blood No Tears*' surface pretence of moral cynicism or indulgence in genre conventions for its own sake, it shares a surprising kinship with the contemporary neo-noirs in which femmes fatales overcome their male antagonists and 'get away with' either murder or loot, or both.[20]

However, *No Blood No Tears* does not push destabilization of male sexuality to the extent that it departs from the heterosexual norm or moves into a feminist direction. Ryoo himself appears indecisive about the extent to which he wants to destabilize Dokbul's character. The climactic, vicious fight between Dokbul and two women is filmed in such a way as to elicit disgust and outrage, rather than pleasure: we are reminded of everyday scenes of domestic violence and patriarchal oppression by this sequence. Ryoo then allows Kyung-seon to use a metal key – a realistic instrument of spontaneous self-defence for women but simultaneously symbolizing dissolution of domesticity and opening of a door to new life – to deal a fatal blow

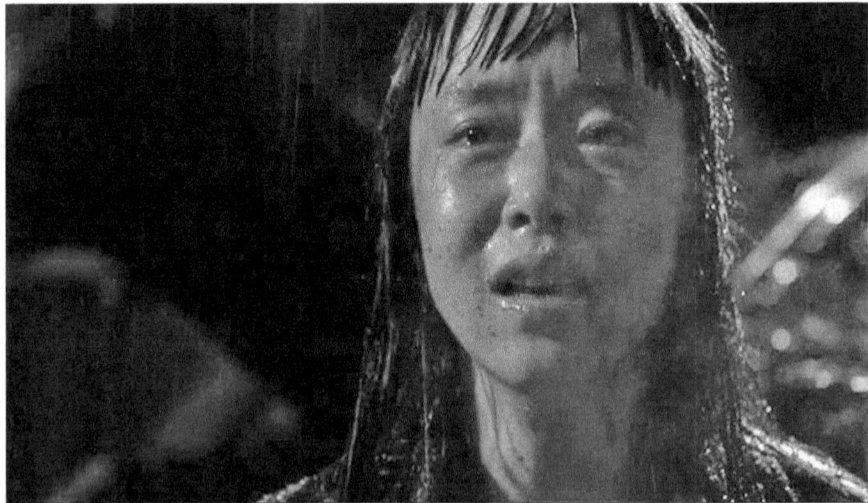

Figure 6.1 In *No Blood No Tears*, Su-jin looks on ambivalently with remorse and disgust as Dokbul bleeds to death

to the raging Dokbul's jugular vein. Here he allows a brief moment of pathos for the character as he mutters a pleading line of dialogue, 'Su-jin, do you hate me so much? Fuckin' bitch', before bleeding to death. But this little aside, a concession to the melodrama of the suffering male body, arrives too late: Su-jin's display of sympathy toward Dokbul lasts only a few seconds of screen time. Viewers are likely to exit this climax exhausted and a bit traumatized, but still repelled by the ex-boxer. He is like Jake La Motta in Martin Scorsese's *Raging Bull* (1980), bereft of Scorsese's semi-anthropological gaze from a black and white camera, maintaining a proper emotional distance from the subject: La Motta as a true loser, hateful and pathetic.

Speaking in retrospect about *No Blood No Tears*, Ryoo explained that for him 'neo-noir was a mountain that I had to climb over once in my life', and in order to challenge this mountain, 'I chose a female protagonist, not femme fatale, but who could stand at the centre of the narrative by herself, and chose as my weapon the "thickness of feeling" instead of coolness'.[21] Despite Ryoo's intent, *No Blood No Tears* is in the end a less stable film than *Die Bad*. If the latter could be characterized as a radical hybrid film that (in a distinctively South Korean manner) recreates in itself the transition from a gangster-action film to a classical-mode film noir, *No Blood No Tears* may be seen as an experimental neo-noir that does not entirely cohere stylistically and formally. It tries to address, not always successfully, diverse and fascinating impulses found in a contemporary neo-noir in relation to the classical noir typologies: why can't the femme fatale get away with it after all? Can characters express genuine affect without resorting to melodrama or conversely abandoning it altogether for 'surface cool'? How much 'realism' can one incorporate into a story while staying true to key genre conventions? Some of these questions, raised in *No Blood No Tears* to not always satisfying resolution, are more effectively addressed in Ryoo's subsequent films.

Nesting Within the Concrete Jungle: *The City of Violence* and *The Unjust*

After the interludes of the martial-arts fantasy *Arahan* (2004) and the pugilist drama *Crying Fist* (2005), Seung-wan Ryoo directed and starred in *The City of Violence* (*Jjakpae*, 2006). Again compared to Tarantino's *Kill Bill* films (2003, 2004) when released, mainly due to its climactic fights taking place in a vaguely Japan-esque setting, the film was welcomed by Young-jin Kim and others as Ryoo's 'return to the form'.[22] A Seoul cop, Tae-su

(Doo-hong Jung), receives the shocking news that his childhood friend Wang-jae (a Seung-wan Ryoo regular, Kil-gang An), a retired gangster, has been stabbed to death by a handful of punks. Tae-su goes back to his hometown, On-seong, to attend Wang-jae's funeral. He finds the town under the thumb of their childhood buddy Pil-ho (played by the excellent comic actor Beom-soo Lee), now a local crime boss involved in a citywide real-estate development scheme. Tae-su reluctantly teams up with the short-tempered civilian Seok-hwan (director Ryoo) to investigate and avenge Wang-jae's death.

Photographed in grainy Super 16mm, *The City of Violence* purposefully returns to a 'classical' mould in characterization and narrative structure. Continuing one of the strategies employed in his previous work, Ryoo updates for contemporary viewers a 1960s or 1970s Korean action film with localized characters (speaking in thick regional accents and dressed in plain clothes unlike the stylized fashions of new-century genre films), localized settings (*The City of Violence* joins a welcome trend of recent Korean crime thrillers increasingly moving away from the decades-old pattern of being set in Seoul, populated by gangsters who speak only in the discriminated Jeolla Province dialect) and clear-cut (relatively speaking) depictions of heroes and villains.

The City of Violence is also clearly the product of the Doo-hong Jung/Seung-wan Ryoo partnership (Jung's stunt/martial-arts company, Seoul Action School, co-produced the movie). Jung, like Ryoo, wants to keep action/martial-arts choreography as closely linked as possible to the corporeality of the actors,[23] but in other important ways prefers the affectation of male melodrama (what Ryoo himself calls 'macho tendencies'). In *Crying Fist*, for instance, the original conception of the character played by Min-shik Choi, based on a real-life Japanese boxer, had a considerable distance from the melodramatic impulse expressed through a 'body of suffering'.[24] Indeed, the character was almost extreme in his disaffect, a 'human sandbag' who would not react emotionally even when punched again and again by his clientele and would not fight back no matter how humiliatingly and brutally he was beaten. In the movie, Choi's 'tough-guy' portrayal of the character and Doo-hong Jung's choreography significantly move him away from such radical characterization. Likewise, Jung's (admittedly charismatic) presence and his characterization in *The City of Violence* push the film toward archetypal poses of heroes and villains, as much reminiscent of a western and a Hong Kong *wuxia pian* film as of an urban crime thriller.

In other ways, however, *The City of Violence* shows evidence of an evolution of Ryoo's engagement with the film noir genre. The film explores more deeply than Ryoo's previous films the environment in which criminal events and the 'investigation' of the truth take place: a South Korean cityscape. The film's fictional city, On-seong, is both a generic and specific environment that invokes the historical modes of urban development and modernization in South Korea since the 1970s. The developmental drive in the film is personified in the character of Pil-ho. He purchases lands owned by residents of the city cheaply and sells them to the bureaucrats, politicians and businessmen operating in Seoul, a metropolitan mega-city whose relationship with smaller, regional cities is comparable to that of an imperialist metropole and its colonies. Pil-ho is extremely recognizable as a peculiarly South Korean villain, a corrupt regional notable saddled with a massive inferiority complex against the wheeler-dealers from Seoul.

In *The City of Violence*, On-seong is a combination of garishly boom-town, neon-lit glamour and a series of deteriorating streets where the young and underprivileged are exploited. The lively dynamism of a civic square is missing in the city, and its gigantic structures are shown to be empty, such as the under-construction hot-springs resort ironically used by Pil-ho almost as a Roman arena in which to threaten and torture his enemies. Tae-su and Seok-hwan are later chased by a group of thugs variously dressed as baseball players, break-dancers and other cultural icons, an homage to Walter Hill's *The Warriors* (1979), which also transformed certain sections of New York City into a non-temporal, fantastic space. Two protagonists must run through what should ordinarily be a busy commercial district but is seemingly entirely populated by these violent gang members, framed by vertical buildings, construction platforms and other 'grids' that constrain them horizontally. They must escape from the 'centripetal space' of the city[25] or be overcome by the deadly mob and crushed.

This sequence is in my view much more effective in conveying the uncanny quality of the threat posed by a modern city and the betrayed promise of the rapid modernization in South Korea than the popular, martial-arts-heavy climactic fight. Indeed, in its attention to the corrupt process of the growth of a city, *The City of Violence* squarely belongs to the genealogy of 'Korean noir' that Han-seok Jeong and Mi-na Shin have traced to *Green Fish*. *Green Fish*'s evocative coda is a panoramic view, a mock-pastoral, of Ilsan, now a suburban 'bedroom community' for Seoul's upper-middle-and middle-class population. Its protagonist Makdong's death is evoked in relation to this view, as one of the sacrificial lambs for the ruthless process of urban development.

Back on track, as far as commercial prospects are concerned, with *The City of Violence*, Ryoo returned to crime-thriller territory in his next film,

The Unjust (*Budang Georae*, 2011). *The Unjust* has a clever plot, developed by screenwriter Hoon-jeong Park, that turns film noir's usual narrative of investigation on its head. We are shown in the very beginning the 'truth', that the top brass of the Korean police have decided to frame an innocent man for the atrocious serial murder of young children. The brass cajoles Captain Cheol-gi Choe (Jeong-min Hwang) to stage the false arrest. When he twists the arm of a gangster-businessman, Seok-gu Jang (Hae-jin Ryoo), to find a fall guy for the con, he inadvertently antagonizes a young, corrupt prosecutor, Yang Joo (Seung-beom Ryoo), who comes to suspect that the highly publicized arrest of the serial rapist-murderer has been staged. The situation becomes even more convoluted and dangerous when the framed 'murderer' suspiciously kills himself, and Seok-gu starts to blackmail Joo and Choe with incriminating photos and video files.

The Unjust is a full-blown film noir. The film amplifies and refines the themes present but not fully explored in *The City of Violence*: a critique of South Korean modernity and modernity's systematic takeover of an individual's everyday life. Jiro Hong's review of the film suggests that it can be best understood as a New Korean Cinema corollary of Fritz Lang's films noirs.[26] Lang's films are sometimes considered too dependent on their characters' unreliability, but the German filmmaker's interest in the 'networks of deception' that collapse moral certainties and in the almost paradoxical rehabilitation of the individual caught in this web of relationships clearly echoes what goes on among the characters in the Korean film. *The Unjust* presents striking inversions of certain situations familiar from such Lang films as M (1931), *Man Hunt* (1941) and *Beyond a Reasonable Doubt* (1956), featuring reversal or overlapping of the identities of the investigators and the ostensible criminals/culprits. In Ryoo's film, this reversal or blurring of identities is shown as a symptom of structural problems that plague South Korean modernity. The film takes place in an urban landscape in which the structural evil has already triumphed and overtaken the everyday reality. The surveillance regimes and the corresponding mob mentality are portrayed as ubiquitous and unavoidable, driving the film's characters into paranoia, anxiety, mutual deception and eventually lethal pathologies.

Visually, Yang Joo, when in his element, is associated with the horizontal space, often filmed talking into a cell phone and moving from one side of the screen to the other, while Cheol-gi and Seok-gu are associated with the vertical, frequently filmed inside a high-rise, conversing or fighting on the rooftop of a building, or on ground surrounded by concrete columns or structures jutting into the sky.[27] When the prosecutor is stifled in his progress, he is filmed descending stairs (and being derided by his colleagues) or looking up at the higher space. Descent for the characters can literally mean their deaths, not merely symbolic downfall. Seok-gu falls to his death in an elevator in a high-rise under construction, normally his domain. Cheol-gi comes down the stairs in a series of dissolves before he is killed. Conversely, prosecutor Joo's ascent of the spiral stairs in his office building at the end of the film suggests that his corrupt behaviour will not be punished. The spatial organizations in the film signify the 'real' class positions (not simply socioeconomic but political and cultural) and hierarchical relationships that do not necessarily match the self-perceptions of the characters and therefore generate anxieties and pathologies. The spatial matrix is enforced to put each character in his 'position', so to speak: any effort to disrupt the matrix generates fear, duplicity, violence and death; that is, the 'film noir situation', as Park calls it.[28]

Hong argues that the film becomes weaker in the third act when Cheol-gi becomes its focus.[29] There is much truth to this claim, but this does not mean that the corrupt cop suddenly becomes a morally rehabilitated hero. The climax and resolution is faithful to the dark moral universe of a film noir. Cheol-gi is eventually shot to death by his own colleagues, who misconstrue the motivation for his crime as desire for self-promotion rather than (itself misdirected) anger, and the ubiquitous news-media reports grasp neither the true meaning of his crime nor of his death. He belongs to the group of doomed noir protagonists embodying unresolvable contradictions, such as the 'inadvertent' murderer Al (Tom Neal) in *Detour* (1945) and the

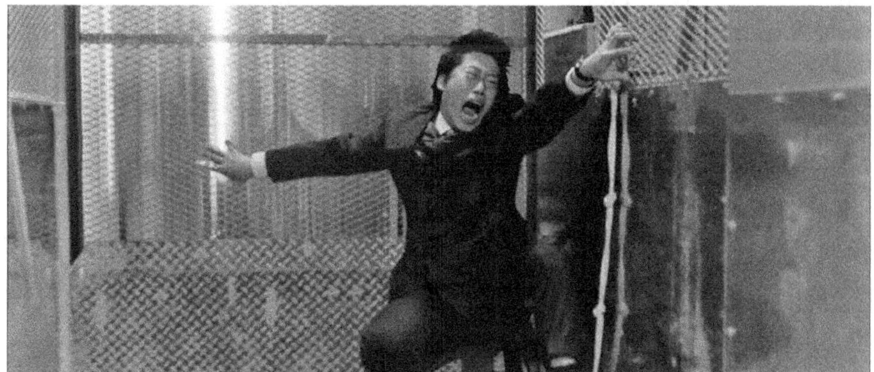

Figure 6.2 In *The Unjust*, Seok-gu realizes to his horror that the elevator is plummeting downward

monstrous yet 'good' cop Hank Quinlan (Orson Welles) in *Touch of Evil* (1958).

The Unjust is anti-Chandleresque in that it refuses to champion a moral hero struggling through the corrupt universe. Everyone, with the exception of a few female characters who exist outside the network of surveillance and administrative relations, is corrupt, seething with anger and anxiety. With this film Ryoo has expunged (the already ambivalent) identification with his childhood Hong Kong cinema heroes as well as his propensity toward male melodrama. This does not mean the quality of emotions in his characterizations or narratives has degraded: it is rather a sign of greater streamlining and refinement.

Conclusion

I have argued here that Ryoo's films have gone through the evolution that turned the gangster heroes into morally compromised, tormented protagonists of the films noirs. The influence on Ryoo of 1980s Hong Kong cinema and 'post-modern' filmmakers such as Tarantino has never been significant, or if one insists, merely transitory. His films effectively address anxieties about industrial modernity, rampant economic growth and rapid social changes, while breaking out in their own direction from the self-conscious modernism of the neo-noirs, including those made by other Korean filmmakers. Jee-woon Kim's *A Bittersweet Life*, to cite one example from the latter group, evokes a form of manufactured nostalgia for the modernity (rather than traditional values or social relations) that had never really existed (or perhaps did not allow contemporary Koreans to acknowledge, as such modernity traces its origins to the colonial past). Ryoo's films for the most part negate this kind of nostalgia, even for the hyper-masculine past of 'youthful days', in which the extremely popular Korean gangster films such as *Friend* (2001) calculatedly indulge (only *The City of Violence* comes close to accepting nostalgia as a central motivation for the protagonists). Likewise, his works sometimes present more profound critiques of South Korean modernity, as represented through its developmental and surveillance regimes, than many of the so-called realist dramas do. Beyond the shallow reading of his films as post-modern pastiches of film genres à la Tarantino, Seung-wan Ryoo is one of the Korean filmmakers to whom we must turn for cinematic explorations into the dark underside of the social and political history of Korea.

Notes

1 Regarding the designation 'New Korean Cinema', see Shin, Chi-Yun and Julian Stringer (eds), *New Korean Cinema* (New York: New York University Press, 2005).

2 Kim, Young-jin, *Ryoo Seung-wan*, trans. Colin A. Mouat (Seoul: Korean Film Council, 2008).

3 Naremore, James, *More Than Night: Film Noir in Its Contexts*, rev. ed. (Berkeley: University of California Press, 2008 [1998]). William Park criticizes Naremore for the latter's diffuse conception of film noir, but it appears that Park's own definition is less concerned with narrative structure or stylistic traits than with certain *orientations* seen in the relevant films. See Park, *What is Film Noir?* (Lewisburg, PA: Bucknell University Press, 2011). The definition of film noir quoted above is found in Park, *What is Film Noir?*, p. 26.

4 Naremore, *More Than Night*, pp. 199–211.

5 Sin, Mi-na, '"Chorok mulgogi" e damgin hangukjeok pillem neuwaru eui teukjing [The Characteristics of a Korean Film Noir Contained in *Green Fish*]', *Seogang keomyunikeishyoenjeu* [Seogang Communications] 1.1 (2000): 211–228; Jeong, Han-seok, '"Hangukjeok neuwareu" e gwanhan bipyeong-damnon jae-jihyeonghwa jeui [A Proposal for Re-Topographification of Critical Discourse on the "Korean-style noir"]', *Yeonghwa munhwa yeongu* [Cinema Culture Studies] 5 (2003): 85–137. All English translations of Korean sources are my own.

6 Jeong, '"Hangukjeok neuwareu"', pp. 107–110; also see An, Jin-soo, '*The Killer*: Cult Film and Transcultural (Mis) Reading', in Esther C. M. Yau (ed.), *At Full Speed: Hong Kong Cinema in a Borderless World* (Minneapolis: University of Minnesota Press, 2001), pp. 95–113.

7 Jeong, '"Hangukjeok neuwareu"', pp. 111–119, 122–127.

8 Cf. Cornell, Drucilla, *Clint Eastwood and the Issue of American Masculinity* (New York: Fordham University Press, 2009).

9 Cf. Yi, Yeong-ju, '*Juggeona hogeun nappeugeona* gijahoegyeon [Press Conference: *Die Bad*]', *Movist.com*, 29 June 2000, <http://www.movist.com/article/read.asp?id=219&type=13>, accessed 4 May 2013.

10 Cf. Bordwell, David, *Planet Hong Kong: Popular Cinema and the Art of Entertainment* (Cambridge, MA: Harvard University Press, 2000).

11 Hirsch, Foster, *The Dark Side of the Screen: Film Noir*, New Edition (New York: Da Capo Press, 2001 [1981]), p. 60. See Warshow, Robert, 'The Gangster as Tragic Hero', in *The Immediate Experience* (New York: Doubleday, 1963) for a classic statement of the gangster as a cinematic hero.

12 Hirsch, *The Dark Side of the Screen*, p. 65.

13 Cf. Collier, Joelle, 'The Noir East: Hong Kong's Transmutation of a Hollywood Genre?', in Gina Marchetti and Tan See Kam (eds), *Hong Kong Film*,

Hollywood and the New Global Cinema: No Film Is an Island (London: Routledge, 2007), pp. 137–158; and Lee, Hyangjin, 'The Shadows of Outlaws in Asian Noir: Hiroshima, Hong Kong and Seoul', in Mark Bould, Kathrina Glitre and Greg Tuck (eds), *Neo-Noir* (London: Wallflower Press, 2009), pp. 118–133.

14 An, '*The Killer*', pp. 102–103.

15 Of course, some contemporary Hong Kong neo-noirs, such as *Infernal Affairs* (2002) or *Mad Detective* (2007), would represent perhaps even more radical cases of departure from the 1980s–1990s model An analyses.

16 Telotte, J. P., *Voices in the Dark: The Narrative Patterns of Film Noir* (Urbana: University of Illinois Press, 1989), p. 30.

17 Kim, *Ryoo Seung-wan*, pp. 35–36.

18 Krutnik, Frank, *In A Lonely Street: Film Noir, Genre, Masculinity* (London: Routledge, 1991), pp. 88–91.

19 Kaplan, E. Ann, 'Introduction', in Kaplan (ed.), *Women in Film Noir*, rev. ed. (London: British Film Institute, 1998 [1978]), p. 10 (emphasis in original).

20 Williams, Linda Ruth, 'A Woman Scorned: The Neo-Noir Erotic Thriller as Revenge Drama', in Bould, Glitre and Tuck (eds), *Neo-Noir*, pp. 168–175.

21 Ryoo, Seung-wan, *Ryoo Seung-wan eui bonsaek* [True Colours of Ryoo Seung-wan] (Seoul: Maum Sanchaek, 2008), p. 20.

22 Cf. Kim, *Ryoo Seung-wan*, pp. 47–51.

23 In 2004, Jung debuted as a boxer at the age of 40, partly to test the limit of his ability as a stuntman, partly to truly 'embody' his philosophy that cinematic 'action' should be as grounded in the human body as possible. See Yi, Hae-jun, 'Aeksyeonbaeu Jeong Du-hong peurobokseo debwi [Action actor Doo-hong Jung debuts as a pro boxer]', *Ilgan seupocheu* [*Sports Daily*], 4 July 2004.

24 Ryoo, Seung-wan, DVD Commentary for *Crying Fist* (Enter One DVD, South Korea, 2005).

25 See Dimendberg, Edward, *Film Noir and the Spaces of Modernity* (Cambridge, MA: Harvard University Press, 2004), pp. 87–114.

26 Hong, Jiro, '*The Unjust*' (film review), *koreanfilm.org* (2011), <http://www.koreanfilm.org/kfilm10.html#unjust>, accessed 4 May 2013. For a different interpretation of the film see Elley, Derek, '*The Unjust*' (film review), *Film Business Asia*, 19 February 2011, <http://www.filmbiz.asia/reviews/the-unjust>, accessed 4 May 2013.

27 Dimendberg, *Film Noir and the Spaces of Modernity*, pp. 87–98.

28 Park, *What is Film Noir?*, pp. 24–25.

29 Hong, '*The Unjust*'.

Chapter 7

A Mess of Contradictions?: Korean Noir in Myung-se Lee's *Nowhere to Hide* and *Duelist*

Daniel Martin

> Almost every critic has his own definition of *film noir*, and a personal list of film titles and dates to back it up. Personal and descriptive definitions, however, can get a bit sticky. A film of urban night life is not necessarily a *film noir*, and a *film noir* need not necessarily concern crime and corruption. Since *film noir* is defined by tone rather than genre, it is almost impossible to argue one critic's descriptive definition against another's. How many noir elements does it take to make a *film noir noir*?[1]

Debates around definitions of film noir remain unresolved; critics and scholars still disagree about some of the fundamental qualities of noir cinema: is it a true genre or merely a critical category? Is noir quintessentially American, or can its themes and style thrive within the output of other national cinemas? As Paul Schrader argues in the quote above, critics have flexible and differing ways of recognizing and canonizing the films they see as noir. Andrew Spicer notes that:

> film noir is a discursive critical construction that has evolved over time. What must now be acknowledged is that it is a *contested*

> construction. Film noir has been defined as a genre, a movement, a visual style, a prevailing mood or tone, a period, or as a transgeneric phenomenon. [...] Any attempt at defining film noir solely through its 'essential' formal components proves to be reductive and unsatisfactory because film noir [...] also involves a sensibility, a particular way of looking at the world.[2]

Film noir is therefore defined by various criteria according to the particular perspective of the critic, academic or historian in question. Schrader is adamant that noir is not a genre, but is rather defined by stylistics (including expressionist lighting emphasizing the darkness of the city) and themes (paranoia and a fear of the unknown future), and is divisible into three classic phases, from the cycle of 'the private eye and the lone wolf' to postwar films about 'crime in the streets, political corruption and police routine' to, finally, films of 'psychotic action' that interrogate 'the loss of public honor, heroic conventions, [and] personal integrity'.[3] Spicer, meanwhile, uses the term 'cycle' to most aptly define noir, largely agreeing with Schrader on the stylistic attributes and identifying the 'noir universe' as 'dark, malign and unstable where individuals are trapped through fear and paranoia, or overwhelmed by the power of sexual desire'.[4] These attempts to define noir without being too prescriptive offer a loose but working definition of the term, one evocative of the classic mode of the private eye, the femme fatale and a world of crime and betrayal.

For the purposes of mainstream film journalism, however, the term 'film noir' is vastly less ambiguous, and has an instantly recognizable meaning. Critics invoke the term as a way to communicate a film's style *and* genre, as well as to demonstrate their own sophisticated cinematic vocabulary. Spicer argues that 'the term film noir has accumulated [...] high cultural capital' and cites Rick Altman's contention that film noir, as a term, has become 'part of film journalism'.[5] The deployment of the term film noir, then, is a common tactic for film critics, and can be especially useful when providing a familiar contextual framework for foreign cinema.

The international release and reception of two South Korean noir films demonstrates precisely how Western critics define 'film noir' in the context of world cinema. Myung-se Lee's noir thriller *Nowhere to Hide* (*Injeong sajeong bolgeot eobtda*, 1999) was one of the first South Korean films to receive a commercial theatrical release in the UK and USA; his next film, *Duelist* (*Hyeongsa*, 2005), equally evocative of noir, came at the peak of the East Asian cinema 'boom' in the West and also achieved significant visibility. Both films attracted a critical consensus as they were contextualized, categorized and defined on the basis of their relationship to familiar and recognizable genres. The way *Nowhere to Hide* was celebrated as noir – and the aspects of the film that were maligned or ignored as a result – reveals a surprisingly strict definition of the term. In the case of *Duelist*, however, the film's noir elements were often overlooked in favour of a reading of the film that foregrounded its martial-arts and swordplay elements, in keeping with a Western critical perception of what is more conventionally 'Asian'. This chapter examines how critics understand and appreciate *Nowhere to Hide* and *Duelist*, in the process revealing exactly what a Western conception of film noir includes and precludes.

Policing the Boundaries: *Nowhere to Hide*

A pioneer of the Korean New Wave of the late 1980s and early 1990s, Myung-se Lee has been widely acknowledged by critics and scholars as an *auteur*; he writes all his own screenplays, and insists upon a high degree of creative autonomy. Although *Nowhere to Hide* remains Lee's most widely seen film (both inside and outside South Korea), his interest in film noir is evident in much of his other work as well. Lee's films are often described as 'genre-bending', and he himself has described his work as 'melo-action movies' with a 'noir ambience'.[6] A cinephile with a strong interest in silent film and Hollywood's black-and-white classics, Lee has explored noir in many of his works. His most recently completed feature, M (2007), is a romance-mystery-thriller that evokes noir associations in its cinematography and themes, yet is ultimately a tragic melodrama about a heartbroken ghost and a frustrated author. The film he made immediately before *Nowhere to Hide*, *Their Last Love Affair* (*Jidokhan sarang*, 1996), begins with a striking acknowledgement of the director's interest in noir aesthetics. Though a romance with both dramatic and comedic elements, the film opens with a playful attempt to mislead the audience via an emphatically noir-esque shot of dark, wet city streets and the lead character emerging from an implausibly large cloud of steam and fog.[7]

Film noir has been one of several defining threads of Lee's overall body of work, but he has typically made reference to noir in a nuanced manner, contributing in a range of ways to the growing number of contemporary variations on and reinventions of the noir genre. *Nowhere to Hide* is a key example of Lee's approach to noir, as the film both conforms to and contradicts the traditional film noir form in a multitude of ways. Ostensibly a crime thriller (though one of a highly hybrid nature, incorporating comedy and action), *Nowhere to Hide* charts the determined adventures of a team of police officers on the trail of a professional killer. The film self-consciously evokes many of the defining qualities of film noir, but also contains references to recent trends in domestic cinema. Signalling the tone of the film to local audiences, the lead character, Detective Woo, tells a suspect early on that 'this isn't *Two Cops*'. The line is translated into English as 'this isn't a cops and robbers movie', but the original dialogue is a specific metatextual reference to a popular action-comedy film (*Two Cops/Too Kapseu*, 1993), which featured the same two lead actors of *Nowhere to Hide*, Sung-ki Ahn and Joong-hoon Park, as bumbling and comically corrupt policemen (unlike in *Two Cops*, in *Nowhere to Hide* they are pitted against each other). *Two Cops* instigated a domestically popular cycle of light-hearted crime films, and the opening of *Nowhere to Hide* directly acknowledges its intent to explore darker territory.[8]

Nowhere to Hide is reverent to noir forms and traditions, and exhibits many of the familiar qualities of classical film noir. The film's black-and-white opening shows a dirty, rain-soaked city, and even after transitioning into colour, the depiction of Seoul as a neon jungle, full of shadows, dangerous hideouts and labyrinthine side streets, offers a nostalgic invocation of noir. The staple plot devices of hard-boiled detective noir are also invoked as, at one point in the film, Detective Woo follows a lead based on a cigarette lighter bearing the name of a nightclub frequented by his criminal quarry. The climactic fistfight in a downpour of rain became the iconic moment that defined the film (appearing on its posters and marketing materials), and vividly recalls Schrader's assertion that in film noir, 'the rainfall tends to increase in direct proportion to the drama'.[9] Indeed, *Nowhere to Hide* opens with an assassination in a shower of rain and often uses weather to signal the emotional turmoil of its characters.

There are also deviations from, and exceptions to, noir conventions. While film noir typically focuses on either criminals or private investigators (i.e. anti-heroes on the fringes of society, detached from or in direct opposition to 'the establishment'), *Nowhere to Hide* sympathizes firmly with police officers. Indeed, it's primarily through the realization of its protagonist that the film departs from noir traditions. Detective Woo, though tough and dogged like many noir leads, is also relentlessly cheerful; wearing a semi-permanent and half-psychotic grin, he seems to be generally happy, and content with his life of crime-fighting. While classical film noir is also defined by a strongly fatalistic tone, and commonly features protagonists unable to escape their doomed fates, Detective Woo is a chaotic force, controlled by no one and utterly unpredictable. Though the character does have depth and pathos (a strained relationship with his sister and his grief at losing his partner hint at some inner turmoil), he represents a notable departure from the dark anti-heroes of typical noir. *Nowhere to Hide*, then, if it can be categorized as noir at all, is part of the cycle of reinventions that followed both the classical noir of the 1940s that established the form, and the later neo-noir films that expanded the genre.

The categorization and canonization of *Nowhere to Hide* as film noir became an especially contentious issue on the film's international release. The film screened in major cities nationwide in the USA and UK, and was widely reviewed at a time when Korean cinema was still 'new' to most Western critics. Julian Stringer has noted that, especially in the case of the relatively recent cycle of transnational Korean cinema, 'genre classification helps secure comfortable positions of knowledge from which hitherto unfamiliar films can be talked about'.[10] Through this rhetorical recourse, the unfamiliar becomes familiar, and the potentially alienating qualities of foreign cinema are given a context that enables critics to read them with confidence. Thus, with no pre-existing frames of reference, critics labelled *Nowhere to Hide* as noir as a way to understand it, and to assume positions of expertise.

A review of the film in the British magazine *Empire* demonstrates this strategy when it categorizes *Nowhere to Hide* as 'film noir', invoking a classical definition of the genre by describing the film as 'a rain-sodden, neon-lit poem to a world of ugly violence, treachery and despair'.[11] British newspaper *The Times* calls the film 'a modern-noir cop fantasia' and *Time Out*'s London edition mentions 'classic noir' when reviewing the film.[12] However, these critical references to *Nowhere to Hide* as film noir are rarely straightforward. *New York Times* critic Elvis Mitchell sees the film as a 'genre jumble', with film noir the most prominent but not the only generic component.[13] The film's English-language press notes, too, describe it as 'a different kind of detective action film that overrides genre expectations'. For the majority of critics, *Nowhere to Hide* is a noir, but it has strong echoes of other generic templates, as well as some deviations from the expectations of film noir.

The film's unpredictability, its range of influences and generic signifiers, and its stylistic variety made it difficult for critics to draw meaningful comparisons with other work. As the review in the *Miami Herald* notes, it is 'a movie unlike any you've seen before'.[14] The way critics categorize and compare the film, however, reveals a blurring of the boundaries between the specific film noir genre and the more general Hollywood crime thriller. Several critics compare the film to William Friedkin's seminal New

Hollywood detective thriller *The French Connection* (1971), drawing specific parallels between protagonists Detective Woo and Popeye Doyle, both slobbish mavericks willing to break the law in order to uphold it.[15] The protagonist of *Nowhere to Hide* is likewise compared to the eponymous anti-hero of *Dirty Harry* (1971), and one critic even suggests that *Nowhere to Hide* is 'modeled on the American police procedural blueprint, like *Lethal Weapon*' (1987).[16] These references suggest an affinity with a range of American films, none of which would necessarily be defined as film noir. One critic identifies the genre to which *Nowhere to Hide* belongs (and takes its influence from) as 'the hard detective genre', an ambiguous category that neither fully encompasses nor totally excludes film noir.[17] Indeed, what many of these critics agree on is that Myung-se Lee is inspired by specifically American films, and contributes to a distinctly American genre: for example, Mick LaSalle of the *San Francisco Chronicle* observes that '*Nowhere to Hide* is a Korean film that takes an American genre and gets fancy with it'.[18]

However, though the critics viewing *Nowhere to Hide* (and its genre) in terms of Hollywood cinema are in the majority, there are also a significant number of references to specifically East Asian noir (as well as other genres) in reviews of the film. The most common non-American reference point is the Hong Kong director John Woo. Critics both in the USA and UK frequently compared Lee to Woo due to their apparently similar emphasis on balletic visual style and carefully choreographed action scenes. Elvis Mitchell is one of several critics to assume that *Nowhere to Hide*'s Detective Woo was named in homage to John Woo.[19] This was certainly not Lee's intention, and he had no specific desire to associate his film with the Hong Kong director.[20] Yet this was also a major aspect of *Nowhere to Hide*'s UK marketing, with the film's DVD cover boldly featuring quotes emphasizing this association, declaring that the film will be 'A sure-fire hit with fans of *Hard Boiled* [1992]' and asking 'Is Hollywood ready for the next John Woo?' Again, this was unexpected to Lee (he told me that 'it doesn't make sense to me that *Nowhere to Hide* was described as a Hong Kong-style movie'), yet the comparisons with John Woo arguably add to an understanding of *Nowhere to Hide* as film noir. James Naremore has suggested that John Woo is the most noteworthy Hong Kong director to have contributed to the new globalization of film noir, in spite of the director's more obvious associations with action (specifically, the 'heroic bloodshed' genre).[21]

The most contentious and criticized aspects of *Nowhere to Hide*, especially for American critics, involve the way the film supposedly violates the rules of film noir, and represents an affront to their definitions of the genre.

Having identified the film as noir on the basis of the way it visibly conforms to their understanding of the term, critics subsequently become unreceptive to any departures from these generic expectations that disrupt their positions of knowledge, and the film's other elements are judged negatively. One particular talking point reveals what critics regard as inappropriate material for film noir: specifically, responses to one of the film's sentimental interludes. Indeed, melodramatic shifts in tone often baffle unaccustomed Western viewers, yet are a staple of Korean cinema and part of a long tradition of genre hybridity. Dating back to the import of the *shinpa* theatrical style of melodrama during the Japanese colonial period, Korean cinema has had a strong investment in heightened emotion and sentimentality, to the extent that melodrama pervades almost every popular genre to some degree.[22] Indeed, Nancy Abelmann and Jung-ah Choi have noted that melodrama forms a crucial hybrid component of even an urban crime-comedy film such as *Attack the Gas Station* (*Juyuso seubgyuksageun*, 1999).[23]

Nowhere to Hide conforms to domestic expectations by including occasional melodramatic interludes, yet the unfamiliarity of US critics with these cultural conventions leads them to react against these moments. Thus, the obvious and familiar aspects of the film – its noir qualities – are the basis on which its other aspects are judged, in an example of culturally different cinematic expectations. One scene in particular attracted the ire of at least two US critics: an assignment has gone disastrously wrong, and Detective Woo's younger and more conscientious partner has been forced to shoot dead a criminal in order to protect a child held at knifepoint. Stricken with guilt, the younger policeman retreats to a small park, and can only be snapped out of self-pity through a cheering and playful snowball fight instigated by the well-meaning Detective Woo. Elvis Mitchell calls this 'an obscene moment', reacting strongly against the sudden change in tone from the 'joke punchouts and thoughtless pleasure' of earlier scenes.[24] Likewise, Mick LaSalle describes this scene as 'creepy' and 'garbage'.[25]

Similarly, the film's largely comic depiction of police brutality was roundly criticized by American critics, who felt that this was not an appropriate source of comedy. *Nowhere to Hide* features sympathetic characters brutally beating and harassing suspects in order to obtain information; one scene with a comedic tone shows a beaten and dejected criminal in police custody, his face decorated with the clear imprints of boot soles. Elvis Mitchell suggests that the film has 'fascist underpinnings', and several other critics agreed.[26] Armond White expresses the most impassioned outrage at this aspect of the film, accusing Lee of being both 'apolitical' and 'amoral' and arguing that the director 'pays homage to film noir without advancing

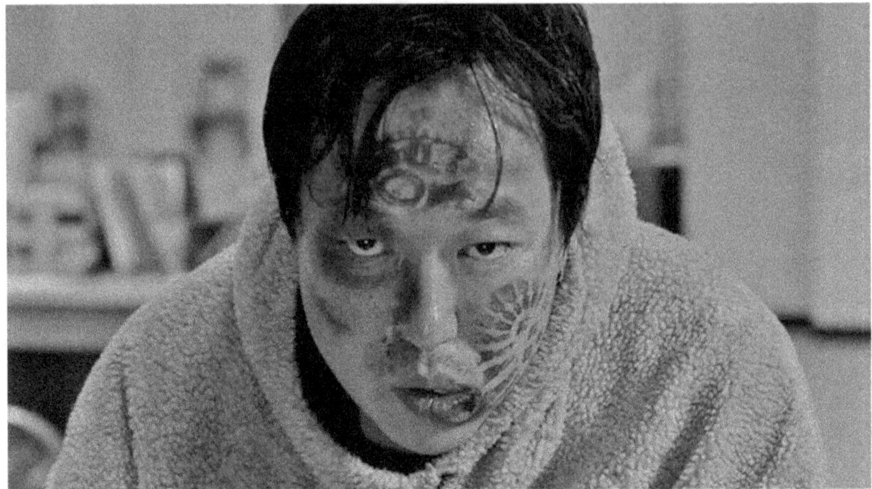

Figure 7.1 Slapstick comedy meets police brutality in *Nowhere to Hide*

understanding of its political and spiritual dynamics. Brutal cops are only exciting and funny if one hangs on to old genre clichés'.[27] White regards the staples of what he calls 'the cop/crime genre' to be 'allied with social hegemony, celebrating police/state power'.[28] It seems, therefore, that Lee is regarded as politically irresponsible by having an outdated approach to film noir. Steve Erickson of the *Chicago Reader* also acknowledges the uncomfortable connotations of the film's mixed tone, quipping that 'this may be the first film to bridge the gap between Buster Keaton and the Rodney King video'.[29] However, Erickson also indirectly took issue with White's attack on the film, suggesting that American critics 'who think it glorifies police brutality [...] are projecting our own problems onto a different culture'.[30] Erickson here essentially argues for an acceptance of cultural difference, advocating constructing different generic expectations of Korean film noir than should be applied to American incarnations of the same genre.

Indeed, the critical reception of *Nowhere to Hide* continually demonstrates the tension between competing frameworks of understanding: the film's generic elements and its regional origin. The vast majority of critics assume that by invoking noir traditions, Lee crafts a reverent reworking of specifically American films, and that on that basis, its depiction of police corruption and brutality (extremely common in the domestic Korean cycle of police comedies and thrillers) is an inappropriate addition, a crass miscalculation. Likewise, the film's melodramatic tone is seen as wholly unbefitting a dark film about cops and criminals. Film noir thus becomes a way to decode the film and ignore its national origin. Unusually, the reception of this East Asian film is not predicated on Orientalist stereotypes of the Far East. Rather, its unfamiliar elements are swept aside, ignored or criticized, in favour of interpreting the film on the basis of its relationship to a familiar Hollywood genre.

One of the consistent themes of *Nowhere to Hide*'s English-language critical reception is that the film's superficial elements – the basics of its plot and its flashy visual style – suggest it should be classified as noir, while the film's tone and theme suggest otherwise. Yet Paul Schrader's seminal and highly influential (though not unproblematic) essay on film noir suggests that qualities of theme and tone are not the essence of noir; that the genre is defined purely by its visual style. In his essay, Schrader complains that American critics fail to recognize and correctly define noir:

> The fundamental reason for film noir's neglect, however, is the fact that it depends more on choreography than sociology, and American critics have always been slow on the uptake when it comes to visual style. Like its protagonists, film noir is more interested in style than theme, whereas American critics have been traditionally more interested in theme than style.[31]

The reception of *Nowhere to Hide* both confirms and denies Schrader's contention: critics discount the visually noir-esque properties of the film because its theme and tone signal other genres more strongly; yet when they do define the film as noir, it is only by ignoring or discounting the thematic properties of the film and focusing purely on its aesthetics. Lee's next feature, when seen by critics, would also have its reception characterized by a critical discourse in which the film's visual properties compete with, rather than complement, its plot, theme and tone.

Lost in the Shadows: *Duelist*

Myung-se Lee's next film, *Duelist*, also received international distribution (not quite on the scale of *Nowhere to Hide*, as although *Duelist* achieved a nationwide cinema release in the UK, it had, more than five years after its domestic release, yet to receive distribution in the USA). The film represents an evolution in Lee's determination to craft new variations on the film noir form. *Duelist* mirrors *Nowhere to Hide* in many ways: its protagonist is, again, a driven detective on the trail of an elusive assassin. Set in the *Chosun (Joseon)* period of Korean history, and with scenes of violence that are at once balletic, poetic and slapstick, the film has been described as a 'fusion period piece': a historical drama, martial-arts action film, comedy and film noir, with deliberate anachronisms in its music and language.[32] Though the film was sold to UK audiences as a 'straight' martial-arts film, it can equally be understood as a film noir, an interpretation supported and encouraged by Lee, who defines *Duelist* as 'a detective story' but admits that it 'looks like a martial arts film'.[33]

Duelist arguably belongs to a tradition of female-centred neo-noir identified by William Covey and exemplified by *Blue Steel* (1989); both films are about a female law enforcer dealing with an obsessive male opponent.[34] *Duelist* reflects the staple visual flourishes of classical film noir, with an emphasis on the play between light and dark, as deep shadows often obscure portions of the frame. The narrative involves a complicated criminal conspiracy, dangerous encounters in dark alleyways and seedy taverns, and a complex web of betrayal and secret loyalties. The film's protagonist, Namsoon, is a female detective frequently undercover, and direct parallels with *Nowhere to Hide* are invoked in the lead performance by Ji-won Ha, who models her acting here after Joong-hoon Park's energetic Detective Woo. The film's central relationship revolves around a mysterious, attractive antagonist who sparks a moral crisis for the film's protagonist. More so than with *Nowhere to Hide*, set in modern-day Seoul, the period setting of *Duelist* makes the noir of the film more recognizably Korean; its colourful costumes and period sets arguably evoke cultural specificity more clearly than the urban labyrinths of Seoul (a city largely indistinguishable, for many Western viewers, from any other Asian metropolis).

Again, as with *Nowhere to Hide*, Lee here plays with genre conventions, and *Duelist* violates many of the generic expectations of classic noir. The film focuses on law enforcers rather than criminals or anti-heroes, and it retains the tonal inconsistency typical of Korean cinema but quite atypical of film noir. The film marks an inventive play on the typical noir gender roles, with many reversals and ironies. Namsoon is far from a seductive femme fatale, and can only be described as a tomboy with a highly repressed femininity: she is clumsy when undercover and wearing a *hanbok* (a traditional Korean dress), and she loses her composure completely during a swordfight when her outfit is ripped and her cleavage is exposed. The film's male villain, meanwhile (simply called 'Sad Eyes'), fits into the femme fatale role in every sense but his gender: he's attractive and mysterious, allied with a criminal and instrumental in a conspiracy, and represents a major

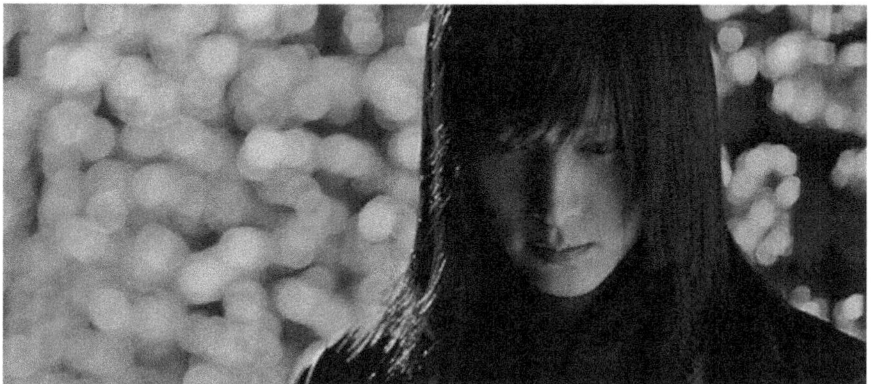

Figure 7.2 The mysterious *homme fatale* stalks and seduces his prey in *Duelist*

distraction to the protagonist as an object of romantic and sexual desire. Overall, *Duelist* exhibits as many traits of contemporary film noir as *Nowhere to Hide*, though the genre to which it ostensibly belongs – the historical martial-arts film – makes the associations less obvious.

Film noir was nonetheless a crucial part of the discourse around *Duelist* on its domestic release. The film was often described in Korea as 'Chosun noir', a term that originated in the film's marketing and was seen as a useful way to express its generic hybridity as both a period film and a noir thriller. Press materials in wide circulation before the film's release made the phrase 'Chosun noir' common, and the phrase was even used as the title for a theatrically exhibited feature-length documentary about Lee's career and the production of *Duelist*.[35] Yet none of these marketing concepts was retained for the film's Western release, as the film's swordplay action was the centre of attention. Indeed, this shift in perspective was invited as soon as the title was translated: the Korean title of the film is *Hyeongsa*, literally 'detective', which invites a reading of the film as noir much more readily than the word 'duelist', which signifies swordfights as the film's central appeal.

It's perhaps still surprising, though, that no Western critics recognized *Duelist* as noir, instead evaluating the film purely as an example of a swordplay film. Just as critics had evaluated *Nowhere to Hide* primarily on the basis of how it reflected the distinctly American detective genre, in the case of *Duelist* the comparisons are primarily made with Chinese *wuxia* films. The reception of *Duelist* arguably demonstrates that iconography and setting are the key aspects that define foreign film. Critics focus entirely on the swords and period costumes, ignoring the film's formal and thematic debt to noir traditions. *Duelist*'s identity as noir is based entirely on a subjective interpretation of the film, yet the question remains: if the film can be read as a noir, and this aspect was central to its domestic consumption, why was noir ignored in both the marketing and reception of the film in the UK? The answer, it seems, is that iconography defines both Asian cinema and film noir. Just as the swordplay film is defined by its period setting and costumes, its inescapable Asian identity, the film noir is defined by its gritty urban setting, and its starkly anonymous metropolis.

On the first international screenings of the film, Derek Elley's review for *Variety* assessed *Duelist* purely as an action film. He characterizes the film as 'a South Korean martial artser that's determined to reinvent the genre every which way'.[36] Elley's chief complaint about the film is typical of how it was read by the majority of critics, when he identifies in the film 'a deliberate disregard for the normal aesthetics of martial artsers'.[37] As suggested above, the film's rejection of the 'normal aesthetics' of martial arts is indeed deliberate, and reflects the much stronger emphasis on the aesthetics of film noir.

Duelist was released in the West at a time when a new wave of Chinese martial-arts films was enjoying unprecedented success. After the breakthrough US–China co-production *Crouching Tiger, Hidden Dragon* (2000),[38] Yimou Zhang's films *Hero* (2002) and *House of Flying Daggers* (2004) saw wide exhibition in the USA and UK in both multiplex and arthouse cinemas. Indeed, on the basis of the assumption that *Duelist* was nothing more than a martial-arts film, and that it aspired to equal Zhang's films in terms of spectacle and action, it was understandably found lacking by British critics. A review in popular magazine *Total Film* criticizes the film's flashy visuals, noting that 'it's rather empty, the total sacrifice of everything to style stopping this from becoming the *Hero* it yearns to be'.[39] Critics typically complain that the film has too much emphasis on expressionist visuals, with too little attention paid to crafting serious and convincing martial-arts action. The *Guardian*'s Xan Brooks suggests that Lee had made a failed attempt to 'fashion a martial arts movie', while the *Independent* grants the film only a two-word review ('completely incoherent').[40]

Tony Rayns offers the most nuanced reading of *Duelist* in his review for the specialist *Sight & Sound* magazine, dismissing notions that Lee was aspiring to mimic the swordplay style of Zhang's films and acknowledging (but neglecting to address in any detail) the aspects of the film that reflect noir. Rayns focuses instead on the film's romantic elements, arguing that love and desire have always been the defining characteristics of Lee's authorship, from his debut film forward. Rayns therefore suggests that in *Duelist* Lee 'develops an erotics of swordplay which is original [and] distinctive' and that the film 'plays more like a rhapsody than either an action movie or the detective thriller suggested by the police-procedural aspects'.[41]

A feature article for the online cult magazine *Firecracker* suggests that *Duelist* is 'difficult to position' for its audiences due its range of styles and generic influences.[42] The film undoubtedly represents a more ambitious fusion of genres than *Nowhere to Hide*, and the film expresses an even stronger connection to – and progression of – the film noir genre. Yet while *Nowhere to Hide* is, ultimately, more of a police procedural than a conventional film noir, *Duelist* is arguably much more a film noir than anything else. Critics viewing *Nowhere to Hide* assumed it was a film noir because it looked like one; likewise, critics responding to *Duelist* simply cannot see past the trappings of costume and setting, the swords and warriors who wield them, to the noir qualities beneath.

Conclusion: Korean Noir as 'Global Noir'

In 1978, James Damico argued that there was an 'urgent need' for 'an examination of film noir which is interested in working from the objects of study outward rather than imposing assumptions upon those which suit such assumptions'.[43] The reception of Lee's two films shows that, more than 30 years later, critics have failed to respond to Damico's call for a reconsideration of how to define film noir. Critics impose a series of expectations and restrictions upon the films they see. The popular critical definition of film noir is revealed, by consideration of the reception of Lee's films, to be fixed and firm. To return to Schrader's rhetorical question – how many noir elements does it take to make a film noir noir? – it's clear that for critics in the West viewing noir of Eastern origin, iconography is everything. In spite of rigorous historical research and multiple academic definitions, the images and characters familiar from the first wave of 1940s crime films are, for critics, the essential ingredient in film noir.

Duelist was unable to achieve meaningful recognition as a noir film because it already fit with a Western perception of what kind of films and genres are conventionally Asian. *Nowhere to Hide*, on the other hand, was easily canonized as noir, but only through a critical discourse that emphasized Myung-se Lee's debt to American cinema and explained or excused how he had misunderstood or misjudged the genre. Film noir may well no longer be an essentially American genre, and, in fact, David Desser has argued that 'to some extent, film noir has always been a global genre or mode'.[44] Desser defines the new mode of 'global noir' in terms of transnational flows of cinema, suggesting that:

> global noir manifests a circulation of imagery and influence across national boundaries [...]. The impulse toward cinephilia – that is, the ability and necessity of acknowledging the intertextual chain of references, borrowings, and reworkings – may be at the heart of global noir. For it involves filmmakers and film audiences in a circuit of acknowledgements – the ability of filmmakers to make references and their confidence in the audience's recognition of them.[45]

It is precisely the ability of the audience, or of critics, to recognize the generic and stylistic influences on these new 'global noir' films that is at stake in the reception of Lee's films. In the case of *Nowhere to Hide*, the borrowed aspects of the text – its debt to American cinema – are hyper-visible to Western critics, while its other elements, deeply rooted in local rather than international film traditions, are an unwelcome and unfamiliar intrusion. In the case of *Duelist*, the non-noir elements were overshadowed by the more familiar generic conventions: critics could easily see the film's connections and formal debt to films from other countries, but they emphasized quite different aspects than were evident in the domestic context. Film noir, then, may have become global, but its critical reception is still rooted in more classical and, crucially, culturally specific definitions of the genre and its style. The next step for global noir will be a revision of expectations in terms of iconography as well as theme and tone, yet with a sense of those qualities that make film noir distinct.

Notes

1 Schrader, Paul, 'Notes on *Film Noir*', in Alain Silver and James Ursini (eds), *Film Noir Reader* (New York: Limelight, 1996), p. 54.
2 Spicer, Andrew, *Film Noir* (Edinburgh: Edinburgh University Press, 2002), pp. 24–25.
3 Schrader, 'Notes on *Film Noir*', pp. 57–59.
4 Spicer, *Film Noir*, p. 4.
5 Ibid.
6 Franklin, Erika, 'Duel Citizenship: Lee Myung-se Interviewed', *Firecracker Magazine* 13 (n.d.), <http://www.firecracker-media.com/interviews/interview1301.shtml>, accessed 15 July 2007; Tony Rayns, 'Rebel Yell', *Time Out* (London), 20–27 June 2001, p. 87.

7 Lee has even turned to noir for inspiration in his non-film projects, in 2008 directing a photo shoot for the Korean magazine *W* that put popular young actress Geun-young Moon, known then for her cheerful and innocent persona, in an unusually dark setting, wearing a man's suit and smoking a cigarette in a way that strongly evokes Hollywood film noir.

8 *Two Cops* inspired a series of imitators and two direct sequels: *Two Cops 2* (1996) and *Two Cops 3* (1998). There has, in general, been a much more successful tradition of police/crime comedies in South Korea than in Hollywood.

9 Schrader, 'Notes on *Film Noir*', p. 57.

10 Stringer, Julian, 'Putting Korean Cinema in its Place: Genre Classifications and the Contexts of Reception', in Chi-Yun Shin and Julian Stringer (eds), *New Korean Cinema* (Edinburgh: Edinburgh University Press, 2005), p. 101.

11 Parkinson, David, '*Nowhere to Hide*' (film review), *Empire*, July 2001, <http://www.empireonline.com/reviews/reviewcomplete.asp?FID=6920>, accessed 15 July 2007.

12 Christopher, James, '*Nowhere to Hide*' (film review), *The Times*, 28 June 2001, Section 2, p. 16; Andrew, Geoff, '*Nowhere to Hide*' (film review), *Time Out* (London), 27 June–4 July 2001, p. 83.

13 Mitchell, Elvis, '*Nowhere to Hide*: Lots of Razzle, Tons of Dazzle and a Genre All Its Own' (film review), *New York Times*, 27 March 2000, <http://www.nytimes.com/library/film/032700hide-film-review.html>, accessed 15 July 2007.

14 Rodriguez, Rene, '"Nowhere" Goes Somewhere Fast' (film review), *Miami Herald*, 25 February 2000, p. 33G.

15 Arnold, William, 'Violent *Nowhere to Hide* Would Be Best Kept Hidden' (film review), *Seattle Post-Intelligencer*, 26 January 2001, <http://seattlepi.nwsource.com/movies/nowhereq.shtml>, accessed 15 July 2007; Andrew, '*Nowhere to Hide*'; Jolin, Dan, '*Nowhere to Hide*' (film review), *Total Film*, July 2001, <http:/ www.totalfilm.com/reviews/cinema/nowhere-to-hide>, accessed 15 July 2007.

16 Erickson, Steve, 'Flashy Trash' (film review), *Chicago Reader*, 1 January 2001, <http://www.chicagoreader.com/movies/archives/2001/0101/010105_2.html>, accessed 15 July 2007; Andrew, '*Nowhere to Hide*'; LaSalle, Mick, 'Korean Film Recycles American Movie Morality' (film review), *San Francisco Chronicle*, 29 December 2000, p. C-1; Walker, Alexander 'Far East Eye-Opener' (film review), *The Evening Standard*, 28 July 2001, p. 30.

17 Stamets, Bill, 'Lee Takes "Nowhere" in Highly Stylized Direction', *Chicago Sun-Times*, 5 January 2001, <http://www.highbeam.com/doc/1P2–4585475.html>, accessed 20 September 2011.

18 LaSalle, 'Korean Film Recycles American Movie Morality'.

19 Mitchell, '*Nowhere to Hide*: Lots of Razzle, Tons of Dazzle and a Genre All Its Own'.

20 I specifically asked Myung-se Lee about this when I interviewed him. All quotes from Lee in this chapter come from this personal interview, conducted in Seoul on 24 April 2009.
21 Naremore, James, *More Than Night: Film Noir in Its Contexts*, rev. ed. (Berkeley: University of California Press, 2008), pp. 228–229.
22 See Paquet, Darcy, '*Christmas in August* and Korean Melodrama', in Frances Gateward (ed.), *Seoul Searching: Culture and Identity in Contemporary Korean Cinema* (Albany: State University of New York Press, 2007), pp. 37–54.
23 Abelmann, Nancy and Jung-ah Choi, '"Just Because": Comedy, Melodrama and Youth Violence in *Attack the Gas Station*', in Chi-Yun Shin and Julian Stringer (eds), *New Korean Cinema* (Edinburgh: Edinburgh University Press, 2005), pp. 132–143.
24 Mitchell, '*Nowhere to Hide*: Lots of Razzle, Tons of Dazzle and a Genre All Its Own'.
25 LaSalle, 'Korean Film Recycles American Movie Morality'.
26 Mitchell, '*Nowhere to Hide*: Lots of Razzle, Tons of Dazzle and a Genre All Its Own'.
27 White, Armond, '*Nowhere to Hide*' (film review), *New York Press*, 22 March 2000, <http://nypress.com/nowhere-nowhere-to-hide-directed-by/>, accessed 15 July 2007.
28 White, '*Nowhere to Hide*'.
29 Erickson, 'Flashy Trash'.
30 Ibid.
31 Schrader, 'Notes on *Film Noir*', pp. 62–63.
32 Myung-se Lee in fact rejected the description of *Duelist* as a 'fusion period piece' in an interview included in the UK Press Notes for the film, distributed by Contender Entertainment Group in 2006.
33 *Duelist* UK Press Notes, Contender Entertainment, 2006.
34 Covey, William, 'Girl Power: Female-Centered Neo-Noir', in Alain Silver and James Ursini (eds), *Film Noir Reader 2* (New York: Limelight, 1999), pp. 311–327.
35 Jae-yong Soh's *Chosun Noir: Lee Myung-se Makes Duelist* was screened at film festivals and some cinemas in Seoul in 2005, and is also included on the Korean DVD release of *Duelist*.
36 Elley, Derek, '*Duelist*' (film review), *Variety*, 31 October 2005, <http://www.variety.com/review/VE1117928646/?refcatid=31>, accessed 15 July 2007.
37 Ibid.
38 Though *Crouching Tiger, Hidden Dragon* is commonly described as a co-production between the USA and China, the film is more accurately a US/China/Hong Kong/Taiwan co-production, involving the talents and resources of three Chinese film industries.
39 Russell, Jamie, '*Duelist*' (film review), *Total Film*, March 2007, <http://www.totalfilm.com/reviews/cinema/duelist>, accessed 15 July 2007.

40 Brooks, Xan, '*Duelist*' (film review), the *Guardian*, 9 March 2007, <http://www.guardian.co.uk/film/2007/mar/09/actionandadventure>, accessed 15 July 2007; Clarke, Roger, 'Also Showing' (film review), the *Independent*, 10 March 2007, Section 2, p. 9.
41 Rayns, Tony, '*Duelist*' (film review), *Sight & Sound*, April 2007, <http://old.bfi.org.uk/sightandsound/review/3771>, accessed 15 May 2007.
42 Franklin, 'Duel Citizenship: Lee Myung-se Interviewed'.
43 Damico, James, '*Film Noir*: A Modest Proposal', in Alain Silver and James Ursini (eds), *Film Noir Reader* (New York: Limelight, 1996), p. 99.
44 Desser, David, 'Global Noir: Genre Film in the Age of Transnationalism', in Barry Keith Grant (ed.), *Film Genre Reader III* (Austin: University of Texas Press, 2003), p. 520.
45 Ibid., pp. 521, 528.

PART III

THREE CHINAS (MAINLAND CHINA, HONG KONG AND TAIWAN), MANY NOIRS

Chapter 8

From Urban Crime Thriller to Silent Ghost Story: *Rebels of the Neon God* and Taiwanese Neo-Noir

Erin Yu-Tien Huang

Taiwanese Urban Drama and De-Spectacularized Crime

Taiwanese-Malaysian filmmaker Ming-Liang Tsai's first feature-length film, *Rebels of the Neon God* (1992), begins with a petty crime. The scene of the crime is a tight and claustrophobic telephone booth in the city of Taipei. Gangster youth Ah Tze and his partner Ah Bing are drilling open the coin deposit of a public telephone. Without telling the audience the narrative cause and effect, the film cuts immediately to another scene and another crime, this time inside the bedroom of teenager Hsiao Kang. Bored by his studies for the college entrance exam, Hsiao Kang discovers a lurking cockroach, one of the most common pests co-inhabiting Taiwan's humid and crowded cities. Rather than resorting to pesticides, Hsiao Kang swiftly pins down the cockroach with one of his study instruments – the compass. After throwing the pest out of the window, the frail-looking teenager discovers it again. Pounding on the window in an attempt to scare the bug away, he accidentally breaks the glass into pieces, an act that greatly upsets his alienated parents. As drops of blood trickle down his wrist, the camera closes in on a bloodstained page of the teenager's textbook, which not coincidentally shows the map of Taiwan. In a film that alludes in its Chinese title to the Daoist and Buddhist deity Nocha, famous for his fiery temper and rebellion against his father, *Rebels of the Neon God (pinyin: Qing shao nian nuo zha)* surprisingly does not open with graphic portrayals of violence, nor the spectacular artistry of theft, but the presentation of mundane, accidental or trivial transgressions. Without a riveting murder or crime mystery that shakes the moral foundation of society, *Rebels of the Neon God*, with its unique vision of a crime cinema of triviality, opens the door to reconsiderations of Taiwanese citizens' affective relationship with one of Asia's rapidly globalizing cities. What makes Tsai's *Rebels* a shocking invention of East Asian urban dystopia and a work of neo-noir, as will be pursued in this chapter, is precisely the lack of psychotic outbursts and moral delinquencies commonly seen in classical Hollywood film noir, elements that signified profound anxieties in the immediate postwar era.

In what follows, my reading of *Rebels of the Neon God* begins by contextualizing a world where the social meaning of violence and brutality has undergone fundamental changes, in what I would call the *de-spectacularization* of crime and violence in Tsai's dystopic portrayal of the rising global city. From a cinema of petty crimes and childish pranks, the urban nightmare collectively dreamed by a group of Taiwanese youths uncovers a violence no longer communicable in terms of physical harm, murder or cruelty inflicted on others. Paralleling the elusive red neon lights that permeate Taipei's empty cityscape, one discovers through the elliptical light a violence not separable from painfully felt and ambivalent desires to maintain relations with a society both endearing and detestable. Through childish pranks and badly planned heists, the de-spectacularization of crime shifts the focus away from the hard-boiled revelation of criminal mysteries that typically characterizes American film noir and neo-noir. This particular trait of putting crime and the city in relation through the de-spectacular has two implications.

First, specifically on the topic of dystopic and noirish urban imaginations in rapidly developing East Asian cities, the cinema of petty crimes and triviality that Tsai's *Rebels* exemplifies provides a microscopic vision of the everyday dimension of the city that does not necessarily involve the familiarized noir landscape of hostess bars, casinos or police stations. In many ways, the film, released in the early 1990s, portrays a much more complicated world intertwined with the city's rationalized and hygienic façade. Represented in terms of a broken elevator rumoured to be haunted, or a clogged drain that seems to have its own will, the city of Taipei is no longer comprehensible in terms of good and bad districts where characters would run into things and people that test the limits of law. On the contrary, the de-spectacularization of crime brings about a species of events and actions that are not explicable through logical rationalization. For example, the elevator in gangster youth Ah Tze's apartment building stops midway and opens its door every time it is in use, although the film never shows anyone pushing the button. Fundamentally changing the definition of mystery, from a cause-and-effect search for the true culprit to numerous inexplicable experiences at the heart of urban modernity, Tsai's brand of urban noir alludes to a larger and more intricate cosmology of the city and its relation to the world, the ecological environment, and the spheres of folktale and religion, all of which have searing presences in modern urban life but remain repressed. If 'noir' could be understood as motion toward trespassing and transgression, what is most disturbing and ground-breaking about Tsai's formative work is an understanding of the everyday, through the mundane and trivial, as losing ground to the absurd and the inexplicable. Life's logical cause-and-effect sequences become literally impossible.

In addition to a unique take on neo-noir through urban spatiality, the second implication of the de-spectacular emerges from the film's focus on Taiwan and East Asia's youth generation. Unlike their cinematic precursors in Taiwan's urban dramas in the 1980s, which I discuss briefly below, Hsiao Kang and Ah Tze have only committed trivial offences that are intriguingly not up to the standard of 'real' rebellion. While the film's Chinese title makes explicit reference to the rebellious deity Nocha, its international title

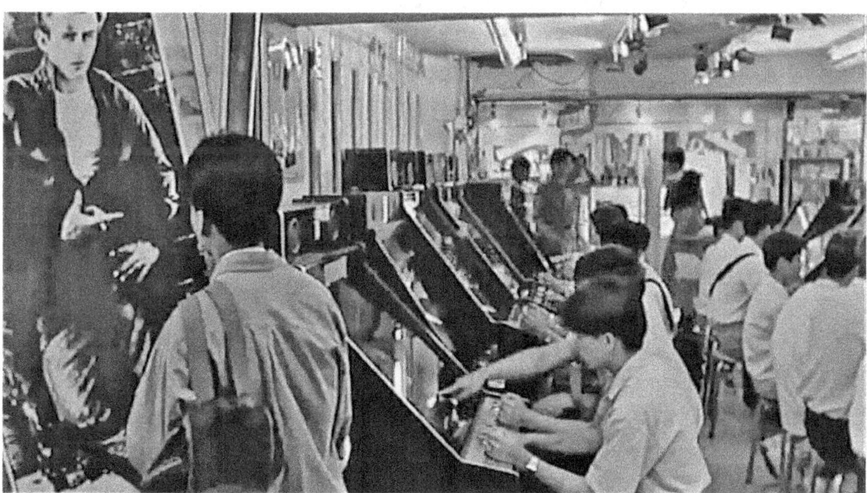

Figure 8.1 In *Rebels of the Neon God*, Hsiao Kang looks at a poster of James Dean from Nicholas Ray's *Rebel Without a Cause*

also evokes the archetype of rebellious youth James Dean, who plays Jim Stark in American filmmaker Nicholas Ray's *Rebel Without a Cause* (1955). However, in the film's depiction of de-spectacularized crimes – for example, when Hsiao Kang seeks revenge on Ah Tze by vandalizing his prized motorcycle, followed by a scene where Hsiao Kang celebrates joyfully by jumping childishly up and down on his bed – the episode of 'revenge' that results from a trivial car accident is portrayed in a drastically different manner when compared with more typical hypermasculinist outbursts used to signify the modern crisis of masculinity. By spying on the initial aggressor Ah Tze and playing a vicious prank, Hsiao Kang plays a game of revenge not separable from a game of desire, in which Hsiao Kang becomes obsessed with Ah Tze and follows him everywhere in the city. In other words, the de-spectacularization of violence in Tsai's neo-noir approach to crime in the city complicates Fredric Jameson's reading of the violent outburst of a middle-aged, middle-class Taiwanese salary man in Edward Yang's *Terrorizer* (1986) as a national allegory of Taiwan's ambiguous geopolitical relation with the rest of the world.[1] If such an outburst can be read allegorically as a sign of national frustration, the allegorical meaning of de-spectacularized crime needs further unpacking, especially if we read crime as a vehicle of social dissent. Before elaborating on the embodied lens of the de-spectacular from an adolescent and young adult's perspective, the de-spectacularized lens of the 1990s should be understood in relation to the depictions of crime and the city in urban dramas of the 1980s, which I briefly discuss below as the evolution of Taiwanese 'urban dystopia'.

I refer to noir and neo-noir as urban dystopia for a specific reason. Under the leadership of the Kuomintang Party after it lost the civil war to the Communist Party in China and retreated to Taiwan, Taiwan was governed by an authoritarian regime that adopted neoliberal economic policies. Based on governmental policies that strongly emphasize economic growth, the Kuomintang Party created an 'economic miracle' that quickly turned Taiwan's agriculturally based economy to one based on industrial outputs. In the presence of a newly established government still at war with its enemy across the Taiwan Strait, Taiwan's domestic film industry, which did not exist until the Kuomintang Party brought along equipment, filmmakers and actors during its retreat, was centralized and operated as a tool of governmental propaganda. While film productions followed strict protocols and the aesthetic principle of healthy realism *(jian kang xie shi)* in the postwar era, films that were made to address real concerns of Taiwan's social reality did not emerge until the 1980s. Edward Yang's *Terrorizer*, for example, portrays Taipei as a prosperous city only on the surface, while a deep, penetrating sense of helplessness and entrapment permeates every dimension of citizens' lives. Hidden under the façade of Taiwan's well-to-do upper-middle class, the terror-ridden city acts like a time bomb that could explode any minute. Any ordinary Taiwanese citizen might act out in sudden outbursts of anger and violence, just like the film's middle-aged male protagonist, who shoots and kills his ex-wife's lover before shooting himself in the head. Given Taiwan's growing economic prosperity, the consequence of rapid modernization is vividly reflected in episodes of sudden outbursts that simultaneously dream and materialize the breakdown of moral boundaries. No longer a uniform and transparent space of rationality, Taiwan's cities transformed into ticking time bombs, ridden with unpredictable crimes committed by the nation's hardworking and prosperous upper-middle class, most of whom felt lost and threatened in a globally competitive economic system. While 'film noir' *(hei se dian ying)* exists in Chinese language as a translated term and refers specifically to American film noir, the Taiwanese New Wave that started in the early 1980s with unprecedented focus on questions of Taiwan as a nation and the Taiwanese identity gave rise to a brand of dystopic urban cinema clearly distinguishable from the detective and crime mysteries in classical Hollywood film noir.

Starting with Yang's *Terrorizer*, a high-modernist text dominated by the realist aesthetics of long takes, the Taiwanese brand of urban dystopia withholds cinematic techniques that would create effects of distortion. These include commonly used first-person voice-over, flashbacks, de-centred and unstable compositions, and dramatic light and dark contrasts. With cinematography presented at a steady angle, in addition to the absence of a male loner's probing eyes, Taiwanese urban dystopias are what could be recognized as crime thrillers where 'crime' or the 'hard-boiled thrill' actually become the films' most unstable and unrecognizable dimensions. Relating back to my earlier point about the disappearance of logical cause-and-effect, where one could still eventually sort out the difference between aggressor and victim, the de-spectacular tendency in Taiwanese urban drama can be read as the demise of crime or moral transgression as we know them. In a society with no shortage of images and representations of violence, and in films where characters still engage in acts of physical violence, the de-spectacular does not suggest the disappearance of dark mirror reflections of social discontents, but a new direction of neo-noir where 'crime' takes on a new social meaning.

If the violent outburst of a middle-class man says something about Taiwan's ambivalent position in the world, being a developing nation without political sovereignty, the infliction of physical injury on the self and on others in *Terrorizer* is an expressive act of revenge committed by the society's frustrated dominant male elite. However, as economic development stalled due to lower costs of production in neighbouring China, Taiwan's youths in the 1990s not only had to carry on the myth and burden of economic growth, but also to face the reality of dwindling opportunities for survival. As I will illustrate in my reading of *Rebels of the Neon God*, the 'rebels' in the film become representative of a generation of Taiwanese and East Asian youths whose acts of 'transgression' do not reflect agitated souls tormented by past traumatic experiences. As seen in the opening scene where Hsiao Kang absurdly turns himself into the victimized by accidentally cutting himself while acting out on a cockroach, the de-spectacularized crime refers to a set of actions that no longer have definite signified consequences. The bleak portrait of the lives of Taiwanese youths that Tsai provides leads the audience to an unfathomable social abyss where even intended acts of rebellion and aggression fail to yield the initially desired result. When intention and consequence are always mismatched, *Rebels of the Neon God* turns a signature chase-and-pursuit detective subplot of film noir into a game of desire, although the true object of desire perhaps remains forever unknown to the pursuer himself.

The Spatiality of the De-Spectacular: Homecoming and Clogged Drains

In this section, I begin with a discussion on the spatiality of the film as the first step toward understanding a world hidden beneath the rational façade of a modernizing city. As mentioned in the first implication of the de-spectacular, I intend to show the de-spectacular as a significant step toward connecting the city dominated by an economic developmental logic and a larger cosmological world of religion, myth and nature. By evoking an aspect of urbanity incommensurable with the homogeneous and progressive logic of modernity, the filmmaker suggests an understanding of urban experience as mythical, unpredictable and inexplicable. Even science and technology can no longer guarantee progress, as we can see in the mundane and annoying glitches of household technologies throughout the film. It is perhaps not a coincidence that the film is made during the urban 'dark age' of Taipei, when the construction of the city's intricate underground metro system tore open miles of underground tunnels. With the whole city and the eyes of the nation on a single urban renewal project, the breakdown of 'modern' living in the characters' apartments serves as an ironic critique of a homogenized view of Taiwan's capital city. In the end of the analysis, I wish to establish the point that Tsai's film sets a new direction for neo-noir, as it is no longer possible to portray an urban dystopia by dividing the city into good and bad, and public and private, spaces. The de-spectacularization of 'crime' means the loss of social significance of previously glamorized spaces that feed on social discontents and harbour moral transgression. What is perhaps more disconcerting is not the loss of such distinction but the embeddedness of what was characterized as the menacing urban environment in every imaginable corner of the city.

In his study of space and its filmic representations in 1940s American cinema, Dana Polan observes that although 'houses' appear occasionally in film noir, there are hardly any depictions of 'homes'.[2] At a time when the reality of the war was too close, the 'home' is its own world and a safe haven separated from the world outside. It is for this reason that home only appears in glimpses in classical film noir. As Polan argues, the spatiality of film noir constitutes a 'negative existentialism' where the external environment resists reflecting the characters' personalities or values, constituting the menacing urban frontier. Building on Polan's observation of an urban spatiality that resists humanistic assimilation, Vivian Sobchack in her study of the relationship between film noir and history further defines a spatiality of transience as a generic characteristic of classical film noir. She writes:

> Such radical externality and resistance can also be found in the cocktail lounges, hotel bars, diners, roadhouses, and motels that spatialize film noir – these rented rooms or tables or counter stools that resist individual particularity and are made for transients and transience, these quasi places that substitute perversely for the hospitable and felicitous places and domesticity of a 'proper' home in which such necessary quotidian functions as sleeping and eating and drinking are secured and transfigured into intimate social communion.[3]

In short, the spatiality in classical film noir, with its emphasis on depersonalized, transient spaces and the avoidance of the space of the home, sets up a clear divide between home as a space of domesticity and the city as the unknown external world. The spatiality of film noir is also related to the gendering of the genre, in stories where a male protagonist gets lost in a city that is both seductively tempting and dangerous, not unlike the femmes fatales in the films. In other words, the obscurity of the 'home' and the engrossing feeling of being lost in the once-familiar urban environment in many ways reflect a historical crisis of masculinity, as women left home and entered the workforce during the war. This in part explains the lack of themes and settings tied to domesticity and domestic life, setting film noir apart from other genres of crime thrillers and melodramas.

However, by focusing on the embodied experience of young adults living in a rapidly modernizing urban space, *Rebels of the Neon God*, or 'Adolescent Nocha' in the Chinese title, brings the menacing urban front and its accompanying lens of reflection inside the space of the home, behind tightly shut apartment doors in densely populated Taipei. Against the backdrop of the city's biggest modernizing construction, the spatiality in Tsai's depiction offers a microscopic view of the most intimate lived environment. In his *Film Noir and the Spaces of Modernity*, Edward Dimendberg draws on the overwhelming presence of the city, especially spatialities that were present but foreign, as he asks a central question about the role and function of American film noir. He says:

> While many historians emphasized the continuity between earlier European cinema and American films noir, I was drawn to ponder the latter's incommensurability with both previous and subsequent cultural moments. How could film noir illuminate the late-modern spaces of the 1940s and 1950s to which it provided unique access?[4]

By dissociating film noir from its European roots, what is most valuable in Dimendberg's methodology is a way of reading film noir not in terms of aesthetic styles and thematic motifs, but as a historical archive of spatial change, and specifically the '"genuine hollow space of capitalism" deployed "without a mask"'.[5] Although not explicitly stated, 'film noir' and its urban settings were always already a historical documentation, seen through the affective lens of alienation, discomfort and at times wonder.

While Taiwan had no shortage of urban representations and urban dramas before the 1980s, the 'urban' never had a menacing effect on viewers, not until a set of modernist texts that set apart the difference between country and city as seen in many of Hsiao-hsien Hou's early films, such as *The Boys from Fengkuei* (1983) and *A Summer at Grandpa's* (1984). Travelling by train, a means of transportation that sustained mobility throughout the small island, characters confront the challenges of life in the city, as well as fundamental social changes brought about by rapid economic development. However, as contextualized in earlier parts of this chapter, *Rebels of the Neon God* presents a documentation of spatiality quite different from earlier spatial binaries of country and city, traditional and modern, low and high culture, and innocent and crime-ridden districts. The 'urban', in this case, is seen not as a symbol of rational and planned progress, but in light of its inexplicable or mythical deterioration. From clogged drains, flooded floor and broken elevator to urban pests, where elements of nature seep into every fundamental aspect of urban life, *Rebels* introduces a temporality and spatiality co-existent with the modern city but repressed in previous representations of urban space. These are spaces of trivial social significance. Yet their presence serves as a constant reminder of dimensions of modern living that exceed rational control. To sum up, the spatiality brought to light by Tsai's de-spectacularizing lens consists of fragments of a city that has its own will, co-inhabited by gods and ghosts and not controllable by human desires. When combined with the sound of pounding rain, evocative of a world larger than and beyond the confined space of the aspiring global city, the spatiality of *Rebels* ironically presents the city's *double* – one that is damp, decaying and rotten from the inside out.

Following the scene that shows Hsiao Kang's bedroom, the next domestic space that we see in *Rebels of the Neon God* is Ah Tze's flooded apartment. After a night out stealing and spending the cash in neon-lit video-game centres, Ah Tze is seen riding on his prized racing motorcycle and cruising the empty streets of Taipei at dawn. However, the atmosphere of the film takes a sharp turn along with the sudden change in the mode of transportation. No longer racing and drifting across the city, Ah Tze returns home by riding an old and dysfunctional elevator rumoured to be haunted by ghosts, as it always stops midway between floors going in both directions. Once he walks into his apartment, the contrast between speed and hampered motion becomes even more prominent. Striding in difficulty on the flooded apartment floor, the sound of splashing water gives a comic-tragic and realistic-absurd portrait of the skilful criminal we see at the beginning. The city as a labyrinth and maze has been one of the central themes in classical film noir.[6] Characters have the appearance of being cool, aloof and detached, as they are regularly seen slipping into cars and taxis and cruising the city in anonymity. Similarly in *Rebels*, we see motifs of drifting around the city in several prominently featured locales that give a local view on young adult life in Taiwan. Not only is Ah Tze constantly seen on his motorcycle, his mind also wanders in the virtual space of video gaming. When the film introduces the central female protagonist, the young and beautiful Ah Kuei who works as a receptionist at a roller-skating rink, the motif of transience and perpetual motion is expertly visualized with shots of teenagers and young adults tirelessly making rounds, circling the confined space, and indulging themselves in intoxicating sensations of detachment.

Against the backdrop of an alienating environment, or the 'negative existentialism' Polan observes, what we see in *Rebels* is a moment of homecoming, in the most literal sense, of an individual on the move returning to the space of the home. Flooded, dilapidated, dark and damp, the space of crumbling apartments is one of the most consistent visual motifs of Tsai's lens of the de-spectacular. Not only is the space of the interior and domesticity at the centre of the filmmaker's portrait of the bare reality of Taipei, so is a unique microscopic lens that dissects trivial domestic details, such as numerous close-ups of the drain in Ah Tze's apartment.

From these close-ups of the clogged drain and Ah Tze's responses to it, the film's de-spectacular magnification of an inconspicuous space of everyday life becomes an allegory of Taiwanese youths' relationship with the urban environment as well as the world. Although not glamorous or beautiful, the drain, very much like the femme fatale, is seen as capricious and unpredictable. With a will of its own, it is first featured in the sequence that shows Ah Tze's homecoming. While the audience has initially seen Ah Bing and Ah Tze working at ease with a drill and screwdriver, here the young adult gives a contrasting image as he laboriously works with a plunger to unclog the drain, but to no avail. After the water mysteriously recedes at the film's midpoint, another striking sequence occurs when the partners in crime get into trouble and are beaten up for selling computer chips that they steal from a video-game centre. Returning home wounded and frightened, Ah Tze soon discovers that water again begins to seep through the drain. Never knowing where it came from, or where it would go, the young adult protagonist is shown stuffing a towel down the drain although the pressure of water immediately pushes it back to the surface. As if choreographing a magic show, the drain functions like a secret tunnel that stages the towel's disappearance and reappearance. Powerless to stay in control, Ah Tze's recurrent struggle with the drain becomes an emblem for the disconnection between action and consequence.

Given the film's title, which evokes images of teenage rebels, Tsai's dystopic depiction of Taipei puts less emphasis on stereotypical portrayals of adolescent delinquency than on the unbearable and overwhelming mismatch between signifying action and signified consequence. For a society that tailors all social, economic and foreign governmental policies for rapid modernization and an outlook toward the future, what remains at stake is the fact that the inexplicable becomes the new normal in Taiwan. The outbursts of violence we see from characters in the earlier decade (for example in *Terrorizer*) are replaced by events where sequentiality and social order lose all possible meanings. Like ripples on water, the decoupling of cause and effect begins to unfold in interpersonal relationships as well as on a societal level. Perhaps just as what Ah Tze says when he complains about a series of unfortunate and incomprehensible events that happen in the course of a few days – 'I must have seen a ghost' – the de-spectacular triviality in *Rebels* surprisingly evokes Taipei's ghostly double, and a spatiality of spectrality. Although always seen on the move on his motorcycle, Ah Tze's mobility is not only hampered by problems at home, but also put into question as the meandering construction sites of Taipei's subway system are everywhere present in the frame, creating a vivid sense of entrapment.

Rebels of the Neon God portrays a city comparable to a giant playground for Taiwan's youths. As the audience follows them through video-game centres, skating rinks and love hotels, teenagers and young adults in the film are frivolous and carefree, just like the deity Nocha who is famous for his fiery temper and swift mobility. Seen as having three heads and six arms, Nocha is often visualized riding on wheels of fire and ready to dash out at lightning speed.[7] Because of his association with mobility, Nocha is also the protective deity of Taiwan's taxi drivers, not coincidentally the profession of Hsiao Kang's father. Before I continue to discuss *Rebels* as a new direction for neo-noir from noir's initial ties with crime thrillers, a final point to make on the spatiality of a Taiwanese neo-noir would be the film's constant evocations of larger cosmological and spiritual worlds that continue film noir's dark reflection on the incomprehensible changes brought by modernity, especially as documented by changes in the urban landscape and remembered by the city itself.

As I have illustrated in this section, *Rebels* highlights through burgeoning urban youth cultures of the 1990s the existence of new, transient spaces such as the video-game centres and skating rinks discussed above. However, the emergence of these spaces in visual representations of Taipei goes beyond proving that these images of the urban stage and construct general feelings of alienation. Rather, the de-spectacular as a visual lens provides microscopic close-ups of numerous literal 'openings' in the city – the drain, the underground tunnels for the city's future subway systems, and the electronic palm reader (or fortune-teller) that Ah Tze once uses – and literally opens up a spatiality and temporality that coexist but are not commensurable with the secularized and rationalized urban landscape, and certainly not with the progressive logic of modernity. Hidden in the most inconspicuous spaces of urban life, *Rebels* points to a direction of neo-noir that literally deconstructs the meaning of the 'urban', while alluding to the *co-presence* of different ethnic groups that crowd urban centres of Asia, to non-human species, and to the world of ghosts and spirits that become central themes in the film-maker's later works. To pave the way for understanding these co-presences, I now turn to a discussion of the teenage 'rebels' in *Rebels of the Neon God*, for a most unusual twist in a post-modern urban ghost story that features rebels.

From Noir to Neo-Noir: Urban Crime Thriller Turns into Silent Ghost Story

As discussed in the introduction, *Rebels of the Neon God* intentionally evokes images of teenage rebels. In addition to the original Chinese title's allusion to the rebellious deity Nocha, the film also makes direct reference to Nicholas Ray's *Rebel Without a Cause* in a scene in which Hsiao Kang looks at a life-size poster of James Dean's character Jim Stark in one of Taipei's video-game centres. After the film introduces its main protagonists Ah Tze and Hsiao Kang, the characters are seen in two separate narrative strands that only have elusive connections. Although the film soon introduces the young and beautiful Ah Kuei who later becomes Ah Tze's girlfriend, what I intend to illustrate in this section is the game of desire that departs from film noir's emphasis on heterosexual and deadly attractions between the male protagonist and the femme fatale. Following Ah Tze like a vengeful and obsessive ghost, Hsiao Kang in *Rebels* plays the teenage detective who spies on his potential enemy. Completely unaware of Hsiao Kang's existence, Ah Tze carries on with his everyday life, stealing money, making love and getting beaten up, without the slightest idea that the same person has been sitting next to him while he plays games, or that his beloved motorcycle has been destroyed by a stranger he has never directly met. As Tsai's *Rebels* explores the intense but indirect relationship between Ah Tze and Hsiao Kang, the film presents a vengeful pursuit that turns out to be a game of desire. The blinking neon light surrounding the endless construction sites that one sees everywhere in the film might be read as a symbol of disconnection and alienation, but they could also mean flickering desires in the city that kindle the darkness of the night.

Compared with traditional crime thrillers that highlight private feelings of unsettlement that seep into the public domain of the urban landscape, Tsai's *Rebels* is perhaps best characterized as a silent ghost story where action, mobility and criminal activities are drastically toned down. At the centre of a Taiwanese production, one does not find teenage rebels making grand heroic gestures of rebellion, like the one we see in the deadly high-speed car race that ends local bully Buzz Gunderson's life in Ray's *Rebel Without a Cause*. In Tsai's version of the 'rebels', the rebellious teenagers are seen committing acts of transgression without any signified meaning. With its young protagonists not making headlines or causing social ripples, *Rebels of the Neon God* resembles a post-modern ghost story without 'ghosts', a full-length game of what seems like childish peekaboo that is in reality a sophisticated orchestration of visibility and invisibility. It is also an emblem for the paradox of seething *invisible presences* of Taiwan's future generation living with shrinking alternatives to survive in Taiwan's economic and political centre.

After setting up two parallel narrative strands at the beginning, *Rebels* follows the lives of Ah Tze and Hsiao Kang respectively. While Ah Tze drifts around the city on his motorcycle and supports himself by making quick bucks through petty crimes, Hsiao Kang is seen discontinuing a normal teenage life by withdrawing and taking a refund from the private tutoring institution where he takes classes and prepares for the college entrance exam. The two young adults first cross paths on what seems to be a good day ahead. Ah Tze has just made friends with the young and attractive Ah Kuei, and Hsiao Kang's taciturn father surprisingly asks his son to take the day off to go watch a movie together. The scene that takes place inside the taxi cab Kang's father drives for a living has striking resemblance to a scene in French director François Truffaut's *The 400 Blows* (1959), where the main character, a 12-year-old boy, is taken by his parents for a fun movie night after almost burning down their tiny Paris apartment. Although not explicitly a noir film, *The 400 Blows* in many ways continues a newly emerged sub-genre of noir at the end of Hollywood's classical noir period. Shifting focus away from distorted angles to realistic compositions, the French production asks a question that goes beyond film noir as an affective record of distorted emotions and surmounting paranoia, by extending the social lens of noir to concrete visualizations of alternative experiences of urban life embodied by other subjects living in the city.

Making *The 400 Blows* a few years after the release of *Rebel Without a Cause*, Truffaut comments specifically on his appreciation of Ray's work:

> In James Dean, today's youth discovers itself. Less for the reasons usually advanced: violence, sadism, hysteria, pessimism, cruelty and filth, than for others infinitely more simple and commonplace: modesty of feeling, continual fantasy life, moral purity without relation to

> everyday morality but all the more rigorous, eternal adolescent love of tests and trials, intoxication, pride and regret at feeling 'outside' society, refusal and desire to become integrated and, finally, acceptance – or refusal – of the world as it is.[8]

In a film that details the semi-autobiographical plight of the young Truffaut in the form of Antoine Doinel, who prefers daydreaming to studying at school, *The 400 Blows* is not merely a domestic French production, but a transnational cousin of film noir that shows an embodied urban angle on intensifying processes of economic integration and globalization. While such an angle proposes questions that are universally linked, by using the turbulent period of young adulthood to re-examine consolidated social norms and structures, Tsai's portrait of Taiwanese young adults presents teenage rebels in Taiwanese bodies as the film visually dissects details of an embodied urban experience of life in Taipei.

Although Tsai's *Rebels* intentionally replicates the happy family outing, the father-and-son trip to the movies is discontinued because of a malicious car accident caused by the motorcycling Ah-Tze. Upset at Hsiao Kang's father who honks at him for blocking the turn lane, Ah Tze smashes the car's side mirror before speeding off and disappearing into traffic. While the scene sets up a stark contrast between Ah Tze as a violent gangster youth and Hsiao Kang as the passive victim sitting in his father's taxi, what the film reveals is Kang's elaborate moves of revenge that turn the city into his private playground. Stalking Ah Tze like a ghostly shadow, Hsiao Kang follows him as the violent young adult traverses through the underground world of Taipei. In this case, the detective 'private eye' does not gaze at the attractive femme fatale. Seen burdened by her own insecurity and desire for love, Ah Kuei is not portrayed any differently from the male protagonists. By redirecting the gaze toward Ah Tze, a total stranger who soon becomes the object of an obsession, Tsai's *Rebels* features a game of desire under the guise of a chase.

However, even in frames where Hsiao Kang and Ah Tze coexist, the two are separated by a physical distance that seems impossible to cross. Rather than presenting the outpouring of desire, whether erotic or a desire for friendship, the film shows the pair's closest contact taking the most unexpected form, which unfortunately only makes the social abyss impossible to cross. Observing details of what Ah Tze eats, where he meets his girlfriend and how he commits petty thefts, Hsiao Kang knows everything about Ah Tze, with whom he has never spoken a word. The climax of their interaction only happens in a violent act of vengeful vandalism. While Ah Tze

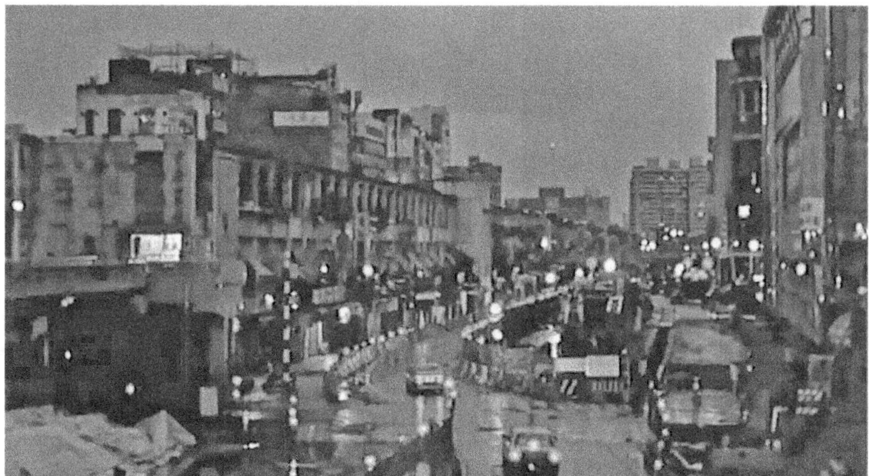

Figure 8.2 Perfectly incremented neon lights in *Rebels of the Neon God*

makes love to his girlfriend in a love hotel, the stranger who has checked into the next room makes his move downstairs, first by sinking a craft knife deep into the seat cushion of Ah Tze's motorcycle, then injecting instant adhesive into the keyhole, and finally spray-painting the letters AIDS onto the side of the cycle. Ironically, the indirect contact works visually like lethal caresses that mimic the steamy love scene happening in the love hotel. Attentively looking out of the window later, Kang jumps joyfully up and down on the bed once Ah Tze discovers the wrecked vehicle. Although Kang is able to hide behind the curtains in his hotel room, he cannot help but approach the initial aggressor and new victim. 'Do you need help?' is the first verbal attempt at communication Hsiao Kang makes in the film as he follows Ah Tze on his way to an auto repair shop. Ah Tze angrily curses at the stranger, convinced that he must have bumped into a ghost on this miserable day. The two are seen going down separate paths, with Taipei's dimly lit skyline and numerous blinking neon lights as the only remaining common ground.

Conclusion

Much like the bloody accident cited at the start of this chapter, where Hsiao Kang accidentally turns into a victim when he acts out on a cockroach, the initial aggressor Ah Tze is caught powerlessly in a loop of events that turns him into one of the victimized. As this chapter has illustrated through the reading of a neo-noir tendency of triviality and the de-spectacular, more emphasis is put on the decoupling of cause and effect, of action and consequence. Although Tsai's *Rebels* presents a cinematic hyperrealism through ample uses of long takes at a fixed angle, the film still evidences film noir's signature aesthetics of distortion and the sense of losing control. If crime is the means of driving characters and the world into a delirious frenzy, de-spectacularized crime in *Rebels* presents an even more overwhelming, all-encompassing loss of control by infinitely expanding the possibility of losing grip with reality in the face of the most mundane details of the everyday. Different from the thrills and actions that usually spring from endangered characters in crime films, the sensation of powerlessness clings to Taiwan's young adults like a slowly paralysing weight, a bitter irony in a society that urges its young generation to chase after speed and upward mobility. Unable to identify the aggressor, Ah Tze remains in the dark throughout the film, not able to see clearly his paradoxical role as both aggressor and victim. Following the attack on Ah Tze, the last sequence features Hsiao Kang walking into a friend-finder calling centre, where one can pay for a one-on-one phone conversation with a 'friend' in small private rooms designed for such intimate exchanges. Returning to another image of the telephone, this time a telephone actually in service, the film ends with Hsiao Kang leaving the phone cubicle, with a sudden cut to Taipei's skyline and an abyss of darkness. The only tangible path is the perfectly incremented red neon lights that surround the meandering subway construction sites.

Another day has ended in Taipei. As the camera refocuses on the cityscape, perhaps nothing of what has happened would be remembered the next day. However, the film's play of visibility and invisibility that literally turns concrete embodiment into ghostly presences serves as a potent reminder of Taiwan's marginalised social groups in the city. These presences exist in paradoxes, as we have seen in Taipei's disillusioned youth living in a rapidly developing as well as decaying urban environment. More precisely, *Rebels of the Neon God* examines, by presenting the bared and mundane everyday life of a group of Taiwanese youths, their spectral presence and invisibility. Therefore, the question is, how does one *de-spectralize*, by giving back flesh, blood and concrete presence to the spectralized? In my reading of *Rebels*, I hope to have shown that Tsai's use of Taipei apartments' interior details on the one hand deconstructs the home as safe haven, and on the other hand gives Taiwan's marginalized youths a concrete footing, even if a most humble one. At last, as neon lights have permeated every major developing East Asian city and form the most common component of the urban landscape, Tsai's de-spectacular lens, an optical unconscious, may be rapidly multiplying. In other parts of Taiwan and East Asia, the same ghostly encounter may repetitively occur, constituting additional ghostly presences that haunt the neo-noir portraits of modern Asia.

Notes

1 Jameson, Fredric, 'Remapping Taipei', in *The Geopolitical Aesthetic: Cinema and Space in the World System* (Bloomington: Indiana University Press, 1995).
2 Polan, Dana, *Power and Paranoia: History, Narrative, and the American Cinema, 1940–1950* (New York: Columbia University Press, 1986).
3 Sobchack, Vivian, '"Lounge Time": Postwar Crises and the Chronotopes of Film Noir', in Nick Browne (ed.), *Refiguring American Film Genres: History and Theory* (Berkeley: University of California Press, 1998), p. 138.
4 Dimendberg, Edward, *Film Noir and the Spaces of Modernity* (Cambridge, MA: Harvard University Press, 2004), p. 3.
5 Ibid., p. 4.
6 Silver, Alain and James Ursini, *The Noir Style* (Woodstock, NY: Overlook Press, 1999).
7 According to *The Investiture of the Gods (Fengshen yanyi)*, written in the sixteenth century, Nezha (Wade-Giles: Nocha) was born during the Shang Dynasty in a military fortress. Nezha's father was the famous military commander Li Jing, who mistakenly believed that Nezha was born a demon. After a pregnancy that lasted for three years and six months, Li Jing's wife gave birth to a ball, which Li split open with his sword. From the moment of his birth, Nezha was on unfriendly terms with his father.
8 Truffaut, quoted in McCann, Graham, *Rebel Males: Clift, Brando and Dean* (London: Hamish Hamilton Ltd, 1991), p. 141.

Chapter 9

Film Noir, Hong Kong Cinema and the Limits of Critical Transplant

Andy Willis

Many national and regional cinemas have long traditions of crime film production. Whilst not all of these have been claimed as having their roots in film noir, from John Woo's urban gangster dramas of the 1980s and early 1990s to the recent crime films of Johnnie To, the idea that the neon-lit, densely populated, high-rise city of Hong Kong is a suitable space for the creation of a contemporary East Asian noir cinema has been a seductive one. However appealing, if rather simplistic, this may be, in this chapter I want to consider what it actually means to label Hong Kong crime films – such as *One Night in Mongkok* (2004), *Divergence* (2005) and *Beast Stalker* (2008) – as film noirs and by extension part of a cinematic style that developed halfway around the world in Hollywood, half a century before.

The dominance of Hollywood cinema globally, and its subsequent focus for much of the critical writing that has been produced in relation to cinema, has led to critics attempting to understand a range of international works by simply transplanting approaches and concepts that have been developed in relation to the products of Hollywood. For example, the *auteur* theory and notions such as genre have been widely applied to films from other national cultural and production contexts. The identification and labelling of some Hong Kong crime films as film noir, or as drawing on the codes and conventions of film noir, is one such example of this critical transplant. This is perhaps not surprising when one acknowledges Steve Neale's argument that '"film noir" as a term is now freely used in reviews and in listings magazines to describe more or less any new crime film on the one hand, and more or less any crime film made in the 1940s and 1950s on the other'.[1] This wide acceptance of the currency of the term film noir as shorthand for a variety of visual motifs and cycles within crime film production has led to an overly simplistic and somewhat problematic appropriation of the term in relation to contemporary Hong Kong crime film productions. With the issue of critical transplant in mind, I want to consider how useful the adoption of the term 'film noir' is in relation to Hong Kong cinema, specifically investigating how the appearance of what seem noir elements in my examples, *One Night in Mongkok*, *Divergence* and *Beast Stalker*, may not ultimately add up to anything like a fully formed 'Hong Kong Noir'. I will also explore how critics' assumption of a mutual, international understanding of the term film noir can lead to an overlooking of the historical and cultural specificity of contemporary Hong Kong cinema. In such instances, the desire to connect Hong Kong crime films to traditions developed within Hollywood can work to dislocate these works from the very particular contexts of their production and, perhaps more significantly, the cinematic traditions from within which aspects of both their form and content have developed. The assertion of links to Hollywood film cycles also results in the privileging of that cinema as the originator of particular styles, and the dismissal of other national and local cinemas as merely derivative and by extension lacking in innovation or originality. By freeing Hong Kong crime films from such reductive perspectives, we can begin to see them as significant films in their own right.

Film Noir and Hong Kong Cinema

In his work on the Hong Kong-based director Johnnie To, Stephen Teo has coined the term 'Kowloon Noir'.[2] As To's international reputation is based around a series of muscular, urban crime films that draw on influences from across cinema history, from Hollywood to France to East Asia, the idea of transplanting versions of a noir style from its origins in US cinema to To's neon-lit streets of Hong Kong is again a seductive one. However, Teo's definition of 'Kowloon Noir' remains somewhat difficult to identify. There are a number of reasons for this; he asserts that '"Kowloon Noir" is perhaps best seen as a sub-category of the action film',[3] before going on to state that such films may also be fruitfully thought of as melodramas. Whilst not advocating a simplistic shopping list of elements that identify what makes a work a film noir, and acknowledging the important work that has been done arguing for the profitability of seeing examples of noir as male melodrama,[4] Teo fails to precisely draw the boundaries of what constitutes 'Kowloon Noir'. Indeed, much of the cinema of Hong Kong displays high levels of melodrama, so the evocation of that genre or mode does not help his cause. Ultimately, Teo's desire to use the term 'noir', but his resistance to directly link it to wider acknowledged ideas of what makes a film noir, becomes unhelpful. This vacillation between genres and styles clearly raises more critical questions than it creates an applicable critical model. This problem is enhanced when Teo goes on to list a number of familiar aspects of film noir that his 'Kowloon Noir' does not include. He says that the category has no discernible *femmes fatales*[5] and that it has 'no flashbacks, no past recollections [...] [and] little of the mood of *temps perdu* which is one of the stylistics of American film noir noted by Paul Schrader'.[6] By critically drawing his 'Kowloon Noir' away from established thinking about film noir, Teo uses the term 'noir' in a manner that is not strongly linked to definitions of film noir.

Whilst Teo's 'Kowloon Noir' may lack critical bite and applicability, the general idea that there is a Hong Kong film noir remains enticing. Writing about Johnnie To's *PTU* (2003), a nighttime-set police procedural that follows one Police Tactical Unit (PTU) squad through a series of scrapes, Michael Ingham cites Teo's notion of 'Kowloon Noir', even though *PTU* has little that connects to the sensibilities or visual style of classic film noir.[7] When addressing the question of film noir in relation to *PTU*, Ingham does not cite any textual moments that might be considered noir-esque.[8] For me, Ingham's evocation of the term, with little evidence for its usefulness in understanding the film's operations, pinpoints one of the main issues with the idea of Hong Kong noir: that it is easy to invoke but much more difficult actually to identify. With this in mind, I want to explore further some contemporary Hong Kong crime films that may evoke the idea of noir in their use of visual, narrative and character codes and conventions but ultimately are more profitably seen as Hong Kong crime films than as fully blown examples of an elusive Hong Kong or Kowloon noir. It is therefore worth taking a moment to revisit the basic elements of film noir.

The widely acknowledged difficulty in defining film noir has led to its becoming something of a critical catch-all term, and one applied to films that show just the slightest hint of noir. However, the easy application of the label has been challenged by a number of scholars in the field. In this regard, Steve Neale usefully states that:

> a number of features said to be characteristic of noir – the use of chiaroscuro, for instance, and the use of flashback and voice-over, scenarios of destructive and murderous passion, an emphasis on perverse forms of character motivation and behaviour and on the

> depiction of extreme mental states, and a stress on suspicion, distrust and deceit in the depiction of relations between male and female protagonists – can all be found in genres and cycles – such as the gothic women's film and Val Lewton's horror series at RKO – that proponents of noir tend to regard as either non-canonical or marginal.[9]

Neale thus suggests that the visual and narrative traits now so closely associated with film noir were in fact present in a number of works that have been more profitably placed in other categories in order to fruitfully explore them critically. Therefore, an overly concrete idea of what constitutes film noir and the subsequent placing of every, even marginal, work into that category due to the identification of particular narrative or visual qualities has the potential to become a critical block. In the cultural context of Hong Kong, the evocation and identification of a noir trend can close rather than open up the ways one might critically approach contemporary Hong Kong crime films.

Noir Tendencies in Contemporary Hong Kong Crime Films

As I have already noted, and whilst acknowledging Neale's observations, many recent Hong Kong crime films could be considered as having touches of noir due to their visual style, narrative structure or characterization. *One Night in Mongkok*, *Divergence* and *Beast Stalker* all offer useful case studies through which one can explore noir tendencies in contemporary Hong Kong crime films, but importantly they also suggest the significant limitations of importing the term wholesale.

One of Hong Kong's most critically acclaimed crime films of the past decade,[10] *One Night in Mongkok* incorporates what can be identified as elements of noir whilst not constituting a wholehearted Hong Kong take on film noir. Somewhat downbeat in tone, the film can be seen as fitting Vivian Sobchack's argument that film noir constituted 'a pessimistic cinematic response to volatile social and economic conditions'.[11] Derek Yee, as both director and scriptwriter, constructs *One Night in Mongkok* around a number of overlapping narrative strands used to highlight the social and economic conditions that form a vital backdrop to the film's stories. These involve the beginning and escalation of a war between two prominent Kowloon street gangs, the Hungs and the Dongs. The outbreak of this street war leads to one of the gangs hiring a mainland hit man, Lai Fu, played by Daniel Wu, to kill the opposition gang leader. Lai Fu is clearly

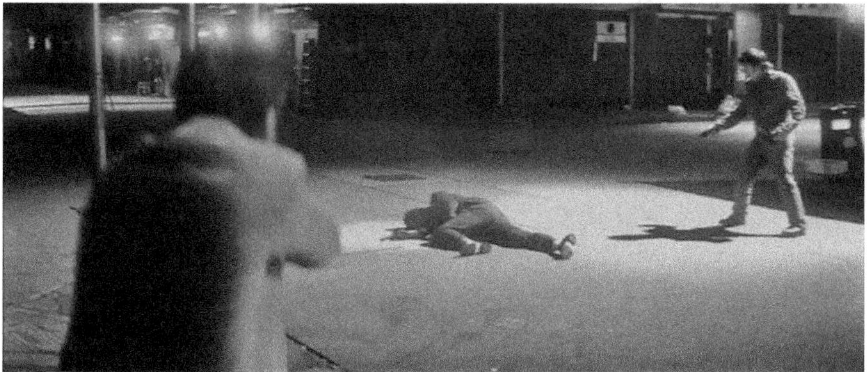

Figure 9.1 The dark and dangerous streets of Hong Kong in *One Night in Mongkok*

shown as coming from a mainland village, which a character later refers to as impoverished. Ultimately, when viewers learn that Lai Fu's desire to go to Hong Kong is driven by a search for his missing girlfriend, it is this grinding poverty that explains why he takes on such a dangerous job; it provides the only opportunity a poor man will get to go to Hong Kong. Made seven years after the handover of Hong Kong to the People's Republic of China, *One Night in Mongkok* uses the character of Lai Fu to highlight the way criminals can exploit mainlanders' poverty and hardship, and their ensuing desire to enter what they see as the promised land of Hong Kong. In addition, the film presents the economic opportunism that this situation offers. This is something of which many mainland migrants to Hong Kong are widely, and not unproblematically, accused. *One Night in Mongkok* explores this tension through the character of Liu (Suet Lam), whose greed is shown through his brokering of deals between Hong Kong gang leaders and desperate men from his own mainland village.

Another element within *One Night in Mongkok* that potentially links it with the conventions of noir is the character of Dan Dan (Cecilia Cheung). A young woman who works as a prostitute in Hong Kong to earn money to take home to the mainland, she provides a further complication for Lai Fu when he arrives in the city and strikes up a friendship with her. This friendship is based on their mutual outsider status, and the film quickly and effectively establishes this connection through their mutual difficulty in speaking and understanding Cantonese, the dominant language in Hong Kong. Their relationship also neatly develops the central idea of the economic exploitation of migrants beyond an individual character and suggests that Lai Fu may be part of a developing mainland migrant underclass within Hong Kong.[12]

The other central characters in *One Night in Mongkok*, Inspector Milo's police squad, are introduced in a series of police procedural-style scenes. When news of the arrival of a mainland hit man filters through, they are assigned the task of hunting him down. This leads to the setting up of operation 'One Night in Mongkok', which will draw the film's characters together as their storylines begin to overlap further and the film moves toward its climactic nighttime sequences. The intersecting of characters' lives in *One Night in Mongkok* focuses on one of the film's other main concepts, fate and its impact on people's lives. This theme is highlighted in the film's opening scene, which takes place at night and frames two men in a medium long shot as they sit outside on some steps with their back to the camera. At this point viewers do not know the characters' identities, and as they share some thoughts, the one positioned on the left states, 'The person you want is never around. The one you don't want to see keeps turning up like a bad penny.' The other replies, 'It is fate. Fate will make it happen.' The film then cuts to a street scene in black and white, a scene introduced with the title 'the day before yesterday'. The importance of the discussion about fate becomes clear when the exchange between the two men reappears later, by which stage the characters' identities – they are Milo and his lieutenant – have been established. Again, the idea that characters are unable to escape their destiny, however bad that might be, can be seen as connecting with broad definitions of the conventions of film noir. Here, however, fate is presented as a factor that affects the lives of everyone in the film, not just the individual at the centre of the story.

Though a number of aspects of *One Night in Mongkok* can be identified as overlapping with definitions of film noir, many elements are more generally drawn from the non-noir, urban crime film. For example, the use of triad street gangs, the realist visual style of the police procedural sequences, and the character of a rookie cop who makes a mistake on his first day on the job all sit comfortably with the broader codes and conventions of the Hong Kong crime film. Therefore, arguing that a film such as *One Night in Mongkok* is an example of Hong Kong film noir privileges some aspects of the film whilst ignoring all the evidence that can be drawn from a detailed textual analysis of the work. Whilst clearly 'a pessimistic cinematic response to volatile social and economic conditions',[13] it is, rather than a work striving to reproduce some of the narrative and visual codes of an American cinema of the postwar era, a contemporary crime film that engages with a number of issues that urgently concern contemporary Hong Kong society.

Whilst at times *One Night in Mongkok* utilizes the codes of social realism, other Hong Kong crime films include some highly melodramatic elements, very much in line with popular East Asian cinema more generally. So, whilst filmmakers do not always wholeheartedly display the kind of visual style associated with film noir, they do often draw on character traits and narrative elements that can be linked to noir's codes and conventions. Such aspects of these films often manifest themselves within their more melodramatic moments. Indeed, the already noted ease with which critics are prone to classify crime films as 'noir' means that many of those produced in Hong Kong can be drawn into such a classification. However, this process involves marginalizing the obviously melodramatic conventions that inform the films' construction. *Divergence* is a good example of a crime film that has such highly melodramatic moments but that also overlaps with the ideas of noir. An illustration occurs near its opening, where the film seems to direct its audience to the visual codes and conventions of noir through shots of rainy, nighttime urban streets washed by neon lighting.

Divergence's complicated narrative and intersecting character storylines also contribute to its possible reception as Hong Kong noir, potentially reflecting Neale's point that '[t]he narratives of film noirs are usually characterized as complex – often confusing – and as frequently entailing the use of flashbacks, and first-person voice-over narration'.[14] However, rather than revealing a desire to reproduce consciously the narrative structures associated with examples of classic film noir, *Divergence* can more fruitfully be linked to trends in Hong Kong cinema. Due to the fast pace of production, short shooting schedules and the noticeable lack of regard for worked-through scripts, particularly in the 1980s and 1990s, Hong Kong cinema has

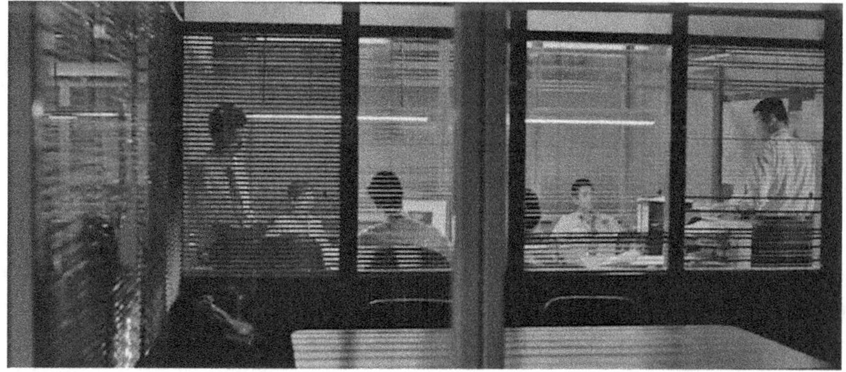

Figure 9.2 Possible shades of noir in *Divergence*

often been characterized by films with confusing narratives. Moreover, one can easily locate a continued presence of 'confusing' narratives in a range of recent East Asian films outside crime genres, such as a number of the historical epics that continue to dominate the Chinese box office.[15]

Divergence contains a psychologically obsessive character who would certainly be at home on the dark streets of a conventional film noir. In an increasingly hysterical performance, Aaron Kwok plays the central role of the highly troubled Suen, a cop fixated on the possibility that his missing girlfriend is still alive. On the surface, the film's story focuses on Suen's role as a member of the Hong Kong police's anti-financial corruption unit. However, director Benny Chan and scriptwriter Ivy Ho push the film away from the procedural and toward a psychological character study. Suen always carries an image of his missing girlfriend and whilst undertaking his investigations begins to think he has found her again in the person of To Hong-sang (Ekin Cheng), the wife of a corrupt lawyer he has under surveillance. His obsession leads to paranoia as he begins to think that everyone is attempting to stop him proving the woman's real identity. He cannot sleep, and flashbacks and slow motion emphasize his ever-present obsession. With its visual style and obsessive lead character, *Divergence* comes close to creating a contemporary Hong Kong film noir. However, it still needs to be considered as a work that not only has a great deal in common with American film noir but also crucially with other Hong Kong crime films, particularly in its exploration of contemporary economic corruption.

Like many Hong Kong crime films, such as *One Night in Mongkok*, fate is also a central concept in Dante Lam's *Beast Stalker*, another contemporary work that utilizes aspects of film noir without belonging exclusively to a Hong Kong noir category. Once again the film operates as a police procedural, highlighted by a handheld, realist style in the opening sequences, before settling on the psychological aspects of the central characters. Particularly in its construction of these main characters, *Beast Stalker* self-consciously utilizes elements associated with the world of noir. These elements consolidate around the character of Hung (played by Nick Cheung), a hired killer with escalating debts who takes his victims to his back-street apartment before killing them and brutally disposing of their bodies. The apartment is shot in a minimal light that draws out shadows and allows for glimpses of his dark, dirt-encrusted sofa and curtains. The *mise-en-scène* of these scenes evokes the desperate world of noir and is enhanced by shots from Hung's point of view being presented in black and white, motivated by his having shards of glass in one eye. To complement such a gloomy view, Hung's continual smoking and drinking, and flashbacks providing some of his backstory, indicate his obsessive behaviour and psychological fragility. However, Hung is made more sympathetic by the fact that he cares for his severely disabled wife in the same apartment in which he commits his crimes. As he feels responsible for the accident that caused her injury, her presence also functions as a constant reminder to him that he has let her down. With the layered construction of Hung's character, the world of *Beast Stalker*, like that of many film noirs, becomes one where the police are as troublesome as the criminals. This aspect of the film is drawn out by a number of scenes that show the police squad leader, Tong (Nicholas Tse), to be in terms of his obsessive behaviour equal to Hung. This character trait is revealed most clearly in those sequences that focus on how his dogged pursuit of criminals regularly puts others in his team in danger.

With its dark characterization and *mise-en-scène*, *Beast Stalker* is in many ways representative of the ways contemporary Hong Kong directors can evoke the world of film noir through stylistic and character traits commonly associated with the form. I would argue, however, that whilst there are elements of noir within these films, they cannot be considered direct adoptions of the style or direct attempts to transplant film noir into Hong Kong cinema. Instead, the films use noir elements sparingly, both as indicators of their directors' cine-literacy and to assist audiences' reading of the films.

These examples show how problematic is the assumption that films with noir traits simplistically constitute a Hong Kong noir. Such assumptions are often built upon a simplistic claim that crime films, particularly those with nighttime settings, are examples of film noir, an assertion often made at the expense of detailed analysis of how 'noir' these works really are. Many crime films do not evoke noir sensibilities at all, and those that do, as I have shown, often do so in a partial and fragmentary way and certainly are not sustained enough to constitute Hong Kong examples of film noir. Film noir remains an attractive term with respect to Hong Kong cinema, and many critics persist in labelling films as noir, however inappropriate such a designation might be. One recent example of such a critical response can be found in relation to Peter Chan's Hong Kong/China co-production *Wu Xia* (2011).

Wu Xia: Critical Divergence and the Idea of a Specifically Hong Kong Film Noir

As already noted, a film's visual style, iconography and certain character traits are often the primary aspects that lead critics to identify a range of different works as having noir tendencies. In a similar way to Neale, Michael Walker notes that these include 'the use of low-key lighting to create unusual shadows and chiaroscuro effects, a high proportion of night scenes, off-angle camera compositions, deep-focus shots framing characters in cluttered, claustrophobic interiors, [and] a greater or lesser sense of expressionist distortion.'[16] However, the identification of films from a wide range of genres as having noir tendencies or being examples of film noir through the slightest hint of these elements is often very superficial. In relation to East Asian cinema, good examples of seemingly random anointing of contemporary works as film noir, or of having noir tendencies, can be found in reviews published around the release of *Wu Xia* in 2011.

Even though the idea of noir was evoked by a number of writers responding to *Wu Xia*, most acknowledged that it is primarily a martial-arts film. The story is set in 1917 and involves an investigation into the death of a wandering bandit in a remote village. This event in turn reveals hidden identities and ultimately unleashes a murderous clan's desire for revenge. The film uses prominent flashbacks to tell its story, as well as a striking visual style with contrasting darkness and light. If one takes Neale's and Walker's descriptions of noir elements at their most general, they could certainly be applicable to a film such as *Wu Xia*. However, as already noted, it is most obviously a martial-arts film, albeit one that, as the title *Wu Xia* suggests, is highly self-reflexive. The knowingness of the title also suggests that the makers of *Wu Xia* are cine-literate enough to use flashes of noir style self-consciously, but without trying to create a work that should be labelled chiefly as noir.

However, in Western journalistic writing, whilst acknowledging the martial-arts aspects of the film, there was a critical acceptance that *Wu Xia* could be referred to as substantially a film noir. The origins of this perspective may well lie in the assertions of Harvey Weinstein, whose Weinstein Company distributed the film in the USA. Whilst acknowledging that there was a high level of self-reflexivity to the film, something he saw as indicating that Peter Chan was a 'true artist', Weinstein argued that this self-reflexivity was manifest most clearly through Chan's use of cinematic genres, forms and cycles. Weinstein claimed of Chan that, 'with *Wu Xia* he has created a dream project, combining two of my favorite genres: film noir and martial arts'.[17] The fact that this labelling came from Weinstein, a master publicist whose primary aim was to attract people from the USA as well as East Asia to the film, is something that critics generally could have been expected to approach with some scepticism. In fact, it seems that Weinstein's remark simply confirmed the film as an unquestioned example of noir.

Rather baldly, Fionnuala Halligan, writing in *Screen Daily*, concurred, exclaiming that *Wu Xia* was, '[n]oirish and very more-ish'.[18] Justin Chang, in *Variety*, was more specific and went even further, identifying a strong noir influence on the film's visual style as well as its inclusion of strong psychological elements. He writes, '[t]he repressed return with a vengeance in *Wu Xia*, a satisfyingly sinewy fusion of martial-arts actioner and brain-tickling noir from busy producer-director Peter Ho-sun Chan'.[19] However, whilst once again Halligan and Chang's positions may appeal on the surface, a detailed textual analysis shows that this embrace of *Wu Xia* as a noir-tinged work needs to be challenged – even if that means arguing with Harvey Weinstein.

The opening sequence of *Wu Xia* emphasizes the simple, idyllic rural life of Liu Jin Xi (Donnie Yen), his wife Ayu (Wei Tang) and their two children. They are shown waking up, washing and cleaning, the children playing, cattle grazing and meals being prepared. This basic existence is shot in a manner that draws out the green and blue hues in the image, creating something of a glow. Liu is then shown walking through the unspoiled countryside to his work at the local paper mill and shop he helped establish in the village and that has brought new visitors and prosperity to the area. This quiet existence is interrupted by the arrival of two strangers who attempt to hold up the local general store, with Liu intervening and killing one with a blow to the head. Whilst the underestimation of Liu, a seemingly peaceful man, is predictable within the martial-arts genre, the film uses it to introduce a strand of detective story featuring a less generically familiar character, the investigator Xu Bai Jiu (Takeshi Kaneshiro). Xu initially stands out due to his appearance: he wears glasses and a panama hat, has short hair without a pigtail, and carries an umbrella. However, the film quickly reveals through Xu's actions that his mindset differs from that of the other officials who have arrived in the village as part of the investigation. He deduces how the events under investigation unfolded by drawing on a logic informed by both traditional Chinese medicine and philosophical thinking. The character's approach to the crime scene uses the traditional in order to create a modern scientific and forensic analysis. The idiosyncratic way he is shown to look slowly and carefully at the crime scene, consider the evidence, and interpret what he finds reveals the methodology of a detective able to decode clues. Detective Xu's methods may be one of the reasons critics were happy to label *Wu Xia* as utilizing the codes of film noir, but such reasoning problematically assumes that all detective stories are in some way classifiable as films noirs. Indeed, with his cold, scientific approach, Xu is in many ways the antithesis of a psychologically troubled film noir detective.

Another element of *Wu Xia* that may have led to critics simplistically labelling it in part a film noir is Xu's voice-over as he undertakes his investigation. However, even this most emblematic of noir elements is used in conjunction with aspects of visual style that are most commonly associated with non-noir styles. On occasion this involves a stark visualization of the attack on the victim's internal organs in a manner familiar from television shows such as *CSI* (2000–); at other moments, such as when Xu reflects on who may have the skills to kill the bandit in the manner he died, a series of horror-film-like scenes show the bloody remains of massacres and utilize shock-inducing jump cuts and a hard-rock score. Whilst these moments do reveal Chan's willingness to pick and mix from various genres and styles, the assertion that some of the elements derive from noir is not enough to justify a fully fledged labelling of *Wu Xia* as a martial-arts film noir. Here, rather than evoking the idea of film noir, the character of Xu gives Chan and scriptwriter Aubrey Lam the opportunity for a meditation on criminality and the possibility of rehabilitation. As the film progresses, it becomes clear that Liu, the gentle family man, had been part of a murderous clan and taken part in some horrendous acts. With China still enforcing the death penalty, *Wu Xia* engages with contemporary issues in Chinese society rather than reproducing styles from US cinema's past.

Like most recent Hong Kong films, *Wu Xia* is a Hong Kong/China co-production, and so works within the context of mainland censorship, which proscribes depictions of the supernatural. Its introduction of the superhuman, highly spiritual, almost supernatural levels of martial-arts skills associated with the *wuxia* film thus has to be handled carefully. In this respect, the film highlights rational thought, manifest in the character of Detective Xu, to offer clearly grounded explanations for anything that suggests supernatural actions. Here, Xu's arch rationality, drawn from traditional Chinese thinking, discourages the belief that anything is possible due to forces associated with superstition. In light of contemporary China's modernization and its film censorship board's distrust of works perceived as encouraging superstition, *Wu Xia*, like the Hollywood films noirs of the post-World War II period, can be seen as a product of a particular set of social, cultural and historical contexts. However, a desire by Western critics to label it, on their terms, as a martial-arts noir markedly undermines the film's complexity and cultural specificity.

Harvey Weinstein's evocation of the term 'noir' in his promotion of *Wu Xia* makes the film more palatable and so more appealing to those in the West not familiar with the codes and conventions of the *wuxia* film.

However, an acknowledgement of the historical specificity of film noir remains important. When one looks at Western critics' acceptance and de-historicized use of the term, the category becomes increasingly unhelpful. The label 'noir' masks the specific 'Chineseness' of contemporary Hong Kong films (or Hong Kong/China co-productions), of which *Wu Xia* is a good example. However, when investigating local responses to *Wu Xia* in East Asia, the critical reference points prove very different. Significantly, writers in East Asia, or those very familiar with Hong Kong cinema, do not transplant critical terms with which Western readers might easily connect. For these critics *Wu Xia* remains a genre film, but the generic labels they invoke demonstrate a different history of popular cinema and a wider pool of references. Many see it, perhaps not surprisingly given their cultural and cinematic contexts and the film's title, as belonging to the *wuxia* genre,[20] a label used to refer to the martial-arts film generally but more precisely identifying the swordplay style of film within the larger martial-arts genre. Writing for the US-based *LoveHKfilm* website devoted to Hong Kong cinema, Kevin Ma is typical when he suggests that:

> *Wu Xia* is a love letter to the genre it tries to renew. In addition to traditional *wuxia* world elements like secret clans and super assassins, Chan also includes subtle references to classic *wuxia* films like *The One-Armed Swordsman*. He even casts genre veterans Jimmy Wang Yu and Kara Hui in small but pivotal roles, representing Chan's love and respect for the genre's history.[21]

Ma reveals both an awareness of the conventions of the *wuxia* film and knowledge of those associated with its production history. For Edmund Lee, writing in *Time Out Hong Kong*, *Wu Xia* drew extensively on the cinema of Hong Kong to the extent that it became something of a celebration. His review, again revealing a broad knowledge of Hong Kong cinema's history, states that:

> The year's runaway winner for the most generic film title, *Wu Xia* is a carnival of pulp cinema clichés, flashy visual effects, fundamental moral torments and brutal, melodramatic excesses that are often worthy of Shakespeare. Under the assured direction of Peter Chan (*Perhaps Love, The Warlords*), what could have seemed chaotic and derivative becomes wildly imaginative and thoroughly compelling. This stylish homage to *One-Armed Swordsman* – Chang Cheh's classic from 1967, which similarly charts a formidable martial arts master's

> struggles to lead a reformed life of domestic bliss – is one of the best Hong Kong films in recent times.[22]

Yi Ho, in the *Taipei Times*, concurs, stating that, '[p]aying homage to Chang Cheh's classic *One Armed Swordsman* series that propelled Wang to superstardom in the 1960s, Chan's martial arts flick recalls the sinewy, visceral and boldly violent works exemplary of the golden age of Hong Kong kung fu cinema'.[23] None of these reviewers refers to film noir in their responses, perhaps due to the term's limited currency among their readership, or more likely because the film itself draws much less on the ideas of noir than the Western critics, or even Harvey Weinstein, would have us believe. For the writers aware of Hong Kong and China's cultural and cinematic history, the occasional, and frankly debatable, noir aspects of *Wu Xia* remain peripheral to their engagement with the film.

The issue of what knowledge may assist an understanding of a film steeped in the conventions and history of Chinese and Hong Kong cinema such as *Wu Xia* was acknowledged by its director, Peter Chan. Interviewed by *Time Out Hong Kong*, Chan explicitly states that Western critics writing about his film's influences lack intimate knowledge of the traditions of Hong Kong and East Asian cinema:

> I started off the creative process by trying to make the simplest, simplest *wu xia* story. A man who's very high in martial arts skill decided to leave his life behind and start a new life, and his past is coming back to haunt him. This is the oldest, most traditional martial arts story [...]. It's exactly what happens in *One-Armed Swordsman*, and it's also exactly what happens in the new *One-Armed Swordsman* with David Chiang and Ti Lung, and it's also exactly what happens in John Woo's – the biggest disciple of Chang Cheh's – *The Killer*. It's the same story! I mean, people say my film is [a reference to David Cronenberg's 2005 film] *A History of Violence*, but I think *A History of Violence* is the fifth or the sixth or the tenth reincarnation of the stuff that we've done for the last 40 years.[24]

Chan's observation highlights the ease with which Western critics locate East Asian films in terms of their own critical knowledge and experiences. Such a process is marked by an assumption that viewers worldwide share an unquestioned mutual understanding of critical terms such as film noir, which can be extremely loose and flexible, and which have been sites of contestation for some time.

The most troubling aspect of this form of critical transplant remains its maintenance of a critical hierarchy that locates Hollywood films and critical responses to them at the top and that marginalizes the significance and specificity of local film cycles. In this light, the idea of a Hong Kong noir needs to be rigorously explored at the level of a film's form and content, not haphazardly attached to a film due to the fact that a detective has walked down a few neon-lit, rain-soaked streets. Indeed, thanks to the local climate and the city's use of light, characters in most Hong Kong films regularly walk such streets. Ultimately, one need not be a devotee of film genres or Hong Kong cinema to know that not every crime film set in contemporary Hong Kong belongs to the loose category of film noir.

Notes

1 Neale, Steve, *Genre and Hollywood* (London: Routledge, 2000), p. 175.
2 Teo, Stephen, *Director in Action: Johnnie To and the Hong Kong Action Film* (Hong Kong: Hong Kong University Press, 2007), p. 11.
3 Ibid., p. 12.
4 Staiger, Janet, 'Film Noir as Male Melodrama: The Politics of Genre Labeling', in Lincoln Geraghty and Mark Jancovich (eds), *The Shifting Definitions of Genre: Essays on Labeling Films, Television Shows and Media* (Jefferson, NC: McFarland, 2008), pp. 71–91.
5 Teo, *Director in Action*, p. 11.
6 Ibid., p. 12.
7 Ingham, Michael, *Johnnie To Kei-Fung's PTU* (Hong Kong: Hong Kong University Press, 2009).
8 Ibid., pp. 22–27.
9 Neale, Steve, 'Noir and Neo-Noir', in Pam Cook (ed.), *The Cinema Book*, 3rd ed. (London: BFI, 2007), p. 311.
10 *One Night in Mongkok* was nominated for a range of local film awards in 2005. For example, it won Best Director and Best Screenplay at the Hong Kong Film Awards, and Derek Yee was named Best Director by the Hong Kong Film Critics Society; see Anon., 'Awards for One Night in Mongkok', *Internet Movie Database*, <http://pro.imdb.com/title/tt0430772/awards>, accessed 20 July 2012.
11 Sobchack, Vivian, '"Lounge Time": Post-War Crises and the Chronotope of Film Noir', in Nick Browne (ed.), *Refiguring American Film Genres: History and Theory* (Berkeley: University of California Press, 1998), p. 130.
12 In recent Hong Kong cinema, Ann Hui's *Night and Fog* (2009) more explicitly explores this subject.

13 Sobchack, '"Lounge Time"', p. 130.
14 Neale, *Genre and Hollywood*, p. 166.
15 Examples of this tendency include *Three Kingdoms: Resurrection of the Dragon* (2008), *14 Blades* (2010) and *White Vengeance* (2011), all directed by Daniel Lee.
16 Walker, Michael, 'Film Noir: Introduction', in Ian Cameron (ed.), *The Movie Book of Film Noir* (London: Studio Vista, 1992), p. 26.
17 Roxborough, Scott, 'The Weinsteins Ride "Wu Xia" For World Outside Asia', *The Hollywood Reporter*, 11 July 2011, <http://www.hollywoodreporter.com/news/weinsteins-ride-wu-xia-world-187374>, accessed 20 July 2012.
18 Halligan, Fionnuala, '*Wu Xia*' (film review), *Screen Daily*, 15 May 2011, <http://www.screendaily.com/reviews/latest-reviews/wu-xia/5027552.article>, accessed 20 July 2012.
19 Chang, Justin, '*Wu Xia*' (film review), *Variety*, 14 May 2011, <http://www.variety.com/review/VE1117945222/>, accessed 20 July 2012.
20 Some noted, though, that for a film titled *Wu Xia*, there was very little swordplay and a lot of hand-to-hand combat.
21 Ma, Kevin, '*Wu Xia*' (film review), *LoveHKfilm*, 2011, <http://www.lovehkfilm.com/reviews_2wu_xia.html>, accessed 20 July 2012.
22 Lee, Edmund, '*Wu Xia*' (film review), *Time Out Hong Kong*, 27 July 2011, <http://www.timeout.com.hk/film/features/44132/wu-xia.html>, accessed 20 July 2012.
23 Ho, Yi, '*Wu Xia*' (film review), *Taipei Times*, 22 July 2011, <http://www.taipeitimes.com/News/feat/archives/2011/07/22/2003508831/1>, accessed 20 July 2012.
24 Lee, Edmund, 'An Interview with Peter Chan', *Time Out Hong Kong*, 20 July 2011, <http://www.timeout.com.hk/film/features/44135/peter-chan.html>, accessed 20 July 2012.

Chapter 10

Life is Cheap: Chinese Neo-Noir and the Aesthetics of Disenchantment

Philippa Lovatt

> One of the facts about China is that life is cheap. To cite a sample case: when China fought its war with Vietnam in 1979, a soldier killed in the war was worth only a few thousand dollars, which was the amount given to his family. The price was such because we have too many people. That's why China has a poor record in human rights, humanitarian issues, or concerns about human beings. It's always been like that.[1]

Tang and Song have a plan. These two itinerant miners drift from mine to mine, murdering their co-workers in cold blood and making the killings look like accidental deaths. After telling the boss the deceased is a relative, they pocket the hush money and hit the road, where they make their way to the next mine and their next unsuspecting victim. It seems like easy money, but when they choose baby-faced teenager Fengming Yuan as their next target, their plan starts to fall apart. Part docu-drama, part noir thriller, Yang Li's *Blind Shaft* (2003) takes place around the unregulated coal mines in north-west China along the border of Hebei and Shaanxi provinces where thousands of reported (and unreported) deaths occur each year. A harsh critique of the political corruption forming the dark underbelly of China's economic miracle, the film is a blazing indictment of what Xiaoping Deng termed 'socialism with Chinese characteristics', exposing the humanitarian

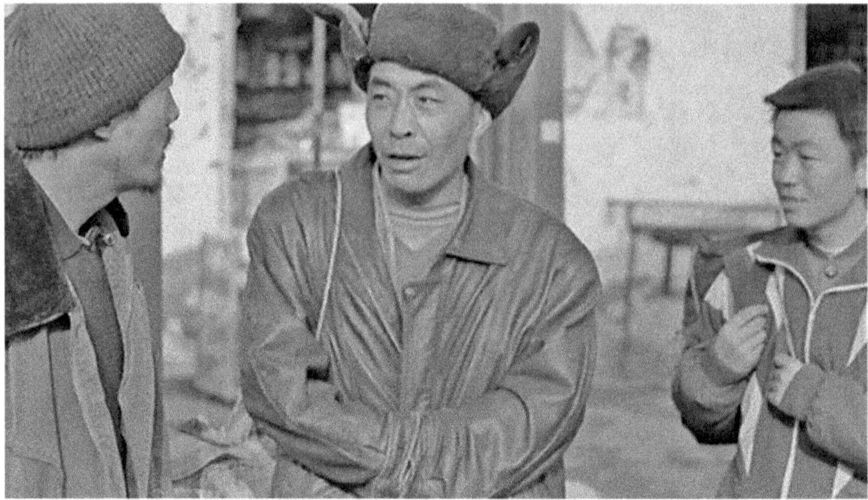

Figure 10.1 Song and Tang meet Fengming in *Blind Shaft*

crisis that the People's Republic now faces. Like several other independent Chinese films produced at the turn of the millennium, Li's tense, morbidly witty drama is reminiscent of the classic American film noirs of the 1940s and 1950s but strongly expresses the cultural and political malaise of its time.

This chapter is a genre study that discusses *Blind Shaft* in terms of the transnational, transhistorical relationship between two very different eras: post-socialist China and postwar America. *Blind Shaft* belongs to a small group of films that emerged in the late 1990s and early 2000s that included *Postman* (*Youchai*, 1995), *Xiao Wu* (1997; aka *Pickpocket*), *Rainclouds Over Wushan* (*Wu shan yun yu*, 1997), *So Close to Paradise* (*Biandang guniang*, 1998), *Lunar Eclipse* (*Yueshi*, 1999), *Scenery* (*Fengjing*, 1999), *Suzhou River* (*Suzhou he*, 2000) and *Missing Gun* (*Xun qiang*, 2003). While each of these films draws differently on the formal aspects of film noir, they share a fascination with China's 'black economy', explored through subjects and themes such as organized crime, mystery and surveillance. These mainland neo-noirs appeared around the same time as a group of Hong Kong productions that Joelle Collier has termed Hong Kong 'Noir East'. Films such as *Intruder* (1997), *The Longest Nite* (*Am faa*, 1998), and *Sleepless Town* (*Fyyajo*, 1998), she claims, while heavily influenced by Hollywood films noirs, 'reconfigured the genre so as to reflect the anxieties of post-modern Asia, not postwar America, thereby transmuting the film noir into something new: the Noir East'.[2] Important differences exist between the geopolitical situation of Hong Kong and Mainland China, particularly with regard to Hong Kong's post-colonial status. However, the year 1997, when the earliest of these films was released, was pivotal across the region as a whole. As the year that saw the official handover of Hong Kong back to China, as well as the Asian financial crisis, 1997 sets in motion a grouping of profoundly cynical neo-noir films that reflect the political, social and economic instability of this historical moment in Hong Kong and the PRC.

Discussions of the impact of Hollywood cinema on other non-Western modes of filmmaking have inevitably fed into arguments around cultural imperialism. However, the complexity of film and video's present-day global circulation undercuts the notion that the traffic of film between Hollywood and developing countries is a straightforward process of economic and ideological domination. In the Chinese context, even though censorship and economic constraints restricted Chinese audiences from viewing Hollywood cinema until 1995 (when the government-owned China Film Export and Import Corporation became China Film Group Corporation), the circulation of pirated films – with DVDs, VCDs and VHS tapes being sold on roadside stalls or viewed at informal video clubs – means that Chinese audiences still had access to American movies. This alternative model of cultural consumption and circulation is treated ironically in Zhangke Jia's later film *Unknown Pleasures* (*Ren xiao yao*, 2002): when one character unsuccessfully attempts to buy the banned film *Xiao Wu* from a street vendor, he takes instead a contraband copy of Quentin Tarantino's *Pulp Fiction* (1994). It is this quintessential Hollywood neo-noir that the central protagonists in *Unknown Pleasures*, Bin Bin and Xiao Ji, watch and model themselves on when they attempt to reinvent themselves as gangsters.

Like so many of the noir directors of 1940s Hollywood, Yang Li can be considered an 'émigré' filmmaker, having left China after studying documentary filmmaking at the Beijing Broadcasting Institute in the mid-1980s, to study drama and directing in Germany, eventually taking German citizenship. The transnationalism of Li's biography is mirrored by *Blind Shaft*'s production context. As Li explains in an interview with Stephen Teo, the film's funding came from Hong Kong and abroad, but many of the scenes were shot (without permits) in China. Because Li did not submit the film to China's State Administration of Radio, Film and Television (SARFT) for approval, it is not a 'legal' Chinese film. This status did not restrict its domestic audiences as much as might be expected, as the film became very successful on the pirate market, selling millions of copies.[3] The film also received accolades at international film festivals, including the Berlin Film Festival, winning the Silver Bear award in 2003. Like *Blind Shaft*, another key Chinese neo-noir, Zhangke Jia's *Xiao Wu*, also won international recognition, receiving the 'Dragons and Tigers Award' at the 1998 Vancouver International Film Festival and the 'New Currents Award' the same year at the Pusan International Film Festival, amongst others. Originally trained at the Beijing Film Academy, Zhangke Jia is now recognized at home and abroad as a leading global auteur. Yet because the Chinese Film Bureau banned Jia from making films in January 1999, domestic audiences for his early 'unofficial' films were also restricted to small cinephile film clubs and individuals willing to buy pirated copies on DVD and VCD. The ban was lifted in January 2004 following a shift in film policy.[4]

Significantly, the dystopian vision of *Blind Shaft* and *Xiao Wu* has no precedent in the cinema of the socialist era, or indeed the films of the Fifth Generation, which are characterized by an uncritical attitude toward the state. During the Cultural Revolution, state media and official 'main melody' (*zhuxuanlü*) films adopted a mode of Socialist Realism, a revolutionary aesthetic that combined realism with melodrama. According to Jason McGrath, these films were intended not only to depict 'the raw, visible surface of reality but more importantly an underlying ideological truth composed of class struggle and the inexorable historical movement toward a communist utopia'.[5] By contrast, he suggests, the independent films of the 1990s used a realist aesthetic to expose 'the ideological representations that distort it'.[6] In terms of style, both *Blind Shaft* and *Xiao Wu* shift away from melodrama by combining documentary-style filmmaking reminiscent of Italian neorealism (using location shooting and non-professional actors) with the existentialist mood or 'sensibility' of film noir. Theirs is not a romantic, optimistic vision of life in the People's Republic, but one that is deeply cynical and on the whole pessimistic about the country's future. In the context of the PRC then, the 'noir sensibility' of the films manifests itself in terms of what Zhang Li calls a 'double disenchantment' at the failure of Mao's utopian vision and the promises of Xiaoping Deng's economic reforms. The access that both filmmakers have had to cinema originating from outside of the PRC is extremely significant for their work, which draws directly on the iconography of film noir to communicate disenchantment to the audience, while the films' transnational aesthetics allow their critique of post-socialist China to be accessible to global audiences familiar with the tropes of film noir.

Film Noir's Hybridity

The notion of film noir as a genre has been notoriously unstable over the years. As Paul Schrader argues, film noir 'is not defined, as are the western and gangster genres, by conventions of setting and conflict, but rather by the more subtle qualities of tone and mood'.[7] What James Naremore has called the 'noir sensibility', then, stems from various aspects of the films' make-up, such as their existentialist outlook, their undertones of violence and sexuality, their brooding, dysfunctional protagonists, acerbic dialogue and dark, sardonic humour.[8] While the film noir aesthetic of expressionistic, chiaroscuro lighting and angular framing conveys characters' angst-ridden state of mind, the films' look and feel also powerfully articulate the mood of the era in which they were made. As Andrew Spicer notes, the original films noirs held a 'dark mirror' to society, reflecting widespread concerns over the end of isolationism following America's entry into World War II, moral doubt over the nuclear attacks on Hiroshima and Nagasaki, and fear over the 'red threat' of Communism. Collectively, these factors resulted in an atmosphere of paranoia and insecurity that 'penetrated deeply into popular consciousness'.[9] Previously held certainties about America's place in the world were replaced by anxiety and a sense of alienation, particularly in Hollywood, as the McCarthy hearings testified. While the classic film noir of 1940s and 1950s wartime and postwar America is often described as a 'product of its time',[10] the presence of the 'noir sensibility' in the numerous neo-noirs to emerge transnationally since this time demonstrates the genre's enduring power as part of a much wider cultural force.

The mood and aesthetic of the original films noirs were transnational from the very beginning. Drawing on several cinematic traditions including German Expressionism and French poetic realism, and combining them with the dark humour and brutality of the 'hardboiled' pulp fiction of American writers such as Dashiell Hammett and Raymond Chandler, film noir has always been characterized by a sense of hybridity.[11] This was due, in part, to the transnational status of many of its émigré filmmakers who came to Hollywood in the 1930s or early 1940s, such as directors William Dieterle, Fritz Lang, Otto Preminger, Robert Siodmak and Billy Wilder, and cinematographers Eugen Schüfftan, Rudolph Maté and Franz Planer. Recent globalized neo-noirs, in both film and television, have continued this hybridization by making further transcultural connections, crossing national boundaries and merging with other genres such as science fiction, horror and melodrama.

The films that are the subject of this book demonstrate that film noir resonates not only transnationally but also transhistorically. While ideologically and politically very different, there are striking parallels between the public mood of post–World War II America and that of contemporary, post-socialist China. Specifically, like post-war America, which struggled to come to terms with changes to gender and other social roles, in China the end of socialism destabilized previously held certainties about social codes and values. From 1978 onwards, with the impact of Xiaoping Deng's economic reforms, China experienced 'a radical break' with its revolutionary past, which led to a questioning of the framework of experiences, values and ideologies associated with that past. As Arif Dirlik and Xudong Zhang describe, 'Market, consumption, and media, all conceived in global rather than merely national terms [...] replaced revolutionary mobilization as the dynamizing force of social change, announcing the triumph of the ideology of consumerism.'[12] The reforms of the 'Open Door Policy' eventually led to a total rejection of collective enterprise and the gradual move toward a market economy and privatization. For rural areas, this meant the decollectivization of communes and the refocusing of power onto local government. Zhang Li argues that this was a 'highly uneven and disorientating process' that resulted in large-scale economic inequalities, corruption, and 'profound confusion, anxiety, and spiritual emptiness in some parts of society'.[13] Maintaining that this shift was fundamentally ideological, Li makes the point that as consumerism spread across Chinese society, the moral codes and values associated with the socialist era began to fade. It is this sense of moral dislocation, I argue, that is at the core of the films mentioned above, as many convey the experience of spiritual loss brought about by the fading of social bonds and estrangement from family.[14]

Like the original noir films, these more recent Chinese works similarly reflect the broader social and cultural anxieties associated with living in a time of flux. Looking to the past as a marker of stability has particular resonance here, as *Blind Shaft* and *Xiao Wu* in particular show. What Vivien Sobchack calls postwar America's 'longing for the purposefulness, unity, and plenitude of a mythologized national past' expressed in the original noirs can equally be applied to the nostalgia felt by many Chinese toward the socialist era in the People's Republic.[15] Yet, while both nations share the impulse to mythologize a coherent 'national' past, implicit in both *Blind Shaft* and *Xiao Wu* is the idea that in China this narrative is made all the more complex because any feelings of loss toward the socialist era are inevitably entwined with traumatic memories of the Cultural Revolution. This complex relationship with the past is a central aspect of Chinese neo-noirs, as is a profound sense of anxiety about the future.

Blind Shaft as Social Critique

Blind Shaft in particular paints a bleak and brutal portrait of what it sees as the amorality of capitalism, depicting a system that turns men, women and even children into commodities whose labour can be bought and sold. Adapted from Qingbang Liu's novella *Sacred Woods* (*Shenmu*, 2001), the film tells the story of the humanitarian crisis at the heart of China's corrupt mining industry while also offering a broader critique of the changes in contemporary China following the reform era. As Xiaoping Lin notes, *Blind Shaft*'s depiction of the dehumanization of miners in China's vast coal industry is 'a painful reminder of [the human cost of] new Chinese capitalism', the men themselves becoming the embodiment of 'postsocialist trauma'.[16]

China's mining industry is notorious for being extremely dangerous because of a lack of regulation; yet it is also well known that comparatively speaking, the pay is reasonable, and there is always work available. Consequently, economic migrants from rural areas where farm collectives were closed down after the Cultural Revolution (often referred to as China's 'floating population')[17] tend to make up the main body of the workforce. These men are particularly vulnerable to exploitation because the mine owners are well aware that many are willing to take risks with their lives to secure an income for their families back home. It was not until 2007, four years after *Blind Shaft*'s release, that China's Supreme People's Court issued a legal document outlining the penalties for coal-mine safety accidents in order to curtail illegal mines whose owners, it argued, were making 'a fortune out of blood-tainted coal production'.[18] Previously, unofficial reports had suggested that as many as 10,000 workers died in mine accidents each year, the majority remaining undocumented because of widespread corruption and collusion amongst private mine owners, officials and local government.[19]

Blind Shaft makes explicit reference to the coal industry's disregard for human life by repeatedly connecting Tang and Song's callousness toward their victims with the attitude held by those in power, namely the mine owners, and by inference, the officials who pull strings behind the scenes. The film suggests, therefore, that there is very little difference between the killers and the supposedly more 'respectable' members of society who might be considered examples of China's economic success story. Ironically, while

Tang and Song are willing to 'play the game' with the mine owners, putting on an impressive show of subservience in order not to raise suspicion; away from view, both men express moral outrage when they hear of 'white-collar' corruption. While they eat lunch at a café before picking up Fengming, for example, a television news report about embezzlement can be seen on the small screen behind them. 'He deserves to be executed', Song says with genuine indignation about the official on trial. Interestingly, however, Tang's response reveals that this news is nothing out of the ordinary. Official corruption is endemic in contemporary China: 'That prick was just fucking like our village's Party Secretary.'

While the younger of the two men, Song, still appears to carry some attachment to socialist-era values, the older, Tang, is an archetypal noir villain. Having fully embraced the capitalist worldview, he tells Song at one point: 'Only money fucking matters.' Tang kills without conscience even those unfortunate individuals who find themselves accidently in his way. As Tang says after butchering a miner from whose death he had nothing to gain, 'I just eliminate anyone in the path of my fortune.' By comparison, toward the end of the film Song demonstrates a more nuanced attitude toward their crimes, spurred on by the recognition of inherently 'good' socialist values in Fengming. His reluctance to carry out the plan to kill him is symptomatic of his own inner ideological crisis. As Jonathan Noble writes, 'A key contradiction within the film is Song's struggle to reconcile the commodification of human life with his growing recognition of Fengming's innocence, kindness and generosity. [...] Figuratively, the mineshaft therefore represents a final battleground between innocence and guilt, humanity and commodification, and life and death.'[20] The dramatic crux of *Blind Shaft* lies in Song's insistence on waiting until Fengming has gone through various rites of passage before his murder – losing his virginity, drinking alcohol and shaving his face – in order for it to be 'fair'. Song's adherence to this somewhat arbitrary and outdated code of behaviour is a stalling technique to avoid dealing the fatal blow – a delay that ultimately results in his own death. Frustrated by his hesitancy, in the darkness of the mineshaft, Tang strikes Song over the head with his pickaxe. Song falls to the floor as Fengming watches in horror. Tang turns to the boy, but is stopped as Song gets back onto his feet and hits him over the head. Fengming flees, moments before the mineshaft (thought to have been evacuated) is blown up, crushing Tang and Song's bodies beneath the rubble in a classic noir twist of fate.

By contrast, the mine owners are shown to have no moral compass. When Tang and Song first take Fengming to the mine and introduce him as Song's nephew, the boss asks them why they had left their previous job. Tang tells him that it was because of a cave-in where there had been a number of deaths. 'What's a few deaths?' he exclaims incredulously. 'You shit after eating. You might die down the shaft. If you're afraid then don't work here.' The killers try to reassure him that they agree but that news of the accident had somehow 'leaked out' and that the family of the deceased demanded compensation. They tell him that when the government investigated, they had discovered safety problems, so the mine had to be closed. The boss answers: 'Regulation is not worth a fart. It can't prevent any deaths.' The men then agree to work a few days as a 'trial' for which they will not be paid, but when Fengming complains that this is not fair, the boss answers, 'Take it or leave it. Otherwise, get out of here. China has a shortage of everything but people.' The film thus suggests that while the workers are fully aware that they are being exploited, they are powerless to do anything about it; if they refuse to accept these working conditions, there are many hundreds more who can, and will, take their places. This scene demonstrates Rey Chow's claim that 'if socialism, as a form of modern humanism, is about honoring the contributions and rights – and thus the basic dignity – of the downtrodden classes, *Blind Shaft* is first and foremost a stark portrait of the bankruptcy of Chinese socialism at the turn of the twenty-first century'.[21] In this environment, human beings have no inherent 'worth' other than that associated with their contribution to the labour market.

Blind Shaft as 'Docu-Noir'

One aspect of film noir's hybridity, particularly in relation to *Blind Shaft*'s social critique, is the notion of the 'docu-noir'. Docu-noirs were an important feature of the original film noir cycle, appearing toward the end of the 1940s as filmmakers influenced by Italian neorealism, and working on similarly tight budgets, began to film on location, swapping the sleek, expressionistic look and feel of the earlier studio films for gritty, documentary-style street realism.[22] Docu-noirs move away from the introspective psychodramas of the earlier films toward what Jim Hillier and Alastair Phillips describe as 'a greater investment in notions of truthfulness and actuality and a closer proximity to life "as it is"'.[23] Docu-noirs offered therefore a 'broader ethical revision of film noir's conventional cynicism'.[24]

The 'ethical' aspect of film noir's legacy has particular resonance with Yang Li's film. Like the early work of his 'Sixth Generation' counterparts Zhangke Jia, Yuan Zhang and Xiaoshuai Wang, *Blind Shaft* blurs the boundary between documentary and fiction filmmaking by using non-professional actors and shooting on location with minimal artificial lighting.[25] Li's film also has several aesthetic and thematic links with China's 'New Documentary Film Movement', an extremely influential body of work that emerged as a response to the social and political changes of the reform era. Chris Berry observes that while the reforms of the 1980s and 1990s created a 'sense of new possibilities', they also led to 'increased frustrations with the new social inequalities that soon emerged'.[26] Enabled by the increased availability (and affordability) of digital-video recording technology, this mood of contestation provided the momentum for people to start making films, motivated by a 'commitment to record contemporary life in China outside any direct control of the state.'[27] Thanks to changes in technology (as well as in the legal requirements for gaining shooting permits), filmmakers were now able to be much more spontaneous in what and where they chose to film and, like the 1950s US docu-noir filmmakers, took their cameras into the street.[28] Often dealing with politically sensitive material, telling stories invisible in mainstream and official media, new documentaries offered a rough and spontaneous feel sharply at odds with the highly controlled sounds and images of the revolutionary period's Socialist Realism and the epic style of the Fifth Generation. Instead, not just their look and feel, but also their social critique, shares a lineage with the 1950s films noirs and docu-noirs. The films also share an interest in ethical storytelling, a mode of filmmaking that encourages viewers to engage with the often difficult questions raised by the social and political inequities presented on screen.

The Idea of 'Home' in *Blind Shaft* and *Xiao Wu*

Reminiscent of the original films noirs, *Blind Shaft*'s *mise-en-scène* expresses a particular mood, often using patterns of light and dark to communicate a Manichean conflict between good and evil. Lit only by the narrow beams of light emitted from the miners' helmets, several of the film's most dramatic scenes take place in the pitch-black depths of the mineshafts, filmed 700 metres below ground by Li and his crew. While in practical terms the darkness is useful because it conceals the murders, these spaces also have powerful resonance as the symbolic site of a broader ethical or ideological struggle. As Jonathan Noble writes,

> Figuratively, the depths of the coalmines are [...] ritualised spaces, in which lives are sacrificed for the sake of the pursuit of money and

> social status. They represent a lawlessness in which [...] morality and humanity are sacrificed in the pursuit of avarice. The figurative space of the mines extends beyond their depths and motivates the actions of the characters above ground.[29]

Other interior scenes take place in low-ceilinged offices, dingy hotel rooms and the cramped interiors of a brothel. These smoky, gloomy spaces, like the mineshafts, suggest liminality and an ideological no-man's-land where previously held certainties have become hazy and indistinct.[30] In addition, and again like the original films noirs, *Blind Shaft* communicates the characters' interiority through the *mise-en-scène*. The oppressive monochrome of the dusty landscape, the unsteady, constantly moving camerawork of the *xianchang* (shooting live) aesthetic, and the uneven location sound mirror the instability of the migrants' lifestyle as they roam the countryside in search of a living, wiring their meagre earnings to their families back home at the end of each grim week. Just as the *mise-en-scène* of the original films noirs expressed the psychic trauma of postwar America, the nomadic aesthetic of *Blind Shaft* similarly articulates psychic and social dislocation, here associated with the contingency of the migrant workers' existence.

Vivian Sobchack argues that the sense of dislocation implicit in the original films noirs can be detected through their use of the recurrent motif of 'home', or more accurately, the absence of home. As she writes, 'in noir, homes are given to us only in glimpses – as something lost or something fragile and threatened'.[31] The films convey this sense of loss by replacing domestic spaces in the films with temporary, partial substitutes: 'the rooms of hotels and motels and boarding houses' that are ubiquitous in the genre 'figur[ing] as spaces of social dislocation, isolation, and existential alienation'.[32]

The 'idea of home' and the notions of domesticity and family life associated with it also form a structuring absence in *Blind Shaft*, appearing only as an imaginary concept. In Li's film, the 'home' is replaced by a number of 'other' spaces, such as the seedy hotel where Song and Tang take prostitutes and the filthy shack they share at the coal mine, a space decorated only with ragged posters of naked women. Instead of home comforts, they have to hang their food from the ceiling so it does not get eaten by rats, share baths with their co-workers and pay out of their wages for their work shoes and helmets. Furthermore, in dramatic terms, as the relationship between Song, Tang and Fengming develops, they become a kind of dysfunctional, substitute 'family'. This is partly out of necessity, because their story that they are related has to be believable for them to get the compensation money after the boy's death, but also because, put simply, they do not have anyone else. Viewers learn that Fengming's father set off to find work six months previously but never returned (the film suggests that this was the man Song and Tang murdered just before meeting Fengming – a classic noir coincidence), and Tang thwarts any contact that Fengming attempts to make with home. When Fengming writes a letter to his sister, for example, Tang rips it up so as not to leave incriminating evidence after his death. The killers also have very little contact with home; at one point, Song talks briefly on the telephone (presumably to his wife), but Tang shows no interest in contacting his family. Even though viewers know that Song regularly sends money home for his son's education (seemingly this financial need is the main motivator for Song to commit the murders), we never see or hear of this son, nor of Tang's children. These men's disjointed relationships with home foreground the fragmentary nature of family life for the film's migrant workers and heighten viewers' awareness of the characters' dislocation.

The 'idea of home' as an imaginary concept is a powerful driving force in the narrative of *Blind Shaft*. The film repeatedly draws on nostalgia as its dialogue poignantly and ironically references 'home'. Crucially, Tang uses the seemingly innocuous questions 'Are you homesick?' and 'Would you like us to send you home?' to signal (at least to the audience) that he is about to bludgeon his victim with a pickaxe. In these moments, he and Song play on the miners' feelings of homesickness to make them drop their guard – it is the home, therefore, and more specifically the sense of loss caused by the *absence* of home, that becomes the film's central motif and the driving force of its narrative.

Nostalgia for the absent 'home' is also a feature of another Chinese neo-noir, Zhangke Jia's *Xiao Wu*, made six years earlier, in 1997. While the notion of the 'home front' often appears in films noirs as an imaginary construct, the central protagonist in Jia's film is also characterized by a delusional longing for something that no longer exists (if indeed, it ever did). Like *Blind Shaft*, *Xiao Wu* documents a period of turbulent transition in China's recent history and similarly focuses on the 'dark underbelly' of the economic miracle, centring on a murky world of petty criminality, organized crime and prostitution in the small town of Fenyang in Shanxi province of north-east China. Set in the present, *Xiao Wu* follows its title character, a pickpocket in his late twenties or early thirties who is a social misfit in the 'New China'. Xiao Wu is profoundly hurt that he has not been invited to the society wedding of his former best friend, Xiao Yong, once a fellow pickpocket and now a highly regarded 'model entrepreneur' (although ironically, he is also heavily involved in organized crime). Xiao Wu regards this rejection as a betrayal of the filial bond they shared as young thieves in Beijing. Throughout the narrative, the film foregrounds the tension between a rhetoric of progress exemplified by the public's attitude toward 'successful businessman' and local gangster Xiao Yong, and the public rejection of Xiao Wu the pickpocket, whose nostalgic attachment to the past, like Song's in *Blind Shaft*, places him within a temporal and ideological no-man's-land. The irony of this juxtaposition, however, highlights some of the difficulties of China's transition. While Xiao Yong is publicly celebrated, appearing on state television to announce his wedding and his large donation to the 'Hope Project', a local charity, the film insinuates that he is involved with corrupt officials, gaining his wealth from the importation of illegal goods and from the sex industry. Xiao Yong rejects the socialist implications of their 'sworn brotherhood' and embraces the capitalist ideology of individualism, rejecting Xiao Wu in the process. By contrast, Xiao Wu's intransigent refusal to let go of the socialist past is illustrated by his insistence on sticking to the promise of a monetary wedding gift he made to Xiao Yong when they were both poor. This gesture is now meaningless to everyone but Xiao Wu in light of Xiao Yong's abundant wealth and Xiao Wu's own comparative poverty.

Like *Blind Shaft*, *Xiao Wu* uses near-constant movement to foreground a sense of 'homelessness'. Much of the film shows Xiao Wu wandering around the city looking for opportunities to make a bit of money picking someone's pocket. Like Song and Tang, he visits a brothel, but unlike them falls in love with a woman, Mei Mei, and visits her at her home, a modest one-bedroom apartment she shares with other prostitutes. When he goes back later with an engagement ring, intending to marry and 'set up home' with her, she has already left town with a wealthy businessman. Following this disappointment, he returns to his parents, giving his mother the ring as a gift, only later to cause an argument and get chased out by his angry father. The crux of this argument emerges from the fact that even his family home has become 'tainted' by capitalism, as Ban Wang writes:

> The family gathering, chat, and meals – traditionally the most elemental form of communal life – are poisoned by money talk and calculation, by bickering over advantages, by the consumer desire for American goods. Sick of this poisoned atmosphere and driven out by his father, Xiao Wu is once again on his way back to town.[33]

The film expresses the ideological (or moral) dislocation of the reform era through the discordant juxtaposition of sound and image in a scene that

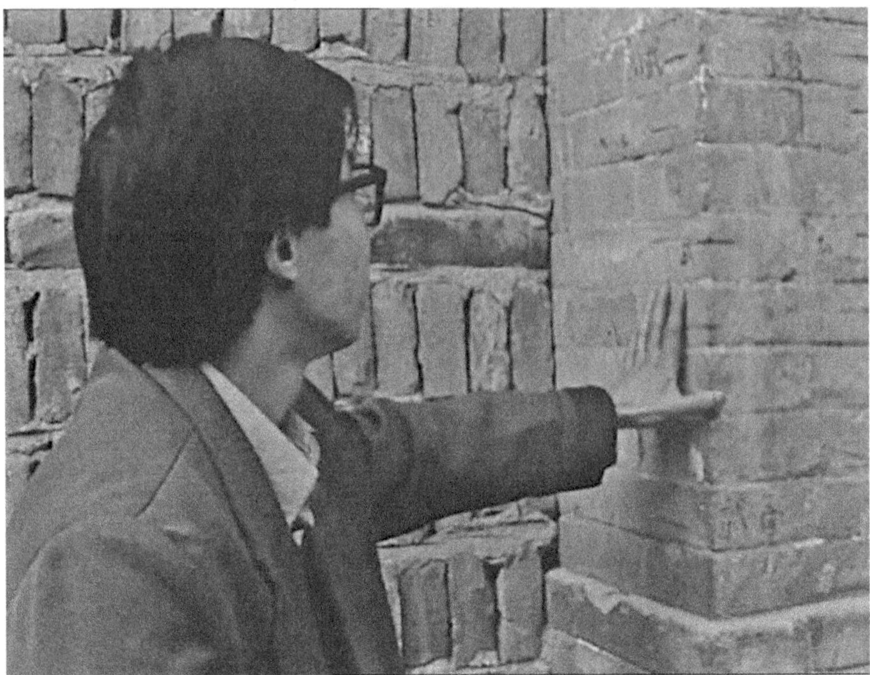

Figure 10.2 In *Xiao Wu*, poignantly, Xiao Wu touches the wall outside Xiao Yong's house, mirroring his friend's gesture moments before

links Xiao Wu and Xiao Yong. The scene, which takes place just before Xiao Yong's wedding, begins with the piercing sound of Xiao Yong's mobile-phone ringtone as a mutual friend calls to try and persuade him to reconsider inviting Xiao Wu. Evidently disturbed by the phone call, Xiao Yong paces back and forth in front of a wall outside his house that has been scored with height lines and inscribed with the date '1982'. As he hangs up, he reaches up to touch the lines on the wall. The film then cuts to a long shot of Xiao Wu sitting in the street, a shot that metaphorically underscores his distance from Xiao Yong's new life, and by association, from the 'new China'.

Juxtaposed against a close-up of his hands, the pop song 'Farewell My Concubine' begins on the soundtrack. The song plays on an old, worn cassette tape, and the distorted quality of the sound suggests time itself is being physically drawn out. While the song's soaring chorus, steady beat and inflated electronic orchestration produce an epic grandeur that on some level emulates the theatricality of public discourse in both the revolutionary period and the reform era, the tape's distorted sound contradicts this feeling, producing a sense of the uncanny. While the song's bombastic quality captures Xiao Wu's perception of himself as morally superior to his former friend because of his 'honourable' commitment to their shared past, the track's distortion registers this perception as delusional. He alone holds onto the outdated moral code. Xiao Wu's nostalgia therefore expresses the wider tension evident throughout the film between the social codes of the communist past and those of the reform era. As Xiao Wu touches the marks on the wall outside his former friend's house, mirroring Xiao Yong's gesture a moment before, he appears trapped by circumstance – unwilling, and like Song in *Blind Shaft*, seemingly unable – to move on.

Blind Shaft and *Xiao Wu*, like the other examples of the East Asian noir phenomenon of the late 1990s and early 2000s mentioned at the beginning of this chapter, foreground the tension between stasis and instability, both thematically and aesthetically, to offer a profoundly disenchanted view of post-socialist China. It is as though the mood of this period is etched onto the surface of the films, just as it had been through the *mise-en-scène* of the original film noir cycle. The transnational and transhistorical resonances among these 'noir East' films and their American counterparts urge a radical reimagining of the ways the concerns of the global and the local manifest themselves in film. Will Higbee and Song Hwee Lim have called for a critical approach to the concept of transnationalism in film studies that 'moves away from Eurocentric approaches to the reading of films'[34] and toward a consideration of broader aspects such as cultural hybridization that inform films' production, consumption and circulation. While this chapter has begun to address some of these concerns (specifically with regards to the films' success at international film festivals and their 'un-approved' status in the PRC), a crucial part of this 'reimagining' must be to consider how intertextual relationships are negotiated, interpreted and used by both global and local audiences, while interrogating the power dynamics that are always part of transcultural flows.

Notes

1 Teo, Stephen, '"There is No Sixth Generation!" Director Li Yang on *Blind Shaft* and His Place in Chinese Cinema', *Senses of Cinema* 27 (2003), <http://www.sensesofcinema.com/2003/feature-articles/li_yang/>, accessed 8 July 2011.

2 Collier, Joelle, 'The Noir East: Hong Kong's Transmutation of a Hollywood Genre?', in Gina Marchetti and Tan See Kam (eds), *Hong Kong Film, Hollywood and New Global Cinema: No Film is An Island* (London: Routledge, 2007), p. 138.

3 Li, Jinying, 'From D-Buffs to the D-Generation: Piracy, Cinema, and an Alternative Public Sphere in Urban China', *International Journal of Communications* 6 (2012), pp. 555–556.

4 See Yuan, Lu, 'Who Framed Jia Zhangke?', 7 June 2007, and Jia, Zhangke, 'A Perplexing Incident', *EastSouthWestNorth* (2007), <http://zonaeuropa.com/20070612_1.htm>, accessed 12 October 2008.

5 McGrath, Jason, *Postsocialist Modernity: Chinese Cinema, Literature, and Criticism in the Market Age* (Stanford: Stanford University Press, 2008), p. 132.

6 Ibid.

7 Schrader, Paul, 'Notes on Film Noir', in Barry Keith Grant (ed.), *Film Genre Reader III* (Austin: University of Texas Press, 2003), p. 230.

8 Naremore, James, *More Than Night: Film Noir in Its Contexts* (Berkeley: University of California Press, 1998), p. 11.

9 Spicer, Andrew, *Film Noir* (Essex: Pearson, 2002), p. 20.

10 Hirsch, Foster, *The Dark Side of the Screen: Film Noir* (New York: Da Capo Press, 2001), p. 200.

11 See Desser, David, 'Global Noir: Genre Film in the Age of Transnationalism', in Barry Keith Grant (ed.), *Film Genre Reader III* (Austin: University of Texas Press, 2003), pp. 516–536.

12 Dirlik, Arif and Xudong Zhang, *Postmodernism and China* (Durham: Duke University Press, 2000), p. 8.

13 Li, Zhang, 'Postsocialist Urban Dystopia?', in Gyan Prakash (ed.), *Noir Urbanisms: Dystopic Images of the Modern City* (Princeton: Princeton University Press, 2010), p. 127.

14 See Chow, Rey, '"Human" in the Age of Disposable People: The Ambiguous Import of Kinship and Education in *Blind Shaft*', in Chow, *Sentimental Fabulations, Contemporary Chinese Films: Attachment in the Age of Global Visibility* (New York: Columbia University Press, 2007), pp. 167–180. See also Weiss, Amanda, '"Family" in Li Yang's *Blind Shaft* and *Blind Mountain*', *Jump Cut: A Review of Contemporary Media* 54, <http://www.ejumpcut.org/currentissue/WeissBlindshaft/index.html>, accessed 13 October 2012.

15 Sobchack, Vivian, 'Lounge Time: Postwar Crises and the Chronotope of Film Noir', in Nick Browne (ed.), *Refiguring American Film Genres: Theory and History* (Berkeley: University of California Press, 1998), p. 133.

16 Lin, Xiaoping, *Children of Marx and Coca-Cola: Chinese Avant-Garde Art and Independent Cinema* (Honolulu: University of Hawaii Press, 2010), p. 24.

17 See Li, Zhang, *Strangers in the City: Reconfigurations of Space, Power, and Social Networks Within China's Floating Population* (Stanford: Stanford University Press, 2001).

18 See Xinhua News Agency, 'New Legal Interpretation Issued to Improve Coal Mine Safety', *China.Org.Cn*, 2 March 2007, <http://www.china.org.cn/english/China/201239.htm>, accessed 12 October 2011.
19 See Tu, Jianjun, 'Safety Challenges in China's Coal Mining Industry', *China Brief*, 15 March 2006, <http://www.asianresearch.org/articles/2997.html>, accessed 12 October 2011.
20 Noble, Jonathan, '*Blind Shaft*: Performing the "Underground" On and Beyond the Screen', in Chris Berry (ed.), *Chinese Films in Focus II* (Basingstoke: Palgrave Macmillan, 2008), p. 34.
21 Chow, *Sentimental Fabulations*, p. 171.
22 These films, including *T-Men* (1947), *The Naked City* (1948), and *Call Northside 777* (1948), were semi-documentaries that drew on factual sources such as news reports and FBI files rather than fiction. See Krutnik, Frank, *In a Lonely Street: Film Noir, Genre, Masculinity* (London: Routledge, 1991), p. 202.
23 Hillier, Jim and Alastair Phillips, *100 Film Noirs* (Basingstoke: Palgrave Macmillan, 2009), p. 41.
24 Ibid., p. 42.
25 See Robinson, Luke, 'From "Public" to "Private": Chinese Documentaries and the Logic of *Xianchang*', in Chris Berry, Xinyu Lu and Lisa Rofel (eds), *The New Chinese Documentary Film Movement: For the Public Record* (Hong Kong: Hong Kong University Press, 2010), pp. 177–194.
26 Berry, Chris and Lisa Rofel, 'Introduction', in Chris Berry, Xinyu Lu and Lisa Rofel (eds), *The New Chinese Documentary Film Movement: For the Public Record* (Hong Kong: Hong Kong University Press, 2010), p. 7.
27 Ibid., p. 10.
28 For a more detailed account of these changes to the production context in China, see Nakajima, Seio, 'Film as Cultural Politics', in You-tien Hsing and Ching Kwan Lee (eds), *Reclaiming Chinese Society: The New Social Activism* (New York: Routledge, 2010), pp. 159–183.
29 Noble, '*Blind Shaft*', p. 34.
30 This shift in moral codes is articulated on the soundtrack when Tang and Song visit two prostitutes who teach them bawdy new lyrics to the old communist classic, 'Long Live Socialism', which the men then sing with great gusto.
31 Sobchack, 'Lounge Time', p. 139.
32 Ibid., p. 155.
33 Wang, Ban, *Illuminations From the Past: Trauma, Memory and History in Modern China* (Stanford: Stanford University Press, 2004), p. 253.
34 Higbee, Will and Song Hwee Lim, 'Concepts of Transnational Cinema: Towards a Critical Transnationalism in Film Studies', *Transnational Cinemas* 1:1 (January 2010), p. 7.

Chapter 11

Tony Leung's Noir Thrillers and Transnational Stardom

Mark Gallagher

As marketable names, attractive or memorable faces, and sites for affective encounters, film stars play key roles in the regional and global circulation of contemporary East Asian films. Stars can also be instrumental to the worldwide distribution and recognition of particular genres and cycles. Hong Kong star Yun-Fat Chow, for example, served as a de facto global ambassador for the territory's urban crime cinema in the 1980s and 1990s; Toshiro Mifune did the same for Japan's upmarket samurai films in the 1950s and 1960s. This chapter looks at Hong Kong actor Tony Leung Chiu-Wai's transnational stardom through his shared leading role in *Infernal Affairs* (2002), with attention to other roles in contemporary films categorizable as noir thrillers, such as *Cyclo* (1995), *Confession of Pain* (2006) and *Lust, Caution* (2007). Leung has starred in numerous successful thrillers that deploy a refined noir sensibility, and aspects of his star persona contribute substantially to that sensibility.

While Leung's long career includes a substantial range of roles and acting styles, those films that travel internationally showcase a narrow range of characterizations and performance attributes. This circumscribed persona distinguishes Leung in the competitive global market for art and prestige cinema and for niche genre releases. The relative stability of Leung's persona as circulated internationally suits well the commercial needs and signifying practices of films that lend themselves to classification as 'global noir'. Elaborating on this category, David Desser begins with a loose definition of neo-noir composed of diverse narrative and thematic elements, then surveys neo-noir's international scope, taking in 'crime films [...] produced in global cities for global markets'.[1] Delineating films by recurring plots, he identifies three strands of neo-noir, including two with global dimensions: the 'couple on the run' film and the 'heist gone bad' variant.[2] (In his formulation, the third strand, which he calls 'the stranger and the femme fatale', circulates less widely owing to an erotic emphasis unsuited to many conservative cultures.)[3] Desser turns further to narrative structure, visual style and editing as means of categorizing global noir.[4] He approaches global noir in terms of sociocultural concerns and textual meaning but registers as well aspects of a broad-based noir sensibility.

Relatedly, my analysis of Leung's thriller roles follows from an understanding of noir as principally a *sensibility*. As Desser and others such as James Naremore argue, this sensibility has historically been called into existence by critics and audiences as well as filmmakers, and noir films have often been recognized as such only retrospectively.[5] I argue that films manifest a noir sensibility through downbeat narratives and thematic emphases on fatigue, cynicism and paranoia. Narrative doses of romantic desire – obsessive or unrequited love, and triangulated or otherwise complicated romance – also routinely contribute to noir films' appeals and to their fatalistic moods. The noir sensibility takes further shape through aesthetic registers, with production design and lighting emphasizing urban density, shadow and literal or metaphoric darkness. Because this sensibility involves a particular way of viewing and experiencing the world, it often relies too on highly stylized, anti-realist elements: subjective or otherwise expressive camerawork, editing and sound; and psychologically layered but highly mannered performances. As such, particular actors can be said to be co-constituents of noir texts, especially as aspects of their star personas create viewer expectations across a body of films. Viewers exposed to Leung's work circulating internationally in the 1990s and 2000s see a reasonably consistent trajectory for his characters: he will mope, desire, suffer, engage in morally dubious acts or even outright criminal ones, and more likely than not die ignominiously. (Films with his frequent collaborator Kar-Wai Wong – particularly *Chungking Express* [1994], *Happy Together* [1997], *In the Mood for Love* [2000] and *2046* [2004] – withhold only the crime and death.)

Performance style, representation and reception of constructs of masculinity and Chinese ethnicity, and intertextual and intergeneric attributes of Leung's stardom also facilitate his films' circulation across regions and film cultures. In the dramatic thrillers in which Leung appears – virtually all of which belong to the broad constellation of global noir – narrative, cinematography and performance construct his characters as archetypal noir heroes or antiheroes. While numerous generic and other descriptors accompany these films in reception discourse in print journalism, speciality online forums and mass internet commentary, the terms 'noir' and 'thriller' appear repeatedly (and often interchangeably) for all of them. In what follows, I investigate numerous films' uses of Leung to convey thematic meanings and to create points of entry for international viewerships. As for other film stars, attributes of Leung's stardom include his embodiment of psychological traits and emotions, his physical presence, and his enactment of performative and kinaesthetic markers for multiple genres. While many works in Leung's extensive filmography have earned exhibition in festivals, arthouses and wider release, the bulk of his international visibility depends on three strands of contemporary East Asian cinema: prestige *wuxia pian* and historical epics such as *Hero* (2002), *Red Cliff* (2008) and *The Grandmaster* (2013); urban action films and thrillers such as *Hard-Boiled* (1992) and *Infernal Affairs*; and moody romantic dramas such as *In the Mood for Love* and *Lust, Caution*. With few exceptions, most of Leung's films in these latter two categories operate as contemporary films noirs narratively, visually and in reception contexts.

Among male stars not associated primarily with action roles, Leung is Chinese diasporic cinema's most successful contemporary transnational star. (In the other category, Jackie Chan, Jet Li and Yun-Fat Chow command greater international recognition than does Leung.) Awareness of Leung is partly complicated by the presence of two prominent Tony Leungs – Tony Leung Chiu-Wai and Tony Leung Ka-Fai – as actors in transnational cinema originating in greater China, compounded by the fact that the men have appeared in many similar films, and even starred together in 1994's *Ashes of Time*. Both men periodically play roles, though not together, in films loosely categorizable as East Asian noirs – crime thrillers and erotic dramas with strong nocturnal ambiance and involving deception, subterfuge, and psychological and physical violence. Hong Kong audiences have long distinguished the two Leungs through their marked height difference, and thus the nicknames 'Big Tony' and 'Little Tony'. The star persona of the diminutive but globally better-known 'Little Tony' shows remarkable portability across genres, national cinemas and production contexts. Chiu-Wai Leung works in a range of genres, including *wuxia pian*, romantic comedies and auteur-designated art films. Like the slightly older transnational star Chow, Leung's career includes many substantial roles in contemporary urban thrillers. In addition to the *Infernal Affairs* series, films co-starring Leung such as the action-intensive *Hard-Boiled*, the lush un-romance *Cyclo*, the bleak cop melodrama *Confession of Pain*, the erotic historical fiction *Lust, Caution* and even the kinetic, avant-pop *Chungking Express* fit broad categorizations of cinematic thrillers or neo-noirs.

Thanks to his Cannes Best Actor award for *In the Mood for Love*, Leung has been most lauded internationally as an art-cinema performer. Taken together, though, his thriller roles have been the most critically successful of his body of work and have earned him repeated accolades at Hong Kong industry awards and international festivals. Many of these films have been among his greatest commercial successes as well, particularly at the local Hong Kong box office. *Infernal Affairs* and its two sequels have been credited with a revitalization of the Hong Kong film industry at the outset of the twenty-first century,[6] and Leung's regional and global star power represent a significant component of Hong Kong cinema's transnational disposition. His noir roles show the greatest portability to international festival and art-house markets. Still, some of Leung's noir-tinged roles target principally local Hong Kong and regional East Asian viewerships. *Infernal Affairs*, for example, played only infrequently outside East Asia; and *Confession of Pain*, which teamed him again with *Infernal Affairs* co-directors Wai Keung Lau and Sui Fai Mak (aka Andrew Lau and Alan Mak) and frequent co-star Takeshi Kaneshiro, received no North American or European theatrical release, appearing only at mid-tier festivals. The film's depiction of night-time Hong Kong as a sea of neon greens and blues, and its stylized flashbacks mixing black and white, colour and sepia tones, offer points of access for overseas audiences. However, its complicated plot, somewhat impenetrable characterizations, and maudlin affect made it a difficult proposition for wider distribution. And until recently, even Mainland China had not been a prime destination for Leung's noir-inflected films. With the exception of the espionage drama and Chinese box-office success *The Silent War* (2012), Leung's noir-based films have also faced cuts or simply gone unreleased in Mainland China, owing to censorship of sexual or crime content perceived as too racy or as not prosocial.[7]

As *Infernal Affairs* and other films reveal, Leung's thriller roles contribute to his twin status as a mainstream star in East Asia and an arthouse figure among Western reception communities. The thriller form encompasses the creative labour of filmmakers identified with the East Asian mainstream (e.g. *Infernal Affairs* series directors Lau and Mak), with the global art cinema (e.g. Hong Kong's Kar-Wai Wong, Vietnam's Anh Hung Tran, Taiwan's Hsiao-Hsien Hou and others), and with figures regarded as both mainstream and auteurist (in particular John Woo, with whom Leung has worked repeatedly, but also Ang Lee, who directs Leung in *Lust, Caution*). In addition, noir-thriller roles position stars such as Leung as simultaneously mainstream and arthouse figures. *Infernal Affairs*, Hong Kong's top-grossing film of 2002, received only a limited release at US and UK arthouse cinemas in 2004. The film, and Leung's stardom within it and across his filmography, demonstrates ways that star casting combines with genres such as the thriller or modes such as film noir to position films for distribution in local markets. By investigating textual features and performances in diverse, noir-inflected films such as *Cyclo*, *Infernal Affairs*, *Confession of Pain* and *Lust, Caution*, we can see how Leung's acting and star persona crystallize particular aspects of global or East Asian noir. As noted, some of these films principally target Hong Kong and the East Asian region, while others circulate to English-speaking countries and elsewhere outside East Asia through festival releases, arthouse engagements and home video. Leung's role and performance in *Infernal Affairs*, and promotion of his efforts in this and other films, highlight overlapping critical and generic categories. Attention to Leung's stardom reveals how international creative workers modulate their activity to suit the needs of producers and receivers in different industrial and cultural contexts. Additionally, figurations of Leung in promotional materials demonstrate aspects of different industries' marketing and distribution practices. Finally, responses to Leung's performances suggest ways film programmers and journalists use stars to create and maintain particular markers of prestige and distinction. All show ways a discernible if porous category such as global noir can organize industrial and institutional activity and steer understandings of textual meaning.

Signposts of a (Sometimes) Noir Star

To proceed, I offer brief descriptions of the four films under consideration and Leung's role in them. In *Infernal Affairs*, Leung plays an undercover policeman, Chen Wing Yan, who infiltrates a Triad gang and whose loyalties remain divided between the opposing groups; co-star Andy Lau (aka Tak-Wah Lau), meanwhile, plays a Triad member, Lau Kin Ming, who infiltrates the police force. At the film's climax, another policeman kills Yan just before he exposes Ming. Leung rejoins much of *Infernal Affairs*' production team for *Confession of Pain*, where he plays another policeman, Lau Ching Hei, also leading a double life, this time as both a mild-mannered husband and a sadistic killer who murders his father-in-law as vengeance for his own family's murder decades earlier, and who stalks and plots to murder his own wife as well. His foil in this film is his alcoholic ex-partner, Yau Kin Bong (Kaneshiro), who investigates the father-in-law's death and solves the case.

Apparently unconcerned with capture, Hei nonetheless kills himself at the film's denouement when he feels regret for orchestrating his wife's death. Leung followed this gloomy effort with the historical drama *Lust, Caution*, playing Mr Yee, a high-level Chinese-government official collaborating with the Japanese occupation in late-1930s and early-1940s Shanghai. He begins an affair with a young activist, Wong Chia Chi (Wei Tang), who he believes to be Mak Tai Tai, the wife of a wealthy businessman. After she alerts him to her comrades' plan to assassinate him, he orders her and their arrest and execution, as he has done for many others across the film. While Wong's story and subjectivity dominate the film, it closes with a scene of Mr Yee alone and disconsolate. Lastly, we can note Leung's earlier role in *Cyclo* as an unnamed underworld figure, identified in the credits as 'Poet', who moves at the margins of the world of the film's title character, a nameless cyclo driver (Le Van Loc). A mass of contradictions, Leung's character recites poetry in voice-over, romances the cyclo driver's sister (Nu Yên-Khê Tran) while also involving her in mildly kinky but mostly sexless prostitution in his apartment, and occasionally ventures out to supervise gruesome acts of knife homicide against criminal adversaries. Before the film's climax, he sets his apartment aflame, perishing (offscreen) in the blaze. All four films, then, show Leung's characters pursuing strongly contradictory activities – policing and crime, sex and killing, poetry and torture – characteristic of noir worlds' ambiguity, irrationality and intensity. In all as well, Leung remains a figure of at least partial sympathy even in the wake of acts of violence and betrayal. Arguably, it is his restrained, interiorized performances rather than narrative machinations that enable the films' affective dimensions. As victimizer and victim, authority figure and malefactor, Leung exudes sexual charisma and psychological energy that radiate out to lend noir texture to these films' surrounds.

Before turning in more detail to Leung's performances, we can address the ways distributors have presented to home-video consumers films in which he appears. The positioning of *Infernal Affairs* in the global DVD market suggests the roles stars play in circulating media texts outside their regions of production. *Infernal Affairs* was released theatrically in Hong Kong in December 2002, with UK distribution rights sold to Tartan Films and US rights to Miramax, with small-scale theatrical runs occurring in the UK and USA in August and September 2004, respectively.[8] Tartan had earlier in 2004 released the film under its 'Tartan Asia Extreme' DVD imprint, although *Infernal Affairs* contains little action or violence. The US theatrical release was comparatively even smaller than the UK's, with the film playing on a total of five arthouse screens in the USA. The later US DVD release came from Dragon Dynasty, the boutique label for East Asian action releases owned by The Weinstein Company (formerly Miramax). In the UK, Tartan's 2004 DVD promotes the film in terms of its stars, prominently showing their names on the DVD box along with titles of other cult action films in which they appear. In the USA, an initial Miramax DVD of 2004 includes images of Leung alongside co-star Andy Lau, the pair bisected by the image of a gun-toting woman in tight shorts who does not appear in the film. The later Dragon Dynasty DVD set of 2007 takes a different strategy, retaining the male stars' faces and adding the tagline 'the motion picture trilogy that inspired *The Departed*', the 2006 US remake of *Infernal Affairs*. Notably, Mega Star's Hong Kong DVD release of *Infernal Affairs* shows the faces of all six of its male stars, representing three generations of regional acting talent and thus presumably magnifying the DVD's appeals to different audience groups. (Notably too, no women appear on the DVD packaging, despite the filmmakers' claim that they built in female characters to maximize the film's potential audience.[9] The top woman in the cast, Kelly Chen, draws out the psychology of Leung's character but earns limited screen time and does not figure in the film's thriller plot involving police and drug traffickers.) Taken together, these releases demonstrate a range of exploitable elements for viewers outside Hong Kong: generic signifiers of guns, scantily clad women and intertextual references to stars' other films; and specific images of the male leads themselves, images not necessarily dependent on consumers' recognition of Leung's or Lau's faces. In this last respect, Leung appears clean-shaven on Dragon Dynasty's DVD box, though he wears a beard in the first and most popular *Infernal Affairs* film. The clean-shaven appearance may aid recognition for viewers who have seen him in other films receiving US distribution.

Promotional materials such as DVD packaging lend emphasis to particular generic or intertextual features of many films featuring Leung, and DVDs often promote features other than the actor's reputation. The home-video release of *Cyclo*, which grants Leung first or second billing depending on release region, demonstrates the resilience of particular marketing strategies for highly aestheticized Asian noir thrillers. English-language critical discourse has repeatedly linked Leung to brand-name East Asian directors, most frequently Kar-Wai Wong given their many collaborations but also Taiwan's Hou and others noted previously. Yet promotional apparatuses can situate Leung's star image, and the films that contribute to that image, in multifarious ways. The video releases of *Cyclo* in different regions exhibit overlapping and conflicting framings that hail varying taste cultures. The cover of Mega Star's Hong Kong DVD of 2000 shows a close-up shot of

Leung embraced by female lead Nu Yên-Khê Tran, beneath the name of director Anh Hung Tran (which appears twice on the cover). Other images on the front and rear similarly foreground tropical romance (though one small still shows a character holding a gun), and the package's jade-green covering links the work to the director's earlier, aesthetically lush *The Scent of Green Papaya* (1993). The North American *Cyclo* DVD, released by New Yorker Films in 2004, shows only a close-up of actress Tran, along with the subtitle 'A Film by Tran Anh Hung', a reference to the film's Venice Film Festival prize, a critic's blurb noting the film's 'passion and poetry', and two references to *The Scent of Green Papaya*. Hence the cover foregrounds the film's auteur-director and festival pedigree, with actor Leung omitted (perhaps surprisingly, given his own Cannes Best Actor standing and the DVD's hailing of art-cinema communities; but foregrounding of both actor and director might create confusion). An earlier release, Entertainment in Video's UK VHS version of the film from 1997, mobilizes noir signifiers in the composite image on the cover, which includes a small view of actress Tran, and behind her a large close-up of lead actor Le Van Loc brandishing a pistol, which dominates the image. The video cover identifies Leung only by showing his name in medium-sized type, suggesting that he had not yet earned robust associations with the field of global noir.

Moving beyond the cover art of its video release, a closer look at Leung's role in *Cyclo* shows varying facets of his acting and stardom put in service of screen art, noir atmospherics and global legibility. His profile in this film sets off his later noir-thriller roles in compelling ways. As in his other noir efforts, he does not play the main character, occupying instead a supporting role that defines the film's project. *Cyclo*'s lead figure is its destitute, toiling cyclo driver, while Leung's poet, pimp and torturer embodies the film's uneasy balance of lush aestheticism and graphic violence. Leung performs amid a Ho Chi Minh City milieu of deep, saturated hues, and he enacts his character's and the film's oppositions with what will become his trademark international performance style, that of passionate detachment. His performance constructs a sombre, withdrawn figure ambivalent about his position in the camps of both art and brutality. (Given Leung's apparent lack of mastery of the Vietnamese language, his nearly wordless performance also conveys the character's detachment, with two poetic voice-overs comprising about half his dialogue in the film.) Leung's casting, here and in later films such as *Hero* and *Lust, Caution*, arguably represents a shrewd manoeuvre on producers' parts, as his minimally demonstrative acting style allows him to serve as a repository for thematic meanings that in other forms could create strong textual incoherence.

The poet of *Cyclo* incorporates character traits that Leung also later displays in more commercially successful films that straddle arthouse and multiplex terrain. The reluctant antihero, skilled in violence but loath to use it even when employed in criminal enterprises, partly defines his characters in *Infernal Affairs* and *Lust, Caution*. Similarly, the poet's longing for romantic happiness matches the outlook of most characters on the dramatic side of Leung's filmography. Acting with little or no dialogue also distinguishes his dramatic roles, in many of which, narrative conditions explain his reticence. Substantive issues remain unarticulated in many of his films, whether owing to social convention (as is the case in *In the Mood for Love*), subterfuge (in *Hard-Boiled* and *Infernal Affairs*), or both (*Confession of Pain* and *Lust, Caution*). We might also attribute a lack of spoken dialogue to characteristic art-cinema ambiguity, as apparent in *Cyclo*, *Flowers of Shanghai* (1998), and even the more cheerful *Chungking Express*. Leung's performances account strongly for the possible categorization of particular films as noir texts. He repeatedly embodies discontented, alienated and psychologically divided male figures who both belong to and define the milieu of contemporary global noir. Along with narrative machinations and formal choices such as lighting, camerawork and sound, Leung's characterizations contribute substantively to the stylized and romanticized but also pessimistic tones of *Infernal Affairs*, *Lust, Caution* and other dramatic crime and thriller narratives in his filmography. This tonality evolves from similar preoccupations in classical US noir, which also depends partly on restrained performances from male stars such as Humphrey Bogart and Robert Mitchum capable of channelling their energies into both action-intensive roles and interiorized, psychological characterizations. In contemporary cinema, the philosophical, romantically inclined (if doomed) man who inhabits a world of violence is a stock figure in films that cross over between festival/arthouse channels and mainstream theatrical release. Even with the limited worldwide recognition of the construct 'film noir', the currency of noir narratives, thematics and imagery locates East Asian and other international noir strongly in this middle category of global film output.

The characters Leung plays in thrillers and dramas routinely behave in ways suiting neo-noir's loosely understood narrative parameters. As the undercover cop Yan in *Infernal Affairs*, Leung must play simultaneously virtuous (his 'real' personality) and criminal (masquerading to maintain the trust of his Triad brethren). He manages these opposing roles through passivity. Yan refrains from explicit violence, and until the film's climax, he never instigates action. Narrative conditions dictating inaction characterize many of Leung's films, even those outside the terrain of noir. *In the Mood for*

Love, for example, shows Leung and co-star Maggie Cheung's characters torn between passionate desire and moral restraint, and their dilated romance achieves no onscreen consummation. Later, an iconic scene in the arty *wuxia Hero* features Leung's character, Broken Sword, writing calligraphy in sand while a rain of arrows besieges his school. In addition, Leung has played many police characters, from virtuous to murderous, as well as numerous roles as men with divided loyalties or ambiguous moral positions. His *Infernal Affairs* role as an undercover cop troubled by his immersion in the criminal world reprises much of the profile of his *Hard-Boiled* character, an assassin who is really a policeman working under deep cover. This thematic thread of psychological duality brings together a substantial portion of Leung's filmography, framing him strongly as a noir protagonist. Psychological characterizations, along with emphasis on interior conflict rather than physical action, fulfil arthouse audiences' expectations for character-based drama rather than propulsive spectacle. At the same time, Leung's performance attributes – for example, his ability to manifest 'presence' with limited or no physical movement – can serve the interests of such varying genres and modes as romantic drama, martial-arts epic and urban noir thriller. Leung's characters can thus occupy both generic categories and those linked to exhibition sites such as art cinemas.

Restrained Performance, Restricted Persona

Genre signifiers facilitate distribution of some of Leung's films globally, though many of his other genre films are restricted to regional, East Asian markets. Long before *Hero* and the historical epic *Red Cliff*, Leung played numerous roles calling for broad physical performance, both in action and comic contexts. Almost without exception, such films did not circulate theatrically outside Asia. *Tokyo Raiders* (2000) and its sequel *Seoul Raiders* (2005), for example, cast Leung as a Jackie Chan-style comic adventurer who leads a team of young, attractive spies; in 2001's *Love Me, Love My Money*, he plays a comic cad in the Hugh Grant mould; in the 1999 Jackie Chan vehicle *Gorgeous*, he plays a supporting role as a flamboyant gay man; earlier in the 1990s, he plays a bumbling swordsman in the martial-arts comedy *The Eagle Shooting Heroes* (1993); and earlier still, Leung gives another slapstick-style performance as a bumbling reporter in the sci-fi comedy *I Love Maria* (1988). More than demonstrating Leung's considerable range as an actor, such roles suggest the limits of intertextuality in global markets. Evidence of Leung's comic and action roles is explicitly suppressed in promotion of films that showcase Tony Leung, soulful romantic icon, for audiences outside Asia. Meanwhile, many viewers in Hong Kong and the Chinese diaspora still associate Leung with his roles in numerous 1980s television series from the popular TVB network, series incorporating generic attributes of *wuxia* action, comedy and drama.[10] Numerous other Hong Kong performers – including Yun-Fat Chow, Stephen Chow and Maggie Cheung – crossed over from 1980s TVB series to feature films. Consequently, Hong Kong audiences' prefigurations of stars such as Leung contribute to diverse reading strategies for contemporary films. Uninitiated viewers outside Asia cannot readily adopt such strategies, as their recognition of Leung may depend principally on the cultural capital his ostensible art-film roles and festival awards provide.

Circulation of Leung's films, while clearly dependent on genre positionings or lack thereof, also reveals preferences for particular acting styles in international markets. Audiences worldwide often respond to straightforward, uncomplex characterizations and performances. At the same time, critical acclaim and sometimes commercial success also accompany performers who can convey ambiguity through facial expressions and a modest repertoire of body language, and who can communicate psychology, emotion and a range of moral positions nonverbally, in ways resonant in different cultural contexts. While prevailing industrial and academic wisdom asserts that action genres travel more widely than other film output, in Leung's case dramatic roles and restrained performances in thrillers have circulated more successfully than his action efforts or other physically demonstrative roles. As I have argued elsewhere,[11] in films receiving festival awards and global distribution, Leung acts principally in what James Naremore terms a 'representational' style, an interiorized style that in stage drama attempts to create the illusion that no audience is present.[12] Meanwhile, in dozens of broad comedies and action films in martial-arts and other genres released only within East Asia, Leung regularly acts in a 'presentational' style that explicitly acknowledges the audience and does not depend on realist psychology. In films such as *In the Mood for Love*, *Infernal Affairs* and *Lust, Caution*, Leung gives highly psychologized, physically restrained performances. *Infernal Affairs* puts him in a climactic rooftop standoff with guns drawn, but no kinetic gunfight occurs; instead, a circling camera emphasizes the protagonists' stasis. *Lust, Caution* shows Leung's character almost entirely in interiors such as parlours and bedrooms. Even in the uncensored version of the film's two lengthy sex scenes, the naked Leung moves very little (partly to shield his genital area from camera view); and his most dynamic physical movement in the film occurs when he rushes into the back seat of a car after learning of a threat to his life. In contrast, in films such as the action-comedy *Tokyo Raiders* or the romantic comedy *Love Me, Love My Money*, Leung's presentational style playfully acknowledges his characters' comic situations with expansive gestures, broad smiles, and continuous and often rapid dialogue.

The global appeal of Leung's illusionistic, representational performances demonstrates not only regional and international taste preferences but also implicit critical patrolling against certain forms of performative expression. In line with implicit preferences for star performances not based on language or speech, Leung remains best known outside Asia for his roles in richly art-directed historical romances such as *In the Mood for Love* and its companion film *2046*. Leung also co-stars in the global blockbuster *Hero*, though its marketing in the USA and UK downplays his role, with theatrical posters and DVD graphics in effect retitling it 'Jet Li's *Hero*'. After *Hero* and *The Grandmaster*, Leung's most successful starring effort in terms of critical recognition and global arthouse circulation may be *Lust, Caution*,[13] the erotic historical drama built on a slow-burning assassination plot and framed in promotional and journalistic discourse in terms of its numerous graphic sex scenes, a rarity in diasporic Chinese cinema. Leung's performance as a sombre man entrapped by his own social position handily merges the lonely, conflicted characters he plays in his many films under director Kar-Wai Wong as well as in genre-driven efforts such as *Infernal Affairs*. Reviewing *Lust, Caution* in the *New York Times*, Manohla Dargis writes, 'Few actors convey desire as beautifully or with such reserve. [...] In his best films, [...] Mr. Leung doesn't do much talking: he looks, he conquers.'[14] One might surmise that Leung has limited vocal gifts, although like many Hong Kong actors, he has pursued a second career as a popular singer, releasing numerous albums and singing the title song on *Infernal Affairs*' soundtrack (in a duet with Andy Lau, also a recording artist). Dargis of course does not call for Asian male stars to be rendered mute in their screen efforts. Instead, her assertion suggests the degree to which restrained performance, characterized by minimal, cinematic expressiveness rather than theatrical gestures or other expansive physical efforts, here registers as more accessible, engaging and overall pleasurable for discerning viewers than do other performance styles. The noir aesthetic of sculpted lighting, dynamic compositions and narratives turning on duplicity and betrayal further promotes restrained, representational performance. Leung's 'soulful' performances – the description appears repeatedly in reviews of his work – can anchor viewers in films

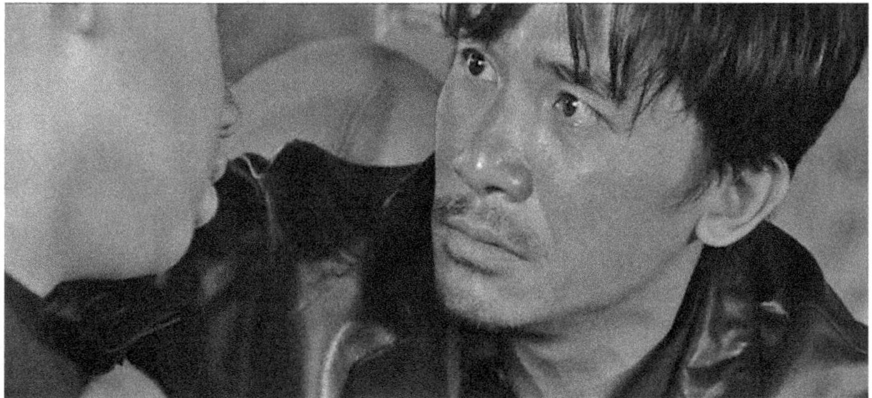

Figure 11.1 In *Infernal Affairs*, an extreme close-up gives prominence to the eyes and face of undercover cop Chen (Tony Leung Chiu-Wai) as he comforts the dying Keung (Chapman To)

dominated by complex narratives or dense images of urban space, whether contemporary or historical.

The Male Face of Melancholic Noir

To highlight the consistency of Leung's performance across films that address their audiences in very different ways, I offer for comparison brief moments from *Infernal Affairs* and *Lust, Caution* that make comparable use of Leung while fulfilling distinct dramatic needs. In *Infernal Affairs*, the character Yan spends most of the film in the company of his fellow criminals, emerging from his cover only for clandestine briefings with Superintendent Wong (Anthony Wong) and therapy sessions with Dr Lee (Kelly Chen). Only his engagements with Triads, then, occur outside institutional settings or power structures. Some of these engagements – particularly a scene in which he uses Morse-code finger-tapping to relay information about a drug shipment while in the Triads' company – involve his tense efforts to maintain his cover. Others, though, show his affable, familiar relations with other men. At the film's second-act climax, Yan sees his friend and superior Wong killed by Yan's criminal partners, then escapes the ensuing melee alongside the slow-witted Keung (Chapman To), who is soon shown to have been fatally shot. Delivering an oblique monologue as the pair drive along a tree-lined country lane and then crash into a ditch, the dying Keung implies that he has known Yan's true identity but kept the secret out of loyalty to his comrade. After this revelation, the film shows Yan in a tight close-up, with

Leung's expressive eyes convening rage, disbelief and sadness, and calling forth a range of signifying possibilities. (As in classical US noirs such as *The Asphalt Jungle* [1950], leaving the city mostly gives male protagonists opportunities to suffer new tragedies.) Leung's face must bear the weight of the scene's (and the film's) complex emotions generated around masculinity and male friendship, around codes of honour and betrayal, around deception and knowledge, and around justice, violence and mortality.

Lust, Caution also puts Leung at the crossroads of intimacy and betrayal, and elements of the film's production focus attention on his expressive eyes and face. Cinematographer Rodrigo Prieto used an amber eyelight on Leung during the film's interrogation scenes: 'We subtly created the effect of embers lighting him during his intense lines. […] It did add a touch of almost terrifying insanity to his gaze.'[15] Technical elements thus steer viewers toward the thematic dimension of Leung's performance, in ways legible without translation. Remarking on another scene, in which Mr Yee acknowledges Wong's love for him solely through facial expression, editor Tim Squyres observes that 'Leung was given the extraordinarily difficult job of portraying this without being able to say it, and the simplicity and effectiveness of his performance is amazing.'[16] Squyres' praise makes a further implicit appeal to prospective viewers to accept Leung's face and eyes, not his voice, as the actor's key performance tool. *Lust, Caution* ends after a brief exchange between Mr Yee and his usually distant wife (Joan Chen), and its penultimate image is also a close-up of the silent Leung. The shot shows Mr Yee alone in the empty bedroom that had been used by his consort, Mak (or Wong), whose offscreen execution he has just sanctioned. The image puts Leung off-centre in the frame, dark shadows engulfing the room but leaving his face visible from the eyes down. Here too, his off-axis glance into space provides the film's final representation of human emotion, his expression acting as the repository for viewer sentiments and interpretive possibilities. (Finally, he steps out of frame, leaving only his shadow set against a rumpled white bedsheet.) Beyond their distinct affective engagements, the two scenes demonstrate that Leung can perform in a similar dramatic register in films pitched to East Asian genre-film viewers as well as those geared to international arthouse audiences.

Lust, Caution is particularly notable in cementing the image of Leung as a soulful romancer trapped in history. Moreover, it extends the darker strand of his persona to depict him as a public and private villain. When not engaged in connotative rape and other sexual encounters relying on disturbing power imbalances, his character supervises interrogations, torture and executions. For international audiences and even members of the

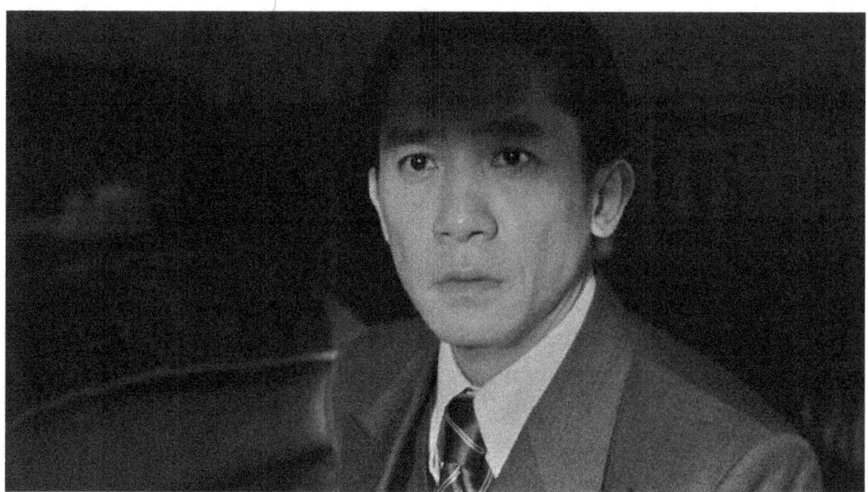

Figure 11.2 In *Lust, Caution's* final scene, Mr Yee (Tony Leung Chiu-Wai) sits alone in shadow on the bed he had shared with Mak Tai Tai (Wei Tang), whose execution he has just approved

production team, Leung's turn in *Lust, Caution* represents casting against type. Interviewed for a DVD supplement, both director Lee and co-writer and producer James Schamus perpetuate the misapprehension that Leung has played mostly virtuous, romantic characters throughout his career.[17] The English-language supplement appears on the film's North American DVD release, so most of its viewers' exposure to Leung's filmography may be insufficient to challenge this view, which is reasonably accurate if only Leung's films distributed to the USA are included. Yet Leung has played numerous villains in Hong Kong films. In 1998's *The Longest Nite*, for example, his corrupt-cop protagonist repeatedly assaults the film's female lead, finally shooting her multiple times in the leg, throwing her from a moving car and running her over. Later, in *Confession of Pain*, Leung's policeman character sadistically bludgeons a criminal in the opening scene as his unnerved colleagues watch; numerous scenes revisit his graphic murder of his father-in-law; and the film devotes extensive screen time to his terrorizing of his innocent wife. Still the film repeatedly invites viewers to sympathize with his plight, representing negative emotions in ways familiar to aficionados of contemporary East Asian cinema though likely baffling to the uninitiated. Correspondingly, in what might seem a counterintuitive inversion of scale, Leung's star persona in Hong Kong admits multiple character types and generic possibilities, while in the global market a far more circumscribed persona circulates, focused around a narrow range of performative signs and psychological attributes. This narrower persona does allow for the marketing of small variations, such as the apparent novelty of Leung playing an irredeemably villainous role. *Lust, Caution*'s historical specificity may strengthen the impression of its singularity in Leung's filmography, as some of his other morally problematic roles have been in highly aestheticized, anti-realist films. In both *Hero* and *2046*, to name just two prominent examples of Leung's films distributed internationally, his characters use sex to exercise power and manipulate others. Presaging *Lust, Caution*'s eroticized murderer, these characters are morally ambiguous if not outright villainous. Still, the notion of Leung as an actor associated with sweet characters such as *Chungking Express*' guileless beat cop or *In the Mood for Love*'s heart-aching writer helps set off his *Lust, Caution* role as daring and remarkable.

The selective deployment of Leung's acting awards in marketing of particular films demonstrates another way multifaceted star profiles are variously reconfigured in transnational distribution according to perceived audience tastes. For example, among his numerous acting awards, Leung's efforts in *Infernal Affairs* won him best-actor awards at 2003's Hong Kong Film Awards and the same year's Golden Horse Film Festival in Taiwan. Theatrical marketing of the film in the USA and UK did not highlight these regional-festival awards, which might be seen to anchor Leung too specifically to the East Asian region rather than to the international art-cinema community. For DVDs, marketed to fans of 'Asian extreme' or action cinema as well as to viewers of the US remake *The Departed*, foregrounding of any critical accolades surrounding acting may detract from implicit promises of exotic spectacle. (Similarly, marketing of Yun-Fat Chow's 1980s and 1990s action films did not highlight his own many acting awards for roles in Hong Kong art-cinema dramas.)

Cases such as Leung's demonstrate that markers of acting prestige may compete with and thus undermine star appeals based on generic associations. At the same time, the flexible space of noir – genre or modality, aesthetic register or sensibility, accumulation of narrative markers and site for particularly coded performances balancing criminality and heart, amorality and devotion, stolidity and sexiness – shows ways critical plaudits and generic structures can consolidate a particular star image. Facilitating his most psychologically intense and interiorized performances while foregrounding his romantic appeals, noir offers a staging ground for much of Leung's work most favoured in global screen cultures. *Infernal Affairs* and other noir thrillers featuring Leung operate at the intersection of global mainstream cinema, transnational genre releases, and implicit arthouse categories of 'foreign' or exotic film. Correspondingly, Tony Leung Chiu-Wai's mutable star persona and the intergeneric apparatuses of cinematic thrillers and neo-noirs speak to multiple constituencies in complex ways. I hope this brief survey of a small number of Leung's many noir-inflected and wider roles has indicated some of the issues raised by regional stars in global circulation.

Notes

1 Desser, David, 'Global Noir: Genre Film in the Age of Transnationalism', in Barry Keith Grant (ed.), *Film Genre Reader III* (Austin: University of Texas Press, 2003), p. 516.

2 Ibid., pp. 522, 523.

3 Ibid., p. 521.

4 While the parameters of film noir or neo-noir are always in flux, many of Desser's examples arguably fall outside even the widest vernacular understandings of noir. He discusses *Natural Born Killers* (1994), *Lock, Stock and Two Smoking Barrels* (1998) and *Run Lola Run* (1998), for example, though I imagine very few critics or viewers would classify those hyper-stylized, frenetic, action-intensive works as strongly noirish. Still, Desser's textual examples contribute usefully to debates over the global expansion of the noir mode and sensibility.

5 See Naremore, James, *More Than Night: Film Noir in Its Contexts*, rev. ed. (Berkeley: University of California Press, 2008 [1998]).

6 For more on the film's local impact, see Marchetti, Gina, *Andrew Lau and Alan Mak's Infernal Affairs – The Trilogy* (Hong Kong: Hong Kong University Press, 2007); Rayns, Tony, 'Deep Cover', *Sight and Sound*, January 2004, <http://www.bfi.org.uk/sightandsound/feature/29/>, accessed 30 June 2008; and Leung, Wing-Fai, '*Infernal Affairs* and *Kung Fu Hustle*: Panacea, Placebo and Hong Kong Cinema', in Leon Hunt and Leung Wing-Fai (eds), *East Asian Cinemas: Exploring Transnational Connections on Film* (London: I.B.Tauris, 2008), pp. 71–87.

7 On the censorship and Chinese reception of *Lust, Caution*, see Chi, Robert, 'Exhibitionism: *Lust, Caution*', *Journal of Chinese Cinemas* 3.2 (June 2009), pp. 177–187.

8 For some release dates and box-office data outside Asia, see the Internet Movie Database listings 'Release dates for *Mou gaan dou* (2002)', <http://www.imdb.com/title/tt0338564/releaseinfo> and 'Box office/business for *Mou gaan dou* (2002)', <http://www.imdb.com/title/tt0338564/business>, both accessed 6 February 2013.

9 Rayns, 'Deep Cover'.

10 These include series such as *Soldier of Fortune* (1982), *Police Cadet* (1984) and *The Duke of Mount Deer* (1984, co-starring Andy Lau), each comprising 40 hour-long episodes.
11 See Gallagher, Mark, '"Would You Rather Spend More Time Making Serious Cinema?": *Hero* and Tony Leung's Polysemic Masculinity', in Gary Rawnsley and Ming-Yeh Rawnsley (eds), *Global Chinese Cinema: The Culture and Politics of Hero* (London: Routledge, 2010), pp. 106–120.
12 Naremore, James, *Acting in the Cinema* (Berkeley: University of California Press, 1988), p. 36.
13 After *Hero*, *Lust, Caution* (a co-production among companies in the USA, China, Taiwan and Hong Kong) stands as Leung's most commercially successful film outside East Asia, narrowly outpacing *The Grandmaster*. According to Box Office Mojo, *Lust, Caution*'s global box office returns to date are in excess of US$67 million (<http://boxofficemojo.com/movies/?id=lustcaution.htm>, accessed 6 February 2013). As verifiable statistics for non-US productions are difficult to obtain, no reliable data exists for the global theatrical grosses of Hong Kong and Chinese productions such as *Infernal Affairs* and *Red Cliff*. The first instalment of *Red Cliff* broke Chinese box-office records in summer 2008 but performed modestly in piecemeal international distribution.
14 Dargis, Manohla, 'A Cad and a Femme Fatale Simmer' (film review), *New York Times*, 28 September 2007, <http://movies.nytimes.com/2007/09/28/movies/28lust.html>, accessed 28 September 2007.
15 Prieto, Rodrigo, 'The Killer Pizza Light', in *Lust, Caution: The Story, The Screenplay, and the Making of the Film* (New York: Pantheon Books, 2007), p. 254.
16 Squyres, Tim, 'Go, Now!', in *Lust, Caution: The Story, The Screenplay, and the Making of the Film*, p. 254.
17 See the supplement 'Tiles of Deception, Lurid Affections', *Lust, Caution* DVD (Universal Studios Home Entertainment, 2008).

Chapter 12

Double Identity: The Stardom of Xun Zhou and the Figure of the Femme Fatale

Chi-Yun Shin

Chinese actress Xun Zhou came into the spotlight in the international art film circuit after starring in Ye Lou's acclaimed *Suzhou River* (2000), winning the Best Actress award at the Paris International Film Festival, where the film also won the Best Film award. In the film, set in contemporary Shanghai, Zhou plays two intriguing heroines – Moudan, a teenage daughter of a shady businessman, who falls in love with a motorcycle courier; and Meimei, a showgirl who performs a mermaid act in an aquarium at a sleazy nightclub. Especially as the world-weary and seductive Meimei, whose past remains unknown, Zhou offers an alluring image of an urban, modern Chinese woman in post-socialist China. In this regard, Zhou's star image marks a stark contrast to those of other contemporary Chinese female stars such as Li Gong and Ziyi Zhang, who have established their stardom in largely historical pieces. Li Gong famously embodied the 'mythic, larger-than-life icons of the repressed peasant woman' in the so-called Fifth Generation films,[1] while Ziyi Zhang's stardom is closely associated with spectacular martial-arts films such as *Crouching Tiger, Hidden Dragon* (2000) and *House of Flying Daggers* (2004).[2]

In her study of *Femmes Fatales*, Mary Ann Doane defines the femme fatale as 'the figure of a certain discursive unease, a potential epistemological trauma. For her most striking characteristic, perhaps, is the fact that she never really is what she seems to be.'[3] Indeed, in her breakout role in *Suzhou*

River, playing both Moudan and Meimei, who might and might not be the same woman for much of the film, Xun Zhou established a femme fatale persona, an elusive double who is not all that she seems. Zhou has continued to develop a star image as a figure of the mysterious, hence unknowable, object of romantic obsession in subsequent films such as *Beijing Bicycle* (2001), *Hollywood Hong Kong* (2002) and *Perhaps Love* (2005). In more recent years, as she is recognized as one of the most famous actresses in China,[4] perhaps not surprisingly, Zhou has appeared in many big-budget historical epics, notably in films such as *The Banquet* (2006), *True Legend* (2010) and *Confucius* (2010), as well as the highly successful supernatural action film *Painted Skin* (2008) and its sequel *Painted Skin: The Resurrection* (2012). Still, in 2010, the CNN chat show *Talk Asia* dubbed her 'China's queen of quirk',[5] suggesting that while Zhou has made some adjustments to her star image, appearing in more glossy mainstream films, she has maintained her 'alternative' image. Reviewing *Painted Skin: The Resurrection* for *Film Business Asia*, Derek Elley also notes that 'Zhou, who since *Suzhou River* has almost had the Mainland patent on sexually ambiguous, seductive roles, dominates the movie, as a demon who wants to be human even if it means pain.'[6]

The sexually alluring figure of the femme fatale is regarded as one of the key features of film noir. However, just as film noir is 'one of the most amorphous categories in film history', a category that 'has no essential characteristics and [...] is not a specifically American form',[7] the figure of the femme fatale needs to be considered beyond film noir, not least because she had existed long before the classic film noirs of the 1940s and 1950s. As Mark Jancovich also points out, the 'vicious women' characters in the postwar period 'were not uniquely associated with an object called *film noir*'.[8] Therefore, this chapter takes the femme fatale as an elastic figure that is not exclusive to noir films. In fact, Zhou's femme fatale persona appears in a range of genres, including realist dramas, historical films and even musicals. The chapter thus focuses on Zhou's roles that have established and developed her femme fatale image. It examines the duality, ambiguity and contradictions inherent in her screen persona against the contexts of China's transformation in the post-socialist era in order to demonstrate how the femme fatale figure is retooled to register conditions of social reality. Considering both historically specific (post-socialist China) and ahistorical (conveying free-floating anxiety) aspects of the femme fatale as embodied by Zhou, this chapter also addresses the critical potential of Zhou's complex, often conflicted, and yet always non-conformist individual who challenges the standardization of the femme fatale character.[9]

Urban Enigmas and Ghostly Doubles

Suzhou River begins in total darkness with a woman's (Xun Zhou) deep and raspy voice, asking: 'If I leave you someday, would you look for me? [...] Would you look for me forever? [...] Your whole life?' These riddle-like words, which will be repeated at the end of the film, foreshadow the film's thematic concerns – 'the nature of romantic pursuit' and associated notions of fidelity and deceit.[10] As the film navigates the rough streets along the waterways of the polluted, murky Suzhou River that runs through Shanghai, the jaded, off-screen narration of the unnamed videographer-for-hire tells of how he first met his elusive girlfriend Meimei. His story starts with a shot of the nightclub boss explaining his mermaid show, which is accompanied by the voice-over: 'I don't believe in mermaids, but then I saw her.' The film then cuts to a shaky and voyeuristic medium close-up shot, peeping through the curtains of a dressing room where Meimei is getting ready for the show. The voice-over announcement that 'she's the mermaid' is followed by a shot of Meimei in red-sequined mermaid costume completed with a long blond wig, swimming around the aquarium in slow motion, waving her arms (at the videographer and the camera) with a bright smile. The voice-over continues to announce: 'I fell in love the first time I saw her in the water.'

These shots introduce Meimei/Xun Zhou as an object of romantic obsession, but already are filled with tension between the subjective voice-over and what is shown (Meimei as mermaid, and Meimei 'performing' a mermaid act). Seen through the videographer's camera for much of the film, Meimei is in fact framed, guided and mediated by his camera and narration. Still, he narrates: 'I didn't know anything about Meimei's past. She didn't say, and I never asked. I just liked to look at her and video her.' Zhou's sensuous performance in the sequence that follows verges on the narcissistic, as the tight close-up shots of her face evidently show her willing submission to the camera, 'acting out' activities such as chewing bubble gum and smoking cigarettes, which are associated with a carefree (childlike) and even decadent (grown-up) attitude, all the while flirting to and with the camera, remaining within touching distance. Her high-spirited smiles, however, soon shift to a subdued expression, as the videographer explains that she would suddenly become sad and would often disappear for days at a time without explanation. Her ambivalence or contradictory traits (happy, then suddenly sad) at least from his perspective are embodied in the hybrid figure of the mermaid (half-woman, half-fish), with its tragic undertone. Her houseboat home, anchored in the river on a crane, also reinforces her rootlessness and ability to leave anytime she wants (as she does at the end of the film).

The videographer next tells us the story of Mardar (Hongshen Jia), a young motorcycle courier in Shanghai. Mardar is hired to escort a teenager, Moudan (also played by Xun Zhou), to her aunt's house whenever her well-to-do father entertains his mistresses at home. Inevitably, as the narrator claims, Mardar and Moudan fall in love, but despite his feelings for Moudan, Mardar takes part in kidnapping Moudan for ransom. Her father, who is in the business of illegally smuggling Eastern European vodka, pays the ransom. Devastated by the betrayal and humiliated by the 'price' tagged on her, though, Moudan jumps into the Suzhou River, clutching her mermaid doll, a birthday present from Mardar. Moudan's body is never found, and Mardar is arrested and sent to prison for several years. After serving his time, Mardar comes back to Shanghai, where he runs into Meimei and becomes convinced that she is his lost love. Seeking redemption in Meimei, Mardar pursues her, turning her into his own obsession. Highly voyeuristic shots of Meimei preparing to appear as the mermaid are offered again, this time in full detail – showing how she puts on her wig and mermaid-tail suit, and so forth. Much of what Zhou as Meimei does in these voyeuristic scenes – carrying on her routine transformation, not knowing she is being watched – presents her as pensive and vulnerable. Although she is seen through Mardar's eyes, hence 'mediated', her indifferent reserve in the scene contrasts with the confident sexuality of her 'performance' to her boyfriend videographer's camera, presenting her character's duality once again. Zhou's elusive Meimei is indeed at the heart of the film – the mystery of the film that both Mardar and the videographer need to decode.

Described as 'a moody exercise in modernist film noir' by one reviewer,[11] *Suzhou River* is a representative work of the new urban cinema that is, in Xiaoping Lin's words, 'obsessed with everyday realities' and 'in general a study of China's painful transformation from a Soviet-style socialist state into a new global capitalist country'.[12] In Zhen Zhang's view, this new cinema is also preoccupied 'with the destruction and reconstruction of the social fabric and urban identities of post-1989 China'.[13] In this regard, the doubling of Moudan (a child abandoned by father figures, and a victim of greed) and Meimei (an alluring showgirl who may be a reincarnation of Moudan who lost her innocence) is resonant with the dual nature of the city of Shanghai – the romantic Westernized glamour and the grimmer reality – that is undergoing a rapid and drastic transformation. With various displacements that undermine boundaries and morality, this urbanization threatens the very possibility of identity, which is embodied in doubles. As

Kelly Oliver and Benigno Trigo point out, 'the uncanny double does not reassure us of our agency or control but, quite the opposite, recalls our feelings of fragmentation and helplessness'.[14]

Suzhou River is indeed filled with doubles and mirror images. The film itself can be regarded as a double of Alfred Hitchcock's *Vertigo* (1958). As many commentators have noticed, *Suzhou River* evokes *Vertigo* in many ways – through music (Jôrg Lemberg's Bernard Herrmann-inspired string music), themes (romantic obsession and betrayal), plot (a man searching for his lost love), visual style (voyeuristic camera movements), and motifs (one actress playing two roles). For instance, the short, green dress Meimei dons frequently seems to be a modernized and downgraded version of the green gown Kim Novak as Madeleine wears the first time James Stewart's Scottie sees her. In the end, however, unlike Judy, who was playing Madeleine in *Vertigo*, Meimei turns out to be *not* Moudan. In fact, Meimei seems to be the one most surprised to find out that there was a Moudan. When she identifies the bodies of Mardar and Moudan, who died together, Meimei turns to the camera, shocked and disoriented in the heavy rain. She confesses to have thought that it was her that Mardar wanted. Regarding this twist, Jerome Silbergeld argues that:

> [I]n *Suzhou River*, virtually the entire film is turned into a MacGuffin. We're long interested in the hero's pursuit of the reincarnated heroine before we discover in the last moments of the film that the moral of this tale is best embodied neither by the vanished girl, M[o]udan, nor by the reincarnation she's supposed to be, but instead by someone she evidently was not but *now* becomes.[15]

Meimei's transformation indeed is manifested in her disappearing as Moudan once did, wanting to be the object of the pursuit again, as she asks: 'if I left you someday, would you look for me forever?'

The high romantic ideals are, however, offset by the weary voice-over narration (the videographer's almost callous reply is 'yes'), as well as by her muted response ('you're lying'). In fact, the voice-over narration is highly unreliable throughout the film; the videographer seems to be looking out of his window and makes up or imagines the stories as he watches people passing by. Yet the stories he tells are very personal, interwoven with his occupation (recorder of the 'truth') and his obsession (filming Meimei). It is indeed difficult to conclude that the entire story is a figment of the narrator's imagination when Meimei and the narrator stand over the dead bodies of Mardar and Moudan at the end of the film. Until that moment, the film intentionally conflates past and present, reality and illusion, and truth and deception. In particular, Zhou's embodiment of dual personalities – and the film's deliberate confusion of the presumed victim and her living double – indicates ambivalence, alienation, fragmentation and uncertainties, all hallmarks of modernity.

Beyond Male Fantasies

After *Suzhou River*, Zhou appears in a varied group of films, ranging from the documentary-style drama *Beijing Bicycle* and the dark comedy *Hollywood Hong Kong* to the historical piece *Balzac and the Little Chinese Seamstress* (2002) and the film musical *Perhaps Love*. Zhou's roles in these eclectic films, however, overall conform to the template of the strong and alluring femme fatale character. She is often admired and desired by male protagonists, but refuses to 'settle' with any of them, leaving at the end of the film. This characterization significantly deviates from the neo-noir revision of the femme fatale character who 'escapes the "final Justice" of the conventional narrative climax, either through succeeding in her treachery (*Body Heat* [1981] and *The Last Seduction* [1993]) or by deceiving the whole legal system by escaping capture and continuing to exercise her femme fatale sexuality (*Basic Instinct* [1992])'.[16] She is not exactly a victim of lecherous men or circumstances either. This section explores how the associations Zhou brings to the roles, namely ambivalence and seductiveness, are related to the films' articulation or reflection of particular realities of Chinese societies.

In *Beijing Bicycle*, the winner of the Berlin Film Festival's Silver Bear Award, Zhou only appears sporadically in an anecdotal strand, but she plays a significant part as an unwitting participant in the sexual awakening of the film's teenage protagonist Guei, a recent immigrant to Beijing from the countryside. Living in a modern apartment opposite the two immigrants – Guei and his friend, a lowly grocery-store owner of the same rural origin – Zhou's beautiful yet remote 'city' girl (identified as Qin in the credits) is regularly and secretly gazed at and admired by the two neighbourhood boys through a crevice in their courtyard wall. Displayed in a fashion not dissimilar to a shop mannequin (or kept like a princess in a castle or tower), she appears unattainable to the men, who are clearly attracted to her but do nothing but watch her furtively. Discussing the representation of rural migrants in the film, Jian Xu suggests that 'their gaze nevertheless fails to possess her image' because they perceive her as 'the image of the urban Other, the site of plenitude represented by all the luxury and comfort of an urban life'.[17] Often seen in several changes of fine clothes by the apartment window, Zhou's character is indeed an object of romantic fascination, 'out of their league' as Guei's friend later puts it.

This impossible fascination is explicitly demonstrated in the scene where the 'city' girl comes to the grocery store to buy soy sauce. The scene starts with Guei's friend shouting out, 'Listen', which is immediately followed by a shot of an empty alleyway resounding with high-heel footsteps. As he announces, 'Here she comes', the film cuts to a close-up shot of the girl's red high heels and carries on tracking them as she walks toward the store. The combination of the image of the empty alleyway accompanied by the sound of her shoes and the long tracking shot illustrates the men's excitement and anticipation of seeing her in the flesh in close proximity. Clad in a red dress, Zhou's character exudes both confidence (in her strides) and indifference (to the boys). As she notices Guei's intense stare, she looks straight back at him, and he immediately turns away from her gaze. Guei's actions illustrate the tension between his (sexual) attraction to her and the warning against such attraction – according to his friend, city girls are wasteful, and even staring at them too long is not good for one's health. Her slightly bemused facial expression as she leaves the store clearly indicates that she is in control, all the time subtly presenting her own ambivalent attitude towards Guei's attention.

The fact that the 'city girl' never speaks in the film adds to her character's mysteriousness. Even when she regains her consciousness in the store after Guei (on a bicycle) accidentally collides with her and knocks her over, she gets up, packs her things and leaves without a word. In another scene, she barges into the store and frantically but in total silence begins to search the place. She is clearly looking for something, but completely ignores Guei, who is almost paralysed by her sudden appearance. Her silence, however, is soon revealed to be linked to her true identity; as the immigrant boys find out, she is in fact a housemaid from the countryside who had liked to dress up in her employer's clothes and had even sold some of them. It turns out that she was practising the very advice Guei's friend gave him earlier in the film: 'The trick is not to let anyone know you're not from here.' Not giving away her accent and origin, she was indeed able to 'trick' the boys. In this sense, her silence and indifference to the boys – ostensibly femme fatale behaviour – can function as a defensive response to the prejudices and inequities prevalent in the big city. After learning that she has been fired and that she disappeared after being found out, Guei's friend ruefully comments: 'If only I'd known that she is from country too!' *Beijing Bicycle* registers the changing dynamics of contemporary Beijing life, and the immigrant boys' misconception of Zhou's character illuminates 'the beguiling nature of surface images and material possessions'.[18]

Continuing the trope of the girl who is not quite who she appears to be, Zhou moves on to the figure of the more predatory and calculated temptress in the Hong Kong independent film *Hollywood Hong Kong*, directed by Fruit Chan. Going by the names Tong Tong and Hung Hung, Zhou plays a prostitute from Mainland China whose seemingly carefree playfulness enchants the residents of the Kowloon shantytown of Tai Hom. The first victim is Keung, a young, local pimp who comes across the picture of Hung Hung while advertising his own (and only) girl on the internet. Instantly attracted to the 'mainlander' (she advertises herself as 'Shanghai Angel'), he pursues her and willingly pays to spend the night with her in the bushes outside Plaza Hollywood, a large apartment and mall complex that overshadows the shantytown. Soon afterwards, Zhou's character, this time called Tong Tong, appears in the shantytown and befriends the Chu family – Mr Chu, the obese owner of a pork barbeque stall, and his equally obese sons, Ming and Tiny. Although the large family of Chu seem content running the pork business, it is clear that Tong Tong's pretty and easy-going character provides a refreshing, joyful presence in their dull lives. The pleasure of having her in their lives is most evident in the swing-set sequence in which all three family members break into big smiles watching her riding high on the swing

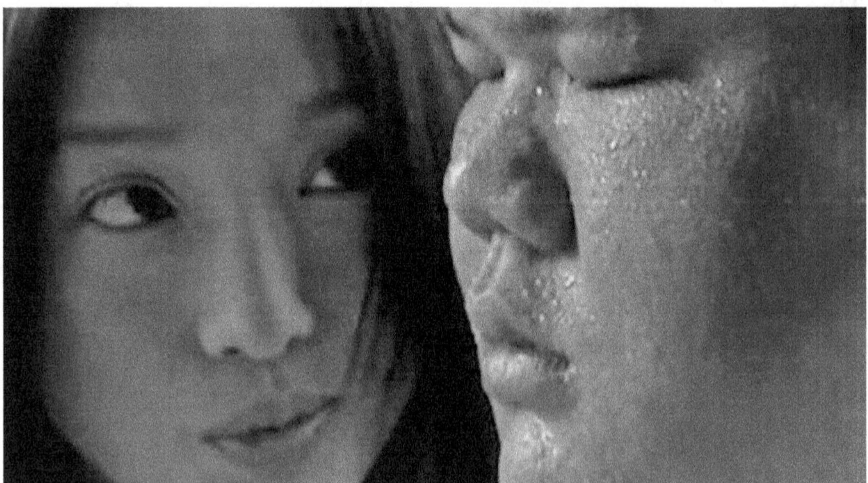

Figure 12.1 Tong Tong provides the cool breeze to Ming in Fruit Chan's *Hollywood Hong Kong*

in their shabby courtyard. Her body going back and forth on the swing here is seen from the men's vantage point. The swing ride motif is repeated in a dream sequence in which Ming and his father 'dream' her gliding by on the swing, just outside their windows, in a red dress. Unlike Tiny, with whom Tong Tong forms a real bond in the film, Ming and his father appear to be fantasizing about, and lusting after, her.

Tong Tong's real reason for being very friendly with the large and unattractive men is the enigma of the film, but even as her sexuality becomes apparent when she seduces reticent Ming, Chu's older son (the film later reveals the she had sexual intercourse with his father too), the exact nature of her intent is not yet clear. In all of her encounters, Zhou's character skilfully balances a genuine friendliness toward strangers with a strong sensuality. Tong Tong soon disappears from the town, however, and her attorney sends letters to the three men – Keung, Ming and Mr Chu – who have come under her spell, asserting that she is 'underage' and threatening to sue them for statutory rape. As it turns out, Tong Tong and her pimp Peter run an extortion scheme whereby her clients pay up to avoid legal repercussions and jail sentences. When Keung refuses to or cannot pay, he is chased down by gangsters who chop off his hand (the source of much of the film's subsequent dark humour). By the time Keung (now with two left hands after someone else's hand is reattached to his arm) and Ming join forces and track her down in Plaza Hollywood, Tong Tong is long gone. It transpires that she has gone to the real Hollywood at the end of the film.

Escaping Hong Kong without being punished, Zhou's character appears to fit well into the neo-noir revision of the femme fatale character. More than that, however, the implications of her 'northern' origin – as a mainlander who takes advantage of the crumbling old Hong Kong (Tai Hom is earmarked to be demolished) – present the facets of the new socio-political landscape after Hong Kong's 1997 handover to China. As Wimal Dissanayake notes, Hong Kong auteur Fruit Chan's films are 'intimately related to the historical moments of their production'.[19] In this sense, *Hollywood Hong Kong* is an example of how the sensuality and ambivalence Zhou brings to the role are used to articulate the tensions generated by the changing Hong Kong social environment following the union of Hong Kong and China.

Zhou's next film, *Balzac and the Little Chinese Seamstress*, stands out as an anomaly in the sense that the film is set in a remote mountain village, during the Cultural Revolution. Playing the Little Chinese Seamstress of the title – an illiterate granddaughter of a tailor in the village – Zhou's character seems far from the enigmatic urban image she had established in previous roles. As the film progresses, however, Zhou's Little Seamstress becomes more associated with the city and more importantly *changes* as she comes in contact with the two 'city' boys, Luo (played by Kun Chen) and Ma (Ye Liu), sent to her village for 're-education'. Fascinated by her beauty and her inquisitive mind (in one scene, she takes apart their alarm clock), the boys decide to educate the Little Seamstress while they are being 're-educated' themselves, mainly assigned to do manual labour such as mining and carrying buckets of excrement to the field. (Indeed, this is a highly repressive and absurd situation where the illiterate educate the literate.) Eventually they steal, at the Little Seamstress' suggestion, a suitcase full of banned books belonging to another exile, the intellectual Four Eyes. The Seamstress also comes up with an idea of performing for Four Eyes as a distraction while the boys search his house. As the boys read these forbidden Western books to her, she is transformed à la Pygmalion.

Her transformation is first noticed by her grandfather, Tailor (Zhijun Cong). Filled with anxiety, Tailor expresses to the boys his fears for his granddaughter in a flashback that portrays him witnessing the Little Seamstress donning a bra for her peers, clearly fashioned by her, inspired by the Western novels. Explaining her new undergarments to her girlfriends (she is the first in all of Phoenix Mountain to have a bra); she also discusses the idea of being civilized, citing Balzac. Tailor confides to the boys: 'I was so frightened of her that my hands shook. Sometimes a book can affect your whole life.' As Michelle Bloom points out, 'this fashion statement anticipates Ma and Luo's complete and pygmalionesque success [...] when she gets her hair cut short, wears tennis shoes and, thus transformed, leaves (her lover Luo, as well as Ma and her grandfather) for what her grandfather identifies vaguely as "a big city"'.[20]

When the two now middle-aged men meet up after 20 years toward the end of the film, their reminiscence turns to the last time they saw the Little Seamstress. The flashback shows Luo trying to persuade her not to leave, but Zhou's character ventures into the unknown world, refusing to compromise (i.e. she leaves the people she loves and the people who love her, and practically disappears from their lives). Tearful Luo confesses to Ma that he looked in vain for the Little Seamstress; he heard that she was working in Shenzhen but could not find her there. He presumes that she must have moved to Hong Kong. Even off-screen, the Little Seamstress, associated with the big cities, clearly belongs to the modern, urban world. The fact that the director of the film, Sijie Dai, cast Zhou after seeing her in *Suzhou River* underlines that Zhou represents a cosmopolitan Chinese image.[21] As such, even playing this relatively straightforward character (i.e. one without a dual identity) in a historically based piece, Zhou projects an aura of mystery – after all, nobody knows where she is and what has become of her.

'Vicious Women'

From the mid-2000s, Zhou's roles expanded into high-profile mainstream films, both in Hong Kong and Mainland China.[22] In 2005, Zhou appeared in the big-budget Hong Kong musical *Perhaps Love* as a driven-for-success actress, Sun Na. She is a leading lady and partner to an acclaimed film director, Nie Wen (played by Jacky Cheung), who is under pressure to make a financially viable film after his recent flops. A bankable Hong Kong movie star, Lin Jian-dong (Takeshi Kaneshiro), who joins the production as the male lead, turns out to be Sun's former lover. In Beijing ten years before the film's present, the two had been lovers, but Sun walked out of Jian-dong's life (when he was a struggling film student) to seek fame and fortune. In the present, she even denies that she ever knew him. Paralleling the love triangle is the film they are making, its story involving an amnesiac female trapeze artist living with the circus director and confronted by her old lover, who is hoping to reignite an old flame. In both stories, Zhou's character is at the centre, caught between the two men – the old sweetheart and the current lover who has made her into a major star. In a film that switches between the past (Beijing) and present (Shanghai) as well as the film-within-the-film circus setting, Zhou plays in effect multiple roles with different looks and styles – from the loving and pixie-like youngster to the glamorous, attention-demanding actress to the singing trapeze artist. Ultimately as a kind of woman who will stop at nothing and seizes on every opportunity, Sun in *Perhaps Love* extends the woman-with-a-past persona that Zhou established with Meimei in *Suzhou River*.[23] The film is also significant in terms of Zhou's stardom, as Sun is a character that viewers can imagine the Little Seamstress or the housemaid from *Beijing Bicycle* could have become. As such, Zhou projects the femme fatale screen persona beyond film noir, at times inverting elements of the classical or neo-noir version of the femme fatale.

Diverging from roles as the object of romantic obsession, in *The Equation of Love and Death* (2008), Zhou plays a chain-smoking taxi driver, Li Mi, who looks for her missing boyfriend in the city of Kunming (the capital of Yunnan Province in south-west China).[24] She keeps in her car a magazine full of photos of her enigmatic boyfriend, who had vanished four years previously but has nevertheless continued to send her letters without revealing his whereabouts. Li Mi shows his picture to her passengers in the hopes that someone will be able to tell her where he is. She narrates: 'I just have to find him, and say it out loud, "Why don't you go screw yourself!"' Living in limbo, her view of Kunming is that 'nothing has changed', while rapid urbanization is evident around her. All she wants is to find her boyfriend. In a film that is full of noir aspects – obsessive love, criminal schemes gone wrong and characters on the social margins – Zhou herself lends a connection to noir by her presence (via *Suzhou River*) not so much as a femme fatale but as a fast-talking, hardened, brooding and obsessive 'private eye' trying to solve a mystery (at least until a real police detective takes over the case). Sharing thematic concerns of love and illusion with *Suzhou River*, the film takes an introspective view of the alienation and ultimate loneliness of life in the big city.

In her next film, *Painted Skin*, Zhou plays her deadliest femme fatale. Set in ancient China, the film introduces Zhou's character, just barely covered with a fur drape and with her legs fully exposed, surrounded by wild bandits. Clinging onto the drape, she looks vulnerable, yet her sexually provocative gaze back at the men also suggests that she is in control. Once the leader of the group picks her up and retires to a separate tent, her true power is revealed; as he offers his heart as a figure of speech, Zhou's character literally rips out his heart. It transpires that Zhou's character, Xiao Wei, is a fox spirit or demon that has taken on the form of a human, who needs to consume human hearts to maintain this new shape ('skin') as well as her beauty and youth. Sexually alluring and dangerous, Zhou's Xiao Wei is the ruthless temptress – a femme fatale who literally rips out men's hearts. Clearly an object of desire, she has no shortage of admirers. There is even a chameleon spirit called Xiao Yi who carries out a series of murders to provide her with fresh human hearts in his attempt to prove his love for her. Zhou's Xiao Wei, however, falls for a human: Commander Wang Sheng (played by Kun Chen), who leads his troops in a raid on bandits in the desert and 'rescues' her. The enchanted troops bring Xiao Wei home with them, and she stays with Wang Sheng and his dutiful wife, Peirong (Wei Zhao), who starts to suspect Xiao Wei and links her to a spate of brutal killings that started with Xiao Wei's arrival in town. Actively plotting to become Wang's wife, Xiao Wei comes between the man and wife, and eventually persuades Peirong to take poison to turn into the 'demon'. In the end, both Peirong and Wang kill themselves to save each other. As she realizes that Wang would never betray Peirong, Xiao Wei gives up the powers she has cultivated over thousands of years, to bring Peirong and Wang Sheng back to life.

Playing the temptress role to perfection, Zhou is bewitching in her ability to switch from sensuous and kindhearted to ruthless, scary demon and back to touchingly generous spirit. However, there is no actual mystery to her character in this film; Zhou's Xiao Wei is clearly laid out from the beginning to be a human-heart-consuming demon. Nonetheless, Xiao Wei is complex and conflicted, finally giving up something precious for the sake of love. As such, Zhou's character does not take on femme fatale attributes for malicious pleasure or great riches but rather to desperately attain love. Indeed, her character's 'change of heart' brings romantic subversion to a film set up as a supernatural horror piece. In the sequel, *Painted Skin: The Resurrection*, which became China's highest-grossing domestic film on its release in 2012,[25] Zhou reprises the role of fox spirit. After being imprisoned for centuries under a frozen lake as punishment for violating the laws of the demon world, Xiao Wei breaks free and transforms again into a beautiful seductress. Once again, she reveals herself to another woman, the badly scarred Princess Jing (played by Wei Zhao) who wants to become beautiful again to get close to her love, Captain Huo Xin (Kun Chen). Xiao Wei is willing to trade her looks for the princess's willing heart, which would enable her to become a mortal and experience 'true' life. Similarly to the previous film, what she ardently wants in this sequel is to become a human. As they experiment

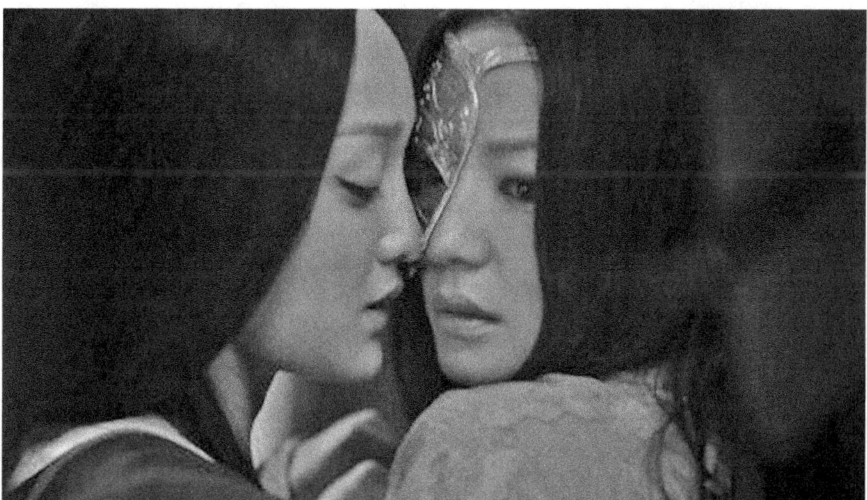

Figure 12.2 'What men care about the most is a woman's beauty' – fox demon Xiao Wei persuades Princess Jing to switch bodies in *Painted Skin: The Resurrection*

with shape-changing, the two switch bodies, the two actresses in effect playing each other (with doubling thus coming back to Zhou in a most strange way). Even in explicitly commercial films, Zhou embodies the intriguing female character whose nuance and manipulation suit the fox demon convincingly.

Conclusion

Xun Zhou took her first step into Hollywood with *Cloud Atlas* (2012), joining big names such as Tom Hanks, Halle Berry, Hugh Grant and Susan Sarandon. In a sci-fi film that spans centuries, Zhou plays three distinctive characters – a blue-eyed tribal woman in the year 2346, a genetically engineered clone in 2144 and a male hotel manager in 1973. Zhou's first major film outside Asia certainly raises her profile,[26] and it is quite fitting that she plays multiple roles in the film. Following the release of the film, in an interview with the *Wall Street Journal*, Zhou remarked: 'the prototype of all the characters I've played so far is Hans Christian Andersen's "Little Mermaid" – someone with a great heart to sacrifice'.[27] Zhou's take on her own screen persona as the 'Little Mermaid', with a particular reference to her breakout role in *Suzhou River*, is highly perceptive in its reference to her frequent dual-identity roles. Zhen Zhang asserts that the 'dubious double is symptomatic of uprootedness and fragmentation, and occasionally split personality or multiple personality disorders that often beset the modern individual'.[28] Indeed, often embodying uncanny doubles, Zhou has acquired a screen persona that articulates the ambiguity of societies undergoing drastic and relentless changes – namely Mainland China in the age of transformation and Hong Kong after the 1997 handover. More importantly, however, the figure of the Little Mermaid is not what she seems; she is an illusion. Combining the sensuality and enigmatism evident in the femme fatale figure, Zhou's screen persona adds another layer to the ambivalent figure of the femme fatale far beyond the films associated with film noir.

Notes

1 Zhang, Zhen, 'Introduction: Bearing Witness: Chinese Urban Cinema in the Era of "Transformation"', in Zhang (ed.), *The Urban Generation: Chinese Cinema and Society at the Turn of the Twenty-First Century* (Durham: Duke University Press, 2007), p. 3.

2 It is interesting to note that Ziyi Zhang plays the characters who lead double lives in these films, but their other, 'hidden' identities are explained during the course of the narrative progression. They also function as significant plot twists in both films. The chief difference between Zhang's star image and Zhou's, however, stems from the historical martial-arts genre films that established Zhang's stardom.

3 Doane, Mary Ann, *Femmes Fatales: Feminism, Film Theory, Psychoanalysis* (London: Routledge, 1991), p. 1.

4 Although not as high profile as Ziyi Zhang on an international level, Xun Zhou is still regarded as one of 'Four Little Fadans' – leading young actresses who dominate the Chinese screen. (*Fadan* refers to the leading actress in a Chinese opera.) The other three actresses are Ziyi Zhang, Jinglei Xu and Wei Zhao.

5 To put her appearance in context, *Talk Asia* is a weekly half-hour interview on CNN International produced from the network's Asia-Pacific headquarters in Hong Kong. According to its website, the programme 'explores the personalities behind the newsmakers in the fields of arts, politics, sports and business'. Past interviewees include sculptor Anish Kapoor, Starbucks CEO Howard Schultz, designer Georgio Armani and South Korean actor Byung-heon Lee.

6 Elley, Derek, 'Painted Skin: The Resurrection' (film review), *Film Business Asia*, 17 June 2012, <http://www.filmbiz.asia/reviews/painted-skin-the-resurrection>, accessed 21 April 2013.

7 Naremore, James, *More Than Night: Film Noir in Its Contexts* (Berkeley: University of California Press, 2008), pp. 11, 5. Steve Neale also argues that the concept of film noir involves 'a set of distinct and heterogeneous phenomena' and any attempt to homogenize it 'inevitably generates contradictions, exceptions, anomalies and is doomed, in the end, to incoherence'. See Neale, Steve, *Genre and Hollywood* (London: Routledge, 2000), p. 154.

8 Jancovich, Mark, '"Vicious Womanhood": Genre, the *Femme Fatale* and Postwar America', *Canadian Journal of Film Studies* 20.1 (Spring 2011), p. 101.

9 Unique among Mainland Chinese stars, Zhou is an outspoken advocate for green issues and is heavily involved in a number of environmental projects. In 2010, she received the Laureate of the United Nations Environment Programme (UNEP)'s Champions of the Earth (Inspiration & Action).

10 Silbergeld, Jerome, *Hitchcock With a Chinese Face: Cinematic Doubles, Oedipal Triangles and China's Moral Voice* (Seattle: University of Washington Press, 2004), p. 13.

11 Scott, A. O., '*Suzhou River*: A Chill Scene for Shadowy Characters' (film review), *New York Times*, 25 March 2000, <http://www.nytimes.com/library/film/032500suzhou-film-review.html>, accessed 4 May 2013.

12 Lin, Xiaoping, 'New Chinese Cinema of the "Sixth Generation": A Distant Cry of Forsaken Children', in Lin, *Children of Marx and Coca-Cola: Chinese Avant-Garde Art and Independent Cinema* (Honolulu: University of Hawaii Press, 2010), pp. 93, 94.
13 Zhang, 'Introduction', p. 2.
14 Oliver, Kelly and Benigno Trigo, *Noir Anxiety* (Minneapolis: University of Minnesota Press, 2003), p. 88.
15 Silbergeld, *Hitchcock With a Chinese Face*, p. 17.
16 Beckman, Frida, 'From Irony to Narrative Crisis: Reconsidering the Femme Fatale in the Films of David Lynch', *Cinema Journal* 52.1 (Fall 2012), p. 30.
17 Xu, Jian, 'Representing Rural Migrants in the City: Experimentalism in Wang Xiaoshuai's *So Close to Paradise* and *Beijing Bicycle*', *Screen* 46.4 (Winter 2005), p. 446.
18 Wright, Elizabeth, 'Riding Towards the Future: Wang Xiaoshuai's *Beijing Bicycle*', *Senses of Cinema* 18 (2001), <http://www.sensesofcinema.com/2001/feature-articles/beijing_bicycle/>, accessed 20 October 2013.
19 Dissanayake, Wimal, 'The Class Imaginary in Fruit Chan's Films', *Jump Cut: A Review of Contemporary Media* 49 (2007), <http://www.ejumpcut.org/archive/jc49.2007/FruitChan-class/>, accessed 28 April 2013.
20 Bloom, Michelle E., 'Contemporary Franco–Chinese Cinema: Translation, Citation and Imitation in Dai Sijie's *Balzac and the Little Chinese Seamstress* and Tsai Ming-Liang's *What Time Is It There?*', *Quarterly Review of Film and Video* 22.4 (2005), p. 314.
21 Xun Zhou in an Interview, Special Feature, *Balzac and the Little Chinese Seamstress* DVD (Optimum Home Entertainment, 2004).
22 In 2004, Zhou starred in Shaohong Li's *Baober In Love*, where she is spirited Baober, who is traumatized by unhappy childhood memories. A bridge between her independent films and mainstream films, the film also utilizes her sensual and conflicted screen persona.
23 Zhou continued to play 'double' roles in the action film *Ming Ming* (2006) – a deadly assassin, Ming Ming; and Nana, a spunky, orange-haired girl who is mistaken for Ming Ming.
24 For most critics, the film belongs to Xun Zhou, who won the Asian Film Award for her performance as Li Mi. For example, Edmund Lee notes that the film 'represents yet another virtuoso performance in the glittering resume of Zhou […] [who] is mesmerizing here'; Lee, Edmund, '*The Equation of Love and Death*' (film review), *Time Out Hong Kong*, 2 March 2009, <http://www.timeout.com.hk/film/features/21150/the-equation-of-love-and-death.html>, accessed 7 May 2013. See also Kozo, '*The Equation of Love and Death*' (film review), *LoveHKFilm.com*, n.d., <http://www.lovehkfilm.com/panasia/equation_love_death.html>, accessed 7 May 2013.
25 Cremin, Stephen, '*Resurrection* Takes China BO Record', *Film Business Asia*, 24 July 2012, <http://www.filmbiz.asia/news/resurrection-takes-china-bo-record>, accessed 4 May 2013.

26 Reporting for the *South China Morning Post*, Mark Graham suggests that the film 'ensures Zhang Ziyi has a potential rival as the Chinese actress of choice for high-profile Hollywood roles'; Graham, Mark, 'Actress Zhou Xun is Having a Moment', *South China Morning Post*, 20 January 2013, <http://www.scmp.com/lifestyle/arts-culture/article/1131002>, accessed 16 April 2013.

27 Zhou in an interview with Tom Orlik; Orlik, Tom, 'Zhou Xun Looks Beyond Borders', *Wall Street Journal*, 14 February 2013, <http://blogs.wsj.com/scene/2013/02/14/a-screen-star-in-china-looks-beyond-her-borders>, accessed 4 May 2013.

28 Zhang, *The Urban Generation*, p. 353.

Index

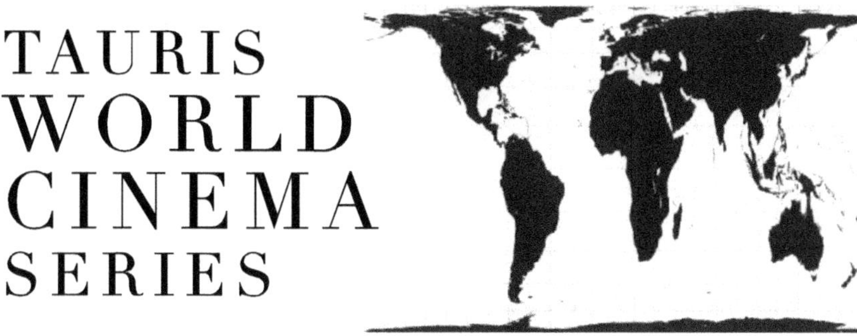

Series Editor: Lúcia Nagib, Professor of Films, University of Reading
Advisory Board: Laura Mulvey (UK), Robert Stam (USA), Ismail Xavier (Brazil)

The *Tauris World Cinema* Series aims to reveal and celebrate the richness and complexity of film art across the globe, exploring a wide variety of cinemas set within their own cultures and as they interconnect in a global context.

The books in the series will represent innovative scholarship, in tune with the multicultural character of contemporary audiences. They will also draw upon an international authorship, comprising academics, film writers and journalists.

Published and forthcoming in the World Cinema series:

Basque Cinema: A Cultural and Political History
By Rob Stone and Maria Pilar Rodriguez

Brazil on Screen: Cinema Novo, New Cinema, Utopia
By Lúcia Nagib

The Cinema of Sri Lanka: South Asian Film in Texts and Contexts
By Ian Conrich and Vilasnee Tampoe-Hautin

Contemporary New Zealand Cinema
Edited by Ian Conrich and Stuart Murray

Cosmopolitan Cinema: Imagining the Cross-cultural in East Asian Film
By Felicia Chan

Documentary Cinema: Contemporary Non-fiction Film and Video Worldwide
By Keith Beattie

East Asian Cinemas: Exploring Transnational Connections on Film
Edited by Leon Hunt and Leung Wing-Fai

East Asian Film Noir: Transnational Encounters and Intercultural Dialogue
Edited by Chi-Yun Shin and Mark Gallagher

Film Genres and African Cinema: Postcolonial Encounters
By Rachael Langford

Greek Cinema from Cacoyannis to the Present: A History
By Vrasidas Karalis

Impure Cinema: Intermedial and Intercultural Approaches to Film
Edited by Lúcia Nagib and Anne Jerslev

Lebanese Cinema: Imagining the Civil War and Beyond
By Lina Khatib

New Argentine Cinema
By Jens Andermann

New Directions in German Cinema
Edited by Paul Cooke and Chris Homewood

New Turkish Cinema: Belonging, Identity and Memory
By Asuman Suner

On Cinema
By Glauber Rocha
Edited by Ismail Xavier

Palestinian Filmmaking in Israel: Narratives of Memory and Identity in the Middle East
By Yael Freidman

Performing Authorship: Self-inscription and Corporeality in the Cinema
By Cecilia Sayad

Queer Masculinities in Latin American Cinema: Male Bodies and Narrative Representations
By Gustavo Subero

Realism of the Senses in Contemporary World Cinema: The Experience of Physical Reality
By Tiago de Luca

Stars in World Cinema: Screen Icons and Star Systems Across Cultures
Edited by Andrea Bandhauer and Michelle Royer

Theorizing World Cinema
Edited by Lúcia Nagib, Chris Perriam and Rajinder Dudrah

Viewing Film
By Donald Richie

Queries, ideas and submissions to:
Series Editor, Professor Lúcia Nagib – l.nagib@reading.ac.uk
Cinema Editor at I.B.Tauris, Anna Coatman – acoatman@ibtauris.com

www.ingramcontent.com/pod-product-compliance
Lightning Source LLC
LaVergne TN
LVHW050511100826
845148LV00002B/301

* 9 7 8 1 7 8 0 7 6 0 0 9 4 *